IN THE FOOTSTEPS OF THE HOLOCAUST

Dedication / Dédicace

To the memory of Amélie Derrez and her husband, Gaston,
and to all the other people who helped Henny and Hermann,
particularly François Casabonne and the Casabonne family.

A la mémoire d'Amélie Derrez et de son mari, Gaston,
et à toutes les autres personnes qui ont aidé Henny et Hermann,
particulièrement François Casabonne et la famille Casabonne.

IN THE FOOTSTEPS OF THE HOLOCAUST

THE STORY AND LETTERS OF A GERMAN JEWISH FAMILY

AINSLIE HEPBURN

PEN & SWORD HISTORY

AN IMPRINT OF PEN & SWORD BOOKS LTD.
YORKSHIRE – PHILADELPHIA

First published in Great Britain in 2025 by
PEN AND SWORD HISTORY
An imprint of
Pen & Sword Books Ltd
Yorkshire – Philadelphia

ISBN 978 1 39903 201 8

A CIP catalogue record for this book is available from the British Library.

Typeset in Times New Roman 10/13 by
SJmagic DESIGN SERVICES, India.
Printed and bound in the UK by CPI Group (UK) Ltd.

The Publisher's authorised representative in the EU for product safety is Authorised Rep Compliance Ltd., Ground Floor, 71 Lower Baggot Street, Dublin D02 P593, Ireland.
www.arccompliance.com

For a complete list of Pen & Sword titles please contact
PEN & SWORD BOOKS LIMITED
George House, Units 12 & 13, Beevor Street, Off Pontefract Road,
Barnsley, South Yorkshire, S71 1HN, England
E-mail: enquiries@pen-and-sword.co.uk
Website: www.pen-and-sword.co.uk

or

PEN AND SWORD BOOKS
1950 Lawrence Rd, Havertown, PA 19083, USA
E-mail: uspen-and-sword@casematepublishers.com
Website: www.penandswordbooks.com

FSC
www.fsc.org
MIX
Paper | Supporting responsible forestry
FSC® C013604

Almost

1.1 million deaths happened in Auschwitz,
1.1 million tales of evil told.
TRUE TALES
Some members of my family were murdered
in this deadly place.
I want to remember…
one untold story of joy, kindness, and cheese.

My great-great-grandparents,
Hermann and Henny Hartog –
a German Jewish couple –
escaped from Germany
(their life).
Nazis were hunting them down.
They stopped in a village called Arette –
which is almost the French for 'stop'.
Almost…

Four generations later,
I discover the crest of Arette:
two hogs and four bulls.
Hogs for bravery, a fight to the death.
Bulls for generosity and courage
in the face of danger.

The story wrote itself:
a beautiful village in the mountains,
the delicious smell of sheep's cheese,
a smiling community welcoming
two refugees who had looked for a sign,
found safety.
Almost…

by Leo Hepburn, 18 October 2020
(then aged 9 years old)

Contents

Introduction

It started with the letters. Quite a lot of them, tightly packed into a large leather wallet and pushed to the very back of a shelf in a bedroom cupboard in a village in Sussex, England. They were all handwritten in German, in tiny writing, on flimsy airmail paper, occasionally on postcards, or (the later ones at the back of the pack) with the stub of a pencil on different scraps of paper.

I was clearing out my mother-in-law's flat as she had gone into long-term care. She had never mentioned these letters, which had been sent to her and her sister from their parents more than seventy years previously. I sat down on the bed and started to look at them and began to realise that I was reading an extraordinary story. It was only after both my mother-in-law and her sister had died that I was able to begin to piece together the story that neither of them had ever been able to talk about themselves.

The letters were from Henny Hartog and her husband Hermann, who were both Jewish and members of strong communities in Germany where Hermann was the teacher and cantor. Anti-Semitism forced them to leave Germany in 1939, but by then they had sent their two young daughters to England. Parents and daughters corresponded frequently and kept the letters.

But the letters didn't complete the story, so I set off with my husband to walk in the footsteps of Henny and Hermann Hartog, who were his grandparents. First, we went to Frankfurt am Main, where Henny had been born and lived until her marriage, and from where her father was eventually deported. It wasn't difficult to catch a glimpse of the accomplished young middle-class woman with her dainty ways and smart clothes, her organisational skills and propriety.

In Aurich, Hermann's birthplace, the memory and understanding of the Jewish community that had once lived there is being kept strongly alive by local people who helped us to understand past events and people of this small town near the Dutch border. Although the serious young Hermann followed a career in teaching, his family was part of the large contribution made to the town's economy through cattle-trading and the butchers' trade. *Stolpersteine*, or stumbling stones, set into the ground guided us through the previously Jewish neighbourhood. Nazi leaders in the area might have declared the town 'Jew free' in April 1940, but nowadays residents, schoolchildren and church members are all involved in vigorously maintaining the legacy of that Jewish community.

Similarly, in Jever we followed Henny and Hermann's life-story in the place where they first lived after their marriage, and where their two daughters were born. We stood in the house where they had lived, and in the room that had once been Hermann's schoolroom at the synagogue, and later met people there who said, 'Oh yes, your grandfather taught my father.' There are many descendants of Jews from Jever who are still drawn back to the town, often by invitation of those leaders in Jever who have worked tirelessly for many years to ensure that the vibrancy of that community and its beautiful synagogue lives on.

As we were guided through Wilhelmshaven and walked through the park where Henny had once played with her little daughters, we were told, 'This would have been the most direct route for your grandfather to take from home to his work at the synagogue.' So we walked the walk and paced the walls of the synagogue that had been outlined on the ground as a memorial. A screech of brakes and a man leapt from a car to introduce himself as the architect of the memorial to the earlier Jewish community and to explain how and why he did it.

But Henny and Hermann had been forced from Germany in 1939, and we followed where they had gone. We picked up their trail in Brussels, where they lived for a few months, and then followed it from there to Paris, and on to the south-west of France. 'It is magnificent here,' wrote Henny to her daughters, as she looked out at the glorious mountains. And so it was for us, as we followed their steps through those same villages at the foot of the Pyrénées.

Like them, we took a long detour to Marseille, where they had tried (and failed) to get on a boat to America. Returning to their safe-seeming village, they were made welcome and helped by the local villagers. We began to understand the quiet and resourceful help that was given by those villagers, who were part of an early resistance in France. The mayor, who made us welcome, had the same name as the mayor who had welcomed Henny and Hermann – he had been a family ancestor. We sat with him in the same farmhouse kitchen as the one where Henny and a few other Jewish refugee women from Germany had spent their afternoons – huddled around the radio together with their French friends in this non-occupied area of France.

These women knew from what they heard on the radio that their village was not really safe, and one day there was the inevitable knock on the door. Their French neighbours recorded Henny's smile and encouragement for her husband, and Hermann's strength of resolve. They were taken to the concentration camp at Gurs. We followed behind them many years later. By then, duckboards had been laid over the mud, so we were able to follow them without needing the clogs that they'd had to telegraph back to the village to request to be sent to them. Henny wrote a strong, loving and practical message to her friends in the village, who were devastated that they had failed to prevent the arrest of the few German Jewish refugees in their village. The last message from Henny to her daughters was written from Gurs, but it was not written by her. She asked the woman next to her in the hut to let her daughters know that they might not hear from her for a while. And both Henny and Hermann sent their love to their daughters.

We followed the trail of Henny and Hermann in their lorry the few miles from Camp de Gurs to the train station at Oloron-Sainte-Marie, where we stared along the track that would have taken them in a cattle truck to Paris. We caught up with them in Paris at the concentration camp at Drancy, from where they were deported to Auschwitz. At Drancy, we said our farewells. We did not follow them.

Unbeknown to us, a 'holiday' that Henny and Hermann's daughters took in France during the early 1970s was in reality an attempt to locate the mountain village where their parents had lived. There were serious communication difficulties for everyone since no one spoke the other's language, but they brought back with them letters that had been carefully stored in the village after Henny and Hermann's departure. Back home in Sussex, these letters were just as carefully and quietly pushed to the back of the cupboard in the bedroom, and no one ever talked about them again.

Finding these letters not only opened up the personal story of Henny and Hermann Hartog, but also facilitated friendships and understanding across countries, faith groups, and small towns and villages. Their story celebrates the strength and resilience of many people at a terrible time in world history – and since. The individual members of the Jewish communities of Frankfurt, Aurich, Jever and Wilhelmshaven might have been largely destroyed and dispersed at a point in time, but their strength and purpose survives and enlightens us all. So many 'ordinary' people have achieved the extraordinary, and this is the story of just some of them.

CHAPTER 1

Frankfurt: Henny's Early Years

Seilerstraβe (Rope Makers' Street) was, and remains, a long straight street towards the north of the city of Frankfurt am Main. It lies just inside the area that had once held the medieval city walls, which were demolished at the beginning of the nineteenth century. The making of ropes here had once been a noisy and flourishing business, and part of the process of the manufacture of the early hemp ropes had required an absolutely straight distance of at least 50m. The place where they were made became known as 'Seilerstraβe'.

By the time Henny Scheuer was born, on Wednesday 21 July 1897 in an apartment at Seilerstraβe 11, the area had become more residential than industrial. Ropes were no longer manufactured there and laid out along the length of the street. Rather, public gardens had been landscaped along the line of the ancient walls, giving a ring of greenery that included trees, footpaths and lakes for the enjoyment of the people of the city. This relatively quiet and peaceful parkland was just a few metres away from Henny and her family's front door. It became a magnet for Jewish newcomers to the city.

Henny's parents were Mina and Adolf Scheuer. They already had a son, Arthur, who was 17 months old by the time Henny was born, and the four of them lived together in the apartment at number 11. Adolf worked as a salesman with a shipping business, and it seems they had extra domestic help in the home, which was normal for families of their class at the time.

They lived in an area of Frankfurt that was popular with the orthodox Jewish community and many of their neighbours belonged to that community. It was said by a passer-by that if you walked through this area as a new visitor from the nearby railway station, you would probably have thought that all of Frankfurt must be occupied by Jews. Both of their families were Jewish, but Mina and Adolf were not as strictly religious as some other Jewish families. Very probably they observed the Jewish holidays and the weekly Sabbath rituals, but they might not have attended synagogue very regularly. Many years later, Henny – who by then had been married to a Jewish teacher for several years – wrote to her daughters: 'I wasn't raised religiously myself, and I have done a lot of it for Vati [Daddy's] sake, but I was very happy to do it.'

Adolf was born on 20 June 1864 in Mainz, a large town on the River Rhine, 40km or so west of Frankfurt, where a Jewish community had been established in the tenth century – one of the oldest in the German-speaking world. The Scheuer family followed the trend of many people during the nineteenth century in moving from the smaller towns (or the countryside) into larger towns or cities, searching for a better way of life.

Adolf was the fourth child in his family. When he was 1 year old – by which time a younger brother had been born – his family moved eastwards to Frankfurt am Main. That year, his mother, Regine, was 30 years old. By 1870, when she was 35, and ten years after her marriage, she had borne ten children, four of whom had died in infancy at just a few months old.

This tragic situation was relatively unusual within the Jewish community at this time. The rates of infant mortality were higher in Germany than in several other European countries, but they tended to be lower within the Jewish community. Generally, the smaller numbers of children in Jewish families and the longer gaps between childbearing, as well as the hygiene rituals and high sanitation practised within Jewish homes, meant there were fewer infant deaths. As in most western European countries, if children survived until their first birthday, they had a reasonable chance of living for much longer – as long as an epidemic of an infectious disease was not encountered.

Adolf and his surviving siblings – a brother and three sisters – grew up in Frankfurt. Helene, who was three years older than Adolf, later married and moved away from Frankfurt. Her husband came from Aurich, a small town in the north-west of Germany, near the Dutch border – a fact that would become significant for Henny many years later.

Adolf's surviving brother Julius married Flora Joske, and they lived in Frankfurt with their daughter Bertha. His younger sister, Franziska, lived only about twenty minutes away with her husband, Jacob Cahen, and their daughter Henriette, who was only a year younger than Henny – so Henny had a cousin of a similar age not far away. The youngest of Adolf's siblings, Rosalie, married Sally Seckel Graetz in 1900 when Henny was 3 years old. Uncle Sally and Auntie Rosa were probably the most popular of the Scheuer relatives. Sally and Rosa didn't have any children and lived at Fürstenbergerstraβe 177, less than a thirty-minute walk away from Mina and Adolf's home (towards the wealthier west end of the city).

Adolf's wife Mina was born into the Bodenheimer family, who lived in Heppenheim, a medieval town about 60km south of Frankfurt, which had had an established Jewish community since about 1700. Mina had been born there at

Bergstraße 26. Her parents, and other members of their families continued to live in the town although, during the last years of the nineteenth century, younger members of the wider family (just like the Scheuer family) began to move to Frankfurt and beyond in order to explore greater opportunities in business.

Mina had an older sister, Henriette, and three younger brothers – Leopold, Max and Louis. Mina moved to Frankfurt for her marriage to Adolf on 8 May 1895, when she was 25 years old. Henriette was four years older than Mina and once she also arrived in Frankfurt, she continued to live there throughout her life. Two of Mina's younger brothers (Leopold and Max) decided to join other young men of their time who emigrated to the USA for even greater opportunities than Frankfurt might offer. Leopold left in 1887, when he was 15, and Max in 1892, aged 16. Uncle Max became an important person in Henny's life many years later, as his residence in America offered hope for her own emigration at a time of despair.

Louis remained in Frankfurt, becoming a prosperous businessman dealing in second-hand goods, a popular trade for Jewish men of his class in Frankfurt at that time. In 1908, he married Hedwig Weiler, whose family also came from Heppenheim, but she and Louis lived in Frankfurt with their only child Arthur, who was born in 1909 (when Henny was 12 years old). Although they lived on the other side of the city, Louis' business premises at Klostergasse 34 – 36 (in the centre of the city) were much closer to the Scheuers' apartment. Both Mina and Adolf were close to Louis and Hedwig.

Since Mina's parents remained in Heppenheim, Henny's maternal grandparents lived at some distance, but Adolf's parents were nearby in Frankfurt. However, both grandfathers died while Henny was a young child – Max Scheuer in 1903, when Henny was 5 years old, and Abraham Bodenheimer in 1905, when she was 7. But her grandmothers were part of her life as she was growing up in Frankfurt.

Back in their apartment in Seilerstraβe, Mina and Adolf's firstborn, Arthur, died in May 1898 when he was just 2 years old. At that time, Henny was 10 months old, and her mother was already pregnant again. In January 1899 (when Henny was a year and a half old) Colestina was born – a sister who would become close and who was always called Cilly. By the time she was born, Mina and Adolf had moved with their two little daughters a few streets away to Gaußstraβe 16. This was in an area of substantial houses, mostly divided into apartments, which was becoming home to a large Jewish population of mainly middle-class businessmen and traders with their families.

This new area of Frankfurt, the most northern part of the city, was developed at the turn of the century during the reign of Kaiser Wilhelm II, and the architecture reflects the grandiose aspirations of the time. Families moved into the fashionable Art Nouveau (or *Jugendstil*) buildings just beyond the earlier city boundary, pleased to be part of this affluent, modern, and progressive society. Whole streets became inhabited by Jewish families, who were moving further away from the centre of the city to what was seen as a more prosperous area. But they also wanted to remain within an orthodox community.

The nearest synagogue for the orthodox Jews in this part of Frankfurt at the end of the nineteenth century was in the Schützenstraβe, which was about a twenty-minute walk from the Scheuer home. A large, three-storey school building stood on the corner of the site, with the synagogue at a similar height adjoining it. Maybe Henny and Cilly attended this school when they were very young. The synagogue, built in 1851 under the leadership of the dynamic Rabbi Samson Raphael Hirsch, initially had 500 seats and was then enlarged to accommodate 1,000 seats. Even so, it became too small for the growing Jewish community in the area. This community was asked to donate towards the building of a new synagogue, which would have 1,000 places for men, 600 places for women, and sixty for the singers.

Building began in 1905 and in August 1907, a few weeks after Henny's tenth birthday, the new synagogue was inaugurated. It was much closer to their home – just a five-minute walk away in the Friedberger Anlage, part of the grassy parkland on the site of the old city walls. The design of the synagogue had been decided by an international competition and was deemed by many at the time to be one of the most beautiful Jewish places of worship in Germany.

Certainly, it was the biggest Jewish prayer-house in Frankfurt, and – judging from photographs of the time – it was indeed impressive. Architecturally, it was a mixture of Romanesque, Moorish Revival and Art Nouveau styles. In front of the main building was an atrium with two large portals. There were doors to the men's dressing rooms and to their main room, as well as vestibules leading to the women's rooms. Inside, the rectangular space had a barrel vault, and there were side galleries in the transepts. There were rich decorations in marble and bronze on the walls. At the opening ceremony on 29 August 1907, representatives from the city and from the Prussian government as well as delegates from thirty-five other Jewish communities attended, and the Torah scroll was brought to the new synagogue from the Schützenstraβe. Photographs taken a few years later show a very well-dressed middle-class community mingling outside the synagogue after a service.

There are very few clues to Henny's early life in Frankfurt. We know that a flourishing kindergarten for the Jewish children in the neighbourhood was built in 1906 just around the corner from the Scheuers' home, at Baumweg 5, but there is no record of Henny's educational experiences or achievements – only literally a scrap of information from 1914.

Most girls of Henny's generation did not receive much of a formal education, but Henny became well-versed in subjects considered appropriate for a girl of her class. She was a capable young woman who knew how to organise a Jewish household, including running the kosher kitchen required by orthodox Jews. She could play the piano and was able to speak and write French and English. It is also possible that since there were no surviving sons in the family, Henny and her sister benefited from an education that would otherwise have been denied them as any sons would have been the first to be educated. However, the education for those girls who attended a school was still largely aimed at preparing them to become wives and mothers.

Middle-class young Jewish women in a city such as Frankfurt were trained to run a kosher home, pass on the Jewish faith to younger members of the family, observe the traditions, and acquire those accomplishments that would gain them a good marriage. Running a middle-class household with a kosher kitchen could absorb the time and energies of several women, and usually paid help was required in the form of maids and/or nurses. Shopping, cooking, baking, preserving, and generally maintaining a kosher household with two kitchens – to say nothing of childcare – was time- and energy-consuming. Coal or wood stoves and oil lamps required extra work, and the demands of the Sabbath rituals required particular preparations at specific times, especially since no cleaning or cooking was allowed on the Sabbath itself.

Jewish women were expected to be thrifty, and to keep detailed accounts of household expenditure. Any savings could be put aside for funds for children's education, dowries, or investments. This way of running the household showed that the family valued culture and gentility. It was passed on from mother to daughter – from Mina to Henny, and from Henny to her daughters. When Henny's eldest daughter was 15 years old – and Henny was not able to be with her – she gave clear advice in one of her letters: 'Work hard and make your work tidy and carry out the smallest thing neatly. Hard work and respectability are often as important in life as intelligence.'

An intriguing scrap of paper lies with the family letters that we found. It is small – 12cm x 9cm – and has rounded corners at the bottom of the page. The top of the paper has been torn, as though a piece of paper 12cm x 18cm has been torn in half. On one side, in neat English handwriting, it says:

> *The time has now come when we must say goodbye to each other. But one day I hope we shall meet again, perhaps in Germany, perhaps in England. Meanwhile spare a thought occasionally for your friend who is very fond of you.*

In the bottom left corner the writer has written 'Les… [it is indecipherable], Lausanne'. This has been roughly crossed through, as though not necessary. On the bottom right of the paper is written a name and address: 'Nathalie Laurence, 33 Greville Road, Londres N.W.'

On the reverse of the paper – half-way through the top torn half of the scrap, in German handwriting – is an unreadable signature and beneath it, in the bottom left corner, the same hand has written, 'Lausanne, le 6 Janv. 1914.'

This scrap of paper looks very much like part of a page from the sort of autograph book young people in Germany had at the beginning of the twentieth century, in which they collected messages from friends at significant moments. Very possibly Henny had such a book, which she kept. She valued the friendships and maintained the contacts, and one day – many years later – one of her old friends seemed to offer the possibility of hope and help. She took the page from the book, tore out the useful contact address, scribbled across the unnecessary information, and enclosed this scrap of paper in a letter to her daughter with some instructions.

Perhaps – and there is some other evidence, which comes later in the story of her life – Henny attended a finishing school in Lausanne during 1913, together with other young women from England and Germany. It was customary for girls from middle-class families to be 'finished' during a year's course at a residential establishment, and Switzerland promoted this as part of its tourist industry as well as for educational purposes. Lausanne was the most prestigious centre for such schools at this time, with private boarding schools for foreigners outnumbering private day schools for local children.

For Henny and her friends, their time at 'Les…' in Lausanne came to an end, and on 6 January 1914 they wrote farewell messages in each other's autograph books before returning to their homes.

A few months later, on 11 June 1914, when Henny was back in Frankfurt, and perhaps making plans for the celebration of her seventeenth birthday in five weeks' time, her mother gave birth to a boy at the Koenigswarterstraβe Hospital in Frankfurt. Mina was 44 years old, and her son did not survive the day.

Two months later, Germany was at war, and the next four years were brutal for those who remained at home, as well as for those young men who fought for their country. With minimal government arrangements for the rationing of food and supplies during wartime, many German civilians, especially those in towns, faced hunger and severe difficulties in finding essential goods. There was increasing civil unrest in many cities, including Frankfurt, as people demonstrated against the hardships of war.

Between her seventeenth and twenty-first birthdays, Henny must have known many brothers and fathers of her friends who never returned from the battlefields. This was a war that almost destroyed a whole generation of men. It probably also affected her hopes and expectations for the future. The young people who survived looked ahead to a future in a vastly changed political landscape. For many young women such as Henny, marriage was the expected way forward. But so many men her own age had died during the war. Prior expectations of a suitor, marriage and a family could not be accommodated in the same way.

Henny's prospects otherwise seemed good. She was accomplished and could organise a Jewish home. She was attractive and personable, with a ready smile and a positive attitude. She was petite, standing at about 150cm, and was of slight build. But her smile and her thick, dark wavy hair and large, dark eyes made her quite noticeable.

A year or so after Germany's defeat, on 28 January 1920, Mina died – just a few months short of her fiftieth birthday. Cilly had recently celebrated her twenty-first birthday, and Henny was 22 years old. Their father, Adolf, became a widower at the age of 55.

Much of the lifestyle and events of Henny's youth in Frankfurt shaped her view of the world and how to behave in it. There had been many deaths in her family during her first twenty years – maybe no more than were generally experienced at that time, but they made her fearful of loss and aware of the need to be vigilant about one's health. Writing to her own teenage daughters about her mother's death more than twenty years later, Henny wrote:

> *In my last letter, I said that after the dance you should never go outside immediately where you can cool down quickly. Hopefully you are sensible, because it was through a severe chill that my late mother, who died twenty-one years ago, contracted such a serious illness that she later died as a result. You must understand, therefore, that you must be careful with your health. I beg you to be careful of your health.*

Only a few months after her mother's death, Henny became engaged to be married to Hermann Hartog. The following year, both Henny and her sister Cilly were married. On Thursday 10 March 1921, Henny married Hermann, a Jewish teacher and cantor from north-west Germany. There was a civil marriage in Frankfurt, followed by a celebration in the synagogue on Sunday 13 March. Henny was 23 and Hermann was 34.

It was an accepted convention within German Jewish society of the time that the eldest daughter should marry first. We do not know how or when Henny and Hermann met, or who introduced them, or how the marriage contract was decided. It is possible they knew each other through Adolf's sister, Helene, who had married Ruben Samson from Aurich, which was Hermann's home town. Ruben's name and his family connections suggest a very strong link with the Hartog/Hoffmann/Cosmann families of Aurich, and at this time Jewish families usually married within their faith.

It is also possible (because it was common practice) that the marriage was arranged through a third party who suggested possible suitors and drew up a contract that detailed a financial settlement. We know that Henny took a substantial dowry of 10,000 Marks when she married Hermann, as well as a considerable quantity of linens and jewellery. It would not have been unusual at the time for certain compromises to have been needed – maybe more than had been the case in the past. With the shortage of young men close to her own age, Henny would need to consider marrying a slightly older man. His education and learning and high standing in the Jewish community complemented her middle-class status, fashionable poise, and greater wealth. But anyway, they adored each other, and created a close and wonderful partnership that lasted until the end of their lives. Some years later, when a second war threatened their existence, Hermann wrote to their daughters:

> *Everything is very difficult for us here. But your mother is so courageous and has supported me so well and firmly in every emergency. I have to write this to you, so that you can keep in mind for your whole life what kind of mother you have. She never despairs and bears all difficulties and every emergency with me. You must never forget that, no matter what fate brings, and what else happens with us and with you.*

Seven weeks after the marriage of Henny and Hermann, on Thursday 28 April, Cilly married Fritz Coper, a businessman from Berlin. Their marriage took place in Frankfurt. Afterwards, Cilly and Frank moved to Frank's home in Berlin at Südwestkorso 20, and Adolf went to live with them.

Henny and Hermann set up their new home together at Schlosserstraβe 23 in Jever – 500km north of Frankfurt, and almost on the northern coast of Germany. It was a long way from Frankfurt and Henny was then also about 500km from her sister and father in Berlin. Hermann was already well-known in the local community, and he had brought his bride to Jever to share that life. But the two of them were making a new beginning together.

They had no idea what the future might hold, but they were happy and excited to face it together. They had each other, and they had the support of the Jewish community in Jever. Hermann's family was not far away in Aurich. Whatever the next few years might bring, they were going to be a strong team.

CHAPTER 2

Aurich: Hermann's Family

Hermann was brought up in very different circumstances from Henny Scheuer and her sister.

'Judenstraβe' ('Jew Street') was the nickname given to the street where he had been born and grew up. The street's real name was Wallstraβe and the Hartog family lived at house number 46, in the small market town of Aurich, which stands on the edge of the flatlands and marshes of north-west Germany. He was born there on 22 February 1887 – the seventh child (and second son) of Rachel and Philipp Hartog. His mother was 42 years old when he was born. His father died the following year, aged 50.

Many of the Jewish citizens of Aurich, including Hermann's family, had for centuries depended on the cattle that grazed on the surrounding countryside to bring them, if not great prosperity, a dependable trade and a continuous financial income. When Hermann was born, the Jews in the town did not live in a ghetto, but most of them lived as neighbours in particular streets, such as the Norderstraβe, Marktstraβe, Osterstraβe, and Wallstraβe, which were all within the city limits. This tight network of streets where so many Jews lived was just around the corner from the large marketplace, which was – and remains – in the centre of the town. It was a close community with many inter-married families, and most members of the Jewish community were fairly strict orthodox believers. The Hartogs' neighbours in Wallstraβe included the Cohen, Wolff, Wolffs, Hoffmann, and Samson families – all of whom had family inter-connections.

Hermann's father Philipp was a butcher, a trade with a long tradition in the family. The Hartogs had been well-known for generations in Aurich, as had the family of Rachel Hoffmann, Hermann's mother. Her family originated from Marienhafe, a community about 15km north-west of Aurich, and had long been occupied with the cattle trade. So both families were well-known in the area, in both the town and the countryside.

Philipp inherited the butcher's business at the age of 18 from his father and grandfather. His grandfather's earlier business was probably quite small, since he had paid only a modest amount of the protection money that was required at that time, and which was based on the scale of the business. (During the sixteenth and seventeenth centuries, a Jewish person could be given a letter of protection from the imperial or princely courts, which granted permission to reside in a city. But he could only be given residence permission if he could contribute to the town's economy, and the fee that was required by the emperors – who were always short of money – in exchange for the permission depended on the size of the economic concern.)

Hermann was an infant of 20 months when his father died on 9 October 1888, and he was just 3 years old when his mother died two years later, on 12 March 1890. And then, two years further on, his sister Jettchen also died. She was 13.

The older siblings stepped into their parents' place. Oskar was 11 years old when his father died and – with his mother's guidance – took on the role of breadwinner and head of the household. When Rachel died, Oskar (by then 13 years old) became the head of the family butcher business, with his sister, Berta (aged 18), taking care of the administration of the business. Berta also cared for Hermann and her other younger siblings and earned extra income as a seamstress. Sara, then aged 15, managed the household, and Hermann's other sisters, Gelli and Henny (who were just 6 and 8 years old when their mother died) continued with their schooling for a few more years.

When Hermann's sister Henny left school (at about 14 years old) she moved out of the family home to work as a resident housekeeper for the Polak family in nearby Emden. When the Polaks later moved to Cologne, Henny moved with them and, while the Polaks became to some extent a substitute family for her, she always kept in touch with her own family in Aurich. Gelli died in 1902, aged 18, when Hermann was 15 years old, and she is buried in the Jewish cemetery in Aurich, together with her parents.

The Hartog family butcher business was run from their home at 46 Wallstraβe, with the shop at the front of the house. Berta and any willing helpers made sausages in the kitchen at the rear of the house, and these were also sold in the shop. The slaughterhouse in Aurich was at Breiter Weg 24 – just 800m from the Hartog home and butcher's shop. It consisted of a cold store, two slaughterhouses (one for small animals and one for cattle), a half-timbered building with a saddle roof, another half-timbered building from 1889, and a farmyard. Ruben Samson ran the slaughterhouse until July 1937.

Oskar Hartog grew to become a successful butcher who was also prominent in the public life of Aurich. As a young man, he was active in the work of the Jewish youth organisations that encouraged local social activities and which also supported those youngsters who wanted to take up positions as teachers – one of whom would later be his younger brother.

Christian and Jewish butchers in Aurich belonged to the same trade guild, which traditionally held their meetings at times that respected the holy days of each group. The members came to relevant guild decisions together, and Oskar was active and vocal in these proceedings. The chairman of the Butchers' Guild was Benjamin Samson and Oskar was the secretary.

Berta, Sara, Oskar and Henny never married. They were a very close unit and cared for each other – and for Hermann. Berta owned their house in Wallstraβe, and the siblings put their savings aside to enable Hermann to continue with his education and to pursue a career outside the family business.

Hermann attended school in Aurich at a time when the Jewish school was flourishing. It had been established in 1842 and by 1865 about eighty children attended the school, which at that time had three classes. Hermann became a pupil in about 1893. As numbers fluctuated, the school sometimes had three teachers and sometimes only two. When the school was first founded, lessons were held in the synagogue. But soon it had its premises in two flats in the Kirchstraβe. In 1900, shortly after Hermann had left, a separate school building was inaugurated, and an apartment was provided for the teacher. Parents could still send their children to the municipal elementary school if they preferred. During the time that Hermann attended the school, the senior teacher was (at first) Daniel Fink, and then Heinrich Reuß, who worked with his junior partner, Bernhard (or Benjamin) Wolff.

In 1894 there had been talk of closing the Jewish school and sending all the children to the elementary school, but after talks with the town authorities – who helped with a financial package – the Jewish school was able to remain open. At that time the teacher was Daniel Fink, but he retired in January 1894 and the new teacher and preacher was Heinrich Reuß. He, in turn, retired fourteen years later in November 1908 and moved to Berlin, just a year before Hermann went to Jever as teacher. That year, when the city council set the budget for all the local schools, thirty-eight children from the city plus five from 'abroad' (outside the city) attended the Jewish school. Heinrich Reuß was succeeded by Bernhard (Benjamin) Wolff, who had been the second teacher in the school for some years.

When Hermann was growing up in Aurich, there were about 400 people in the Jewish community there. They were an important part of the town's economic life and were primarily active as butchers (such as his family), cattle dealers, manufactured goods dealers, or shopkeepers – although not many of these Jewish families were particularly well off. By the mid-1920s, of the fifty-eight cattle operations in the city, fifty were operated by Jews, and it was said that in 1927 Aurich had the most modern and the largest cattle market in the German Reich. The local Jews – like their non-Jewish neighbours – spoke standard German, and many of them also spoke the East Frisian Low German. Many of the Aurich Jews included some vocabulary from Western Yiddish, which made their speech particularly colourful and musical.

Until the end of 1811, the Jewish community held their services in a private house on Langen Straβe and then at Wilhelmstraβe 1, but by September of that year they were able to build a modest synagogue at 13 Kirchstraβe. They were helped by other religious denominations in the town who contributed to the funding of the new synagogue. Relationships amongst the different communities were clearly cordial.

A hundred years later, in 1911, the synagogue was renovated, and there was a joyful celebration at its centenary. Services at the synagogue remained well-attended until the late 1930s. In the same year that the synagogue was renovated, the Jewish cemetery on Emder Straβe, which had been used since 1764, was extended.

Hermann stayed at school after the minimum leaving age and then studied to be a teacher and a cantor in the Jewish tradition. His musical abilities enabled him to train to lead the congregation in the singing of the chants and prayers in the liturgy. This role of cantor, or *hazzan*, was also recognised by the secular government as conferring a status similar to a rabbi, and allowed him to officiate, for example, as the legal celebrant of a marriage. Many of the duties of a rabbi were conferred on a cantor if a rabbi lived far from the community.

We do not know where Hermann received his training, but there were local seminaries and yeshivas that offered the necessary theological studies and practical training for him to qualify as a teacher and cantor. Cantors, as a rule, were not ordained, but were invested or authorised by the same seminaries that ordained rabbis, with roughly the same length of training after an undergraduate education. As a teacher and cantor, Hermann was qualified not only to teach the children in the Jewish school, but also to train children and adults in the Jewish musical traditions, and so he was involved with training and leading the synagogue choir as well as officiating at Bar Mitzvahs. His position also often included the duties of *schochet*, upholding and inspecting the proper practice of the slaughter of animals (*schechita*), as defined by Jewish law. During the time that Hermann was growing up in Aurich, the size of the Jewish community in the town allowed for the role of teacher and preacher to be allocated to one person, and that of cantor and *schochet* given to another – at that time, at the turn of the century, to Jonas Wolff.

Hermann was raised within the orthodox tradition of Judaism, as was his future wife, Henny Scheuer. For them, a traditional interpretation of religious practice was important – with its emphasis on the importance of observing the Sabbath, eating kosher, and (for the men) daily prayer and the study of the Torah. However, they were both also relatively open to the ideas of contemporary society, whilst resisting any pressure to become more secularised. The traditions of the synagogue, its prayer rites and observances remained fundamentally important, but at the same time both Hermann and Henny recognised the need to adapt to a modern world that was inhospitable to traditional orthodox practice. This tolerance was later noted by their daughters and by their daughters' friends, as well as by the non-Jewish people amongst whom they later lived. The orthodox Judaism that they practised was entirely a matter of their beliefs. In other ways, they followed modern German norms in dress, and Hermann was clean-shaven. Most of the members of the Jewish community in Aurich at the end of the nineteenth century were strict orthodox believers.

In September 1909, at 22 years old, Hermann Hartog moved away from his home town of Aurich and took up the post of teacher, cantor and *schochet* in Jever, a larger town with a sizeable Jewish community about 35km east of Aurich. He later described his time in Jever as the happiest time in his life – but in many ways it would not to be the easiest.

CHAPTER 3

Jever: Married Life until 1929

After their marriage in May 1921, Henny and Hermann happily set up their first home at Schlosserstraβe 23 in Jever. The town had developed during the middle of the fourteenth century and its castle dates from about a hundred years later. It lies in the *geest* landscape in north-west Germany – an area of dry and infertile flatlands surrounded by marshes and bogs – about 35km east of Aurich and 20km north-west of Wilhelmshaven. The fortified centre of the town of Jever was protected by a ring of earthworks and moats (*grafts*), which also served to drain the area. Some of the *grafts* were filled in and built over in the nineteenth century, but some remain as pleasant, landscaped areas that still indicate the outline of the medieval city walls.

Several Jewish families owned businesses in the commercial and business area only a few streets away from the castle. Henny was probably pleased to discover the large and flourishing fashion shop of A. Mendelsohn, especially if she was apprehensive about her move to a smaller town from the cosmopolitan city of Frankfurt. Good quality clothing, shoes, and accessories were always important to Henny, and she chose carefully and dressed immaculately. The founder of this fashion business, Anton Mendelsohn, had been a prominent member of Jever society, and his son Ludwig (who was running the business by the time Henny arrived in Jever) served as one of the city's four councillors. The Mendelsohn family was one of several socially integrated and assimilated Jewish families in Jever, although they later became targets of anti-Semitism – the same as the rest of the community – even though Ludwig had by then converted to the Protestant faith.

After the period during the eighteenth century known as the 'Enlightenment', or the 'Age of Reason', when intellectual and philosophical ideas in Germany were increasingly focused on the secular world and the pursuit of knowledge through reason, a separation developed between religion and the state. An emphasis on individual liberty and religious tolerance allowed many German Jews to immerse themselves more fully in their country's culture. They became 'assimilated' into the social life of their neighbours and shared their cultural interests and ambitions in wealth, education and the arts.

When Hermann Hartog first arrived as the new 22-year-old Jewish teacher in Jever in September 1909, eight children were attending religious education in the Jewish school, and this increased to about twenty over the following decade as the Jewish community grew. He was employed not only as teacher but also as the community's cantor and *schochet*. As there was no local rabbi, he was also licensed to conduct weddings and funerals. At that time, the community was under the jurisdiction of the rabbi at Oldenburg, nearly 60km away from Jever.

As the nineteenth century turned into the twentieth, the Jewish population of the town was at its height with about 200 members, and many Jewish families were increasingly integrated into urban life. Two Jewish men sat on the city council of twelve members, and there were several Jewish members of the local rifle corps. The Jewish associations, including a women's association, charity relief, a literary association, and a choir, were popular and active. There were several Jewish-owned businesses in the town – including manufactured goods, building materials and coal trades, the tobacco trade and a hotel, and a large number of Jewish families were involved in cattle and horse trading.

The railway arrived in Jever in 1871, and the railway station was built just outside the old town. The railway allowed easier transport for businesses and access to larger markets, which included the rapidly expanding nearby town of Wilhelmshaven with its growing population that needed to be fed by produce from the surrounding countryside. In the same period, there was expansion and improvement to the road infrastructure of the area, especially connecting the places where cattle were reared with their markets and trading places. Trade and commerce began to boom in Jever, new housing was built near the railway station, and the main street leading from the old town to the station (the 'Bahnhofstraβe') was the first continuously metalled road in Jever. Cattle and horse traders in the town found it preferable to move out of their cramped spaces in the older parts of town in order to live and have their businesses in this locality, where the premises were larger and where there was greater space for stables. Schlosserstraβe, where Henny and Hermann first lived after their marriage, was one of those streets and most of their neighbours were engaged in the cattle trade or in horse breeding and trading.

Their house at number 23 was owned by the cattle dealer Louis Josephs, who lived in the downstairs apartment with his wife Ida, while Henny and Hermann lived upstairs. It was a large and spacious house, divided – as was the local custom – for two families, with plenty of space in each apartment for the two kitchens that were necessary for orthodox Jewish families to keep a kosher table.

Max Josephs, with his well-advertised horse breeding business and the extensive stables at the back of his house, lived further along the same side of the road at numbers 15 and 17. The cattle dealer Philipp Sternberg lived opposite at number

22 with his wife Anna Maria and their two young sons Gert and Rolf, who were pupils in Hermann's classroom. A few doors away from the Hartogs, at number 33, on the corner with Bahnhofstraβe, lived another cattle trader, Julius Levy, with his wife Nanny and their son Friedrich (called Fritz).

Further along the street, at number 12, lived Rieka Peiser, who became a member of the synagogue education committee and was thus a frequent visitor to the Hartog household. Next door to the Hartogs, at Schlosserstraβe 25, lived three sisters – Frieda, Jeanette (Netty) and Emma Cohn. Frieda was 59 years old when Henny arrived to live in Jever and for the rest of their lives the 'Aunts Cohn' were special people to Henny, Hermann, and their daughters.

A short distance from Schlosserstraβe, and not far from the synagogue, lived another cattle trader and farmer. Erich Levy – himself the son of a cattle trader – and his wife Ruth lived at Blumenstraβe 2. After his service in the Imperial German Army during the First World War, in which he was injured and had his left leg amputated, Erich married Louise Seecamp. Louise was the daughter of a Protestant merchant, and after her marriage she converted to Judaism and took the name of Ruth.

A few metres away from Henny and Hermann's house – and about half-way from there to the railway station – stood the *Bahnhofshotel* (the Railway Hotel), which was a focal point for the social life of both Jews and non-Jews. Many a game of skat was played there between members of the Jewish community, as well as with their non-Jewish friends.

It was less than a five-minute walk to the synagogue in Grosse Wasserpfortstraβe from the Hartogs' house, and it was in the synagogue that Hermann had his schoolroom. The schoolroom was an annexe to the synagogue, on its south side. It was approached from a small courtyard, reached from the road, Grosse Wasserpfortstraβe, via a passageway (the Tönjes gang) between the synagogue and the neighbouring building – the Haus Tönjes. On this south side of the building was a vestibule with an entrance that gave access to both the women's gallery above the main floor of the synagogue (up a flight of stairs) and to the schoolroom (through a door on the ground floor). There was no direct access between the schoolroom and the synagogue.

The synagogue was built in 1880, ten years after the railway arrived, when the Jewish population was at its height and when development seemed set fair for progress. It stood on the same site as the previous synagogue, which had been built in 1802 and had become too small for the growing Jewish community. Prior to that, in the last years of the eighteenth century, the local Jews had met in a prayer room in a converted barn. The new synagogue, built in the Byzantine architectural style, was known far and wide as one of the most beautiful in the area and it reflected the growing confidence of the local Jewish population at the turn of the century.

The synagogue was built in red brick and was crowned by a dome of glass windows with a Star of David on top. It was set back slightly from the road and had a short front garden. Large stained-glass windows gave light both to the men's space on the ground floor and to the women's gallery above on the first floor. The annexe where the schoolroom was located was also lit by stained-glass windows. And in the basement of the annexe was the *mikveh* – the bath that was used for ritual immersion – which was reached by a short flight of steps from the ground floor.

Within the main space of the synagogue was seating for about 250 people on wooden benches. The walls were plastered and painted, the cast-iron pillars were decorated, and the floor was laid with dark grey tiles. The Torah shrine was richly decorated, and the synagogue community owned many silver religious objects as well as the valuable Torah scrolls. The inauguration of the synagogue had been a splendid occasion, with visitors from not only the nearest Jewish communities and their leaders but also from the local Christian population, who expressed their very favourable impressions of the building and of the event.

In the next few decades, the Jewish community was at the height of its growth, acceptance, and importance in Jever, and in 1910 – a year after Hermann's arrival – the leaders of the synagogue acquired a house a few metres from the synagogue for extra space to serve as a community centre for the Jewish community and a focus for its extended social and cultural life. In 1914, central heating was installed in the synagogue.

In the years prior to Hermann's arrival as the Jewish teacher in 1909, the local Jewish children had increasingly been attending the local public elementary schools, so the Jewish school had become a purely religious school. By the early years of the twentieth century, it was Hermann's job to not only teach the children in the school annexe but also to give lessons in religion to children in the local schools – as he is known to have done in 1924 and 1926 in the Lyzeum (a school that was attended by many girls from the higher social strata in Jever). As the cantor at the synagogue, he was responsible for the music and the chanting at services, as well as the training and performance of the synagogue choir. As the *schochet*, he had to ensure that the ritual slaughter required by Jewish food laws was inspected and carried out according to law. As well as fulfilling these roles in Jever, he also worked with the Jewish communities in neighbouring villages where the communities were too small to support their own teacher, cantor and *schochet*.

One of these communities was at Neustadtgödens, a small town about 20km south of Jever. It was a unique place with the peaceful co-existence of diverse denominations where religious tolerance was broadly accepted. There were Mennonite, Reformed, Lutheran, and Catholic churches – as well as the Jewish synagogue. The Jewish community had grown during the nineteenth century – to the extent that by the 1850s it included about a quarter of the town's inhabitants. The synagogue was built in the years shortly afterwards and attested to the self-confidence and prosperity of this growing community. However, during the 1870s, many people of working age left the area. They were discouraged from staying by the re-organisation of agriculture in the area, which adversely affected local jobs, and they were drawn to leave by the rapid expansion of the nearby city of Wilhelmshaven, which offered better employment opportunities. Most of those leaving found work in the Kriegsmarine shipyard in Wilhelmshaven, which was an armaments operation that favoured members of the National Socialist Party (the Nazis) as workers. For those staying, the largest landowner in the area, Count Wedel at Gödens Castle, was a convinced Nazi. Many men in the region signed up to the National Socialist Party at this time in order to have any livelihood at all. The resulting anti-Semitism was a poor atmosphere for Jews who wished to remain in Neustadtgödens.

In 1924, there were twenty-eight members of the Jewish community living in Neustadtgödens (about five per cent of the population) and Hermann visited from Jever to teach religious instruction to the four children who lived there. The community managed to struggle on for a few more years.

In the mid-1920s, the synagogue management committee in Jever comprised Hermann Gröschler, Joshua Weinstein and Julius Schwabe. A service was held on 29 April 1923 to honour the retiring committee and to introduce and welcome these new board members. Hermann Hartog was responsible for the musical aspects of the service – the introductory chants and the celebratory choral songs – as well as delivering a short address in which he wished for the community to continue to develop in peace and blessing. The local rabbi, Dr de Haas, came from Oldenburg to give a festive sermon.

All three members of the new committee came from the merchant class in Jever. Hermann Gröschler and his younger brother Julius ran a wholesale business in Albanistraβe, and Hermann was also heavily involved in politics and in the social and civic life of the town. Joshua Weinstein was a grain wholesaler and a representative of the manufacturers of milling products. He lived with his wife Anna and their young daughter Liselotte just around the corner from Henny and Hermann at Bahnhofstraβe 39. Julius Schwabe was one of three brothers – the others being August and Moses – all living in Jever. They came from a long-established Jever family and Julius was a successful shoe retailer there for many years. His father Isaak had been a master tailor and Julius's brother Moses continued the business and ran a small textile shop in Mönschwarf, while August was a watchmaker with his shop in Schlachtstraβe. A few years after the inauguration of the new committee, on 27 May 1926, Hermann Hartog also joined the team and took on the duties of secretary to the committee.

When Henny and Hermann married, the new Weimar Republic in Germany was in its infancy, struggling to gain credibility and to maintain law and order. Jever and the surrounding area became a stronghold of the *volkisch* (popularist) movement from the early 1920s, when a young student from Munich brought the programme of the Nazi Party to Oldenburg and founded a first 'Men for Hitler' group. The local population showed its strong support of the National Socialist Party from 1928, and electoral success was achieved in town halls throughout the region long before the party's national political success of 1933. Hitler had risen to power through the Nazi Party – an organisation he had forged after returning from the First World War when he and other patriotic Germans were outraged and humiliated by the harsh terms of the Treaty of Versailles. By 1921 (just three years after the Armistice), the party had a newspaper, an official flag, and a private army – the *Sturmabteilung* (SA). In 1923, the SA numbered 15,000 men and had access to hidden stores of weapons.

During the time of the Weimar Republic (1918 – 1933), German society was in transition in many ways. Throughout that period, life changed dramatically for everyone in the country, and the negative aspects of this change were very evident to Jewish communities in the area of north-west Germany that included Jever and Aurich.

The Reichstag elections of June 1920 brought to the region an increase in anti-democratic and anti-Semitic political activity. After these elections, right-wing political parties represented a worrying 42.7% of the seats.

It became increasingly possible for people to keep in touch with these developments by tuning into their radio sets and listening to the news. Henny and Hermann owned a radio set, for which they had to pay 2 Marks a month to receive transmissions. The medium was booming and wireless sets were being mass-produced for everyone – at the same time as inflation was soaring, and poverty and economic misery were becoming rampant. By 1925, radio in Germany had developed into a state broadcasting medium, and the numbers of people tuning in absolutely rocketed.

The political landscape was changing fast. Two years after Henny arrived in Jever, the first Hitler-flags – the 'swastikas' – appeared in the town. As early as the end of 1923, the miller Schönbohm hung swastika flags on his mill at the train station – only a short distance from where Henny and Hermann were living.

Changes were also noticeable in the print media. Jever's newspaper, the *Jeversches Wochenblatt,* had been a conservative paper that looked back to the days of Bismarck and was loyal to the monarchy, which generally suited its predominantly bourgeois readership. This all changed when a new editor-in-chief, the extremely right-wing Friedrich Lange, was appointed in 1919.

Advertisements in the newspaper now came mainly from predominantly right-wing organisations and parties, and the *Letters* page reflected this readership. The newspaper was highly influential in forming the opinions of local people, and during the time that Henny and Hermann lived in Jever, it moved unambiguously towards support for the National Socialists, particularly after the institution of the local National Socialist group which, on 1 March 1929, had the editor of the paper officially named as one of its founding members.

The paper's editorial team had hitherto maintained a convention of never reporting on trials or accusations against local businessmen, but on 1 February 1924 it broke this convention in order to comment on the minor misconduct of two Jewish cattle traders, Fritz Levy and Philipp Sternberg – both of whom were the Hartogs' neighbours. Non-Jewish businessmen had never before been singled out in this way, and this report showed a new willingness to treat Jewish residents differently.

Hermann Gröschler, as a liberal democrat and as the head of the Jewish community, was vocal in support of his community and against the emerging anti-Semitism in his town during the 1920s. He frequently wrote letters to explain his views to the editor of the *Jeversches Wochenblatt*. Nevertheless, the newspaper became increasingly supportive of the Nazi Party, which could always rely on it to publicise its propaganda.

On 20 November 1924, just before the December Reichstag elections, Henny gave birth to her first daughter Lore. Around this time, the Hartogs moved to Bahnhofstraße 35. Their new apartment was again on the first floor of the house, which was owned by Berlina de Taube. In 1926, Anna Weinstein came to live in the apartment downstairs after the death of her husband, the grain merchant Joshua Weinstein, who had been one of the leaders of the synagogue. Anna herself was the president of the Jewish Women's Association and lived in the apartment with her daughter Liselotte, who not only took over her father's grain business but also worked as the secretary to the Jewish Board in Jever until she emigrated to London in 1939.

Lore (and her sister Inge, who was born two years after Lore, on 4 December 1926) entered a Germany that was in some respects – despite the increasing local anti-Semitism – experiencing a period of general political calm and stability. In the relatively quiet period (politically) between 1925 and 1929, the Weimar Republic enjoyed an economic upswing, and this brought significant advantages to the inhabitants of Jever – such as connection to a local electricity and gas supply, a water supply and a new sports field.

However, the need to pay the huge reparations required after the end of the First World War destabilised the fragile Weimar economy and brought ruinous, runaway inflation and unemployment. In this north-west part of the country, the far-right political parties were also working hard and successfully to increase their membership and influence public opinion in a political atmosphere that had become one that could easily be exploited. The Nazis blamed the Weimar Republic's weakness on the influence of the Jews and the communists and claimed that they were trying to take over the country. Their leader, Adolf Hitler, envisaged history as a racial struggle in which the 'Aryan' race would win. He was, therefore, violently opposed to the Jews.

In the first twenty years of the new century, young Jews had increasingly been emigrating from even the big cities in search of a better future. By 1925, the Jewish population in Jever had shrunk to 118 people – just two per cent of the city's population – and from 1929, the anti-Semitic climate created by the influence and actions of the Nazis, as well as a depleted economy, encouraged even more Jews to leave.

Henny and Hermann were amongst those who decided to live elsewhere. There were several factors that motivated their move. The foremost was an attempt at economic security for their little family. As Jews left their localities and communities became smaller, those communities became financially unable to support a full-time teacher, and Hermann's livelihood in Jever was becoming increasingly at risk as numbers declined. In 1929, the Jewish teacher in the larger Jewish community in nearby Wilhelmshaven, Max Ruda, left Germany for a post in Zurich, Switzerland, and this vacancy was advertised on 3 May in *Der Israelit*. Hermann applied for the job and was successful, with his new job due to start on 1 October 1929. At the same time, Lore was approaching school age, and educational opportunities looked more promising in Wilhelmshaven, with its larger Jewish community, and a rapidly growing officer class of the German Navy resident in the city who demanded excellent schooling for their children. For Jewish parents, the best possible education had long been of particular importance, and both Henny and Hermann wanted the best they could find for their daughters.

It is also likely that the violence and anti-Semitism that the Jewish community was increasingly experiencing in Jever was a factor in their decision to move with their young children away from a small town – where everyone knew who they were – to live in the somewhat more anonymous milieu of the nearby city. In villages and small towns, Jews were more exposed to random attacks and stone-throwing – often from people they recognised – and to the blood-curdling and intimidating anti-Semitic songs from boys in the Hitler Youth as they passed a Jewish home. For many Jews, the political climate in the locality was a valid reason to turn away from Jever. The teachers at the local secondary school, the Mariengymnasium, included the Nazi group leader, another notorious Jew hater, a Nazi district leader, and other active Nazis were members of staff. Teachers were openly anti-Semitic and encouraged anti-Semitic activities from students.

However, the main reason for Hermann taking his new post was that the membership of the Jewish community in Jever had dwindled to the extent that there was no longer sufficient money there to support a teacher. When Hermann started working in Wilhelmshaven, he remained responsible for both communities and the Jewish Board in Jever contributed to his salary when they were able.

A few months before they moved house, there was sad family news from Berlin. On 23 June 1929, Henny's sister Cilly died suddenly and unexpectedly at her home there. She was 30 years old. Henny and Cilly's father, Adolf Scheuer, was still living with Cilly and her husband in Berlin, but after Cilly's death he decided to go to live with Henny and Hermann.

On 10 October 1929, Hermann and Henny, with their two young daughters and – a little later – Opa (Grandfather), moved to Wilhelmshaven and made their home together at Bismarckstraβe 107.

Henny and Hermann always viewed their time in Jever as the happiest time of their lives, where they created a home and started a family, and where they were part of a strong, vibrant and supportive Jewish community. They kept in close touch with their friends in Jever over the next few years, not least because Hermann returned to lead the singing and music in festival services in Jever and in the surrounding Jewish communities. The memories of the place – and, more importantly, the contact with its people – continued to nourish and support them even as they moved to live elsewhere.

CHAPTER 4

Wilhelmshaven: Family Life 1929–1938

Wilhelmshaven was a busy place: a port, an important town, a naval stronghold, a dynamic city that had grown rapidly in recent years. The apartment at Bismarckstraβe 107 the Hartogs entered on 10 October 1929 when they moved to their new home was in a large, solid building. The bustling street was popular with Jewish residents and was in an area where many Jewish traders kept their businesses. There were seventy merchants, eight butchers, and various other professions and traders gathered nearby around Gökerstraße/Bismarckplatz and Marktstraße/Wilhelmshavener Straße. Many local Jewish businesses were engaged in the cattle trade and in butchery.

The landlord of their new property was not Jewish – a fact that would become important a few years later. The apartment was spacious, with plenty of room for the heavy mahogany suites that the Hartogs took with them to furnish the bedrooms, dining room and drawing room. And these large rooms could easily accommodate the grandfather clock, piano and various desks and side tables that they also brought.

Six days after their arrival, Henny's father, Adolf Scheuer, joined them from Berlin. Lore and Inge's grandfather – Opa. He was then 65 years old and a fit and independent man who particularly enjoyed going swimming. While Henny was responsible for the running of the household, she also had help with domestic duties and childcare. A young woman, Alma, came to look after the children, who celebrated their fifth and third birthdays shortly after moving house, and other help was hired for general household cleaning and for some of the cooking. The Hartogs kept a kosher table, so food preparation and cooking were quite time-consuming activities.

Immediately opposite their house in Bismarckstraβe was a park. This large green space had been laid out and landscaped with sweeping ponds, walkways and decorative structures sixty years previously, in 1870. Since then, more trees and bushes had been added, and gates had been set in the perimeter. Two years before the Hartogs moved to Wilhelmshaven, the park had been designated a *Kurpark* (a spa park), suggesting that the city hoped and expected to become a popular North Sea spa town for affluent visitors from the middle classes.

A water tower was built in the park in 1910, just inside the line of trees alongside Bismarckstraβe, and this remains today as part of Wilhelmshaven's water supply. In 1928, the year before the Hartog family went to live in their new apartment, a gate had been constructed on the other side of the park. It was named after the German field marshal and president Paul von Hindenburg. On the side facing away from the park, the brick arched gateway – which is still incorporated into surrounding buildings – is engraved with the words *Hindenburg Tor* (Hindenburg gate), and in a niche above the words is a small bust of this soldier and politician.

The path between the water tower and the Hindenburg Tor formed part of Hermann's short route from his home to the synagogue. This pleasant walk to work took about ten minutes, and during the day the beautiful park was a popular space where Lore and Inge played with each other, and with either Henny or Alma.

During the late 1920s and early 1930s, there were about 100 Jewish people living in Wilhelmshaven, as well as another 100 in the neighbouring community of Rüstringen, and these Jewish families held a significant position in the city's economic life. The Council for the Jewish community in Wilhelmshaven included Julius Margoniner (who had been chairman from 1919 to 1925), Leo Bein and Jacob Strauß. Leo Bein was the chairman from 1925 to 1931, and then at the beginning of the 1930s the Wilhelmshaven-Rüstringen community had a joint board with Jonas Fränkel as chairman. When Hermann's predecessor Max Ruda was the teacher, he taught about twelve children at the Jewish school, and also held Jewish religious classes at the city's Kaiser Wilhelm High School. It can be assumed that Hermann took over these duties for as long as remained possible. Like Ruda, Hermann was the cantor and *schochet,* as well as the teacher.

Wilhelmshaven is a coastal town built in the mid-nineteenth century, when it became the base of the Prussian Navy on the North Sea. A Jewish community gathered there around 1870 and by the beginning of the twentieth century it was flourishing enough to create an independent synagogue and a religious school. A rented room at the Berliner Hof hotel had originally been used as a prayer room until the synagogue could be built. The community did not have its own rabbi, but it came under the rabbinate of the town of Emden, about 80km away – and not far from Aurich. The local community in Wilhelmshaven was at its most flourishing around 1929, when the Hartogs arrived.

At the beginning of the First World War, about 200 – 300 Jewish sailors who were serving with their country's navy were stationed in the town, and so the prayer room at the Berliner Hof was then no longer a large enough meeting place. A new synagogue in Wilhelmshaven, on the corner of Börsenstraβe and Parkstraße, was built in 1914/15 and consecrated on 7 September 1915. It was a square-ish building with a huge dome roof, but otherwise the exterior design followed a style that was common in Germany at the beginning of the twentieth century – although internally there were windows decorated with figural scenes, which was unusual. Because of the need to accommodate the Jewish sailors, and also to provide a place where they could take their oaths, there were 400 seats in the synagogue. Far more than the community otherwise needed. The synagogue also had a schoolroom for forty-two students, and a *mikveh* – a room with the ritual bath. The whole magnificent building cost 130,000 Marks and reflected the self-confidence of the Jewish community leaders and their expectations and hopes for the future.

A few years before the synagogue was built, a cemetery was created (in 1910) in Schortens-Heldmühle, about 14km from the centre of Wilhelmshaven on land that had been acquired by the merchant Magnus Kariel and transferred to the Jewish community. Prior to that, Jews in Wilhelmshaven buried their dead in the Jewish cemetery in Jever.

The wave of nationalist anti-Semitism in Germany after the humiliating defeat of the First World War in 1918 had been particularly noticeable among the residents of Wilhelmshaven which, as a military port, had seen its livelihood damaged by the Treaty of Versailles. The reparations required from Germany at the end of the First World War were mainly dependent on foreign loans, which were called in after the stock market crash of October 1929, which happened just about two weeks after Henny and Hermann moved into their new home. The resultant unemployment and bankruptcy, together with the earlier blaming of the Jews for the country's humiliation after defeat in war, were fertile grounds for the purposes of the National Socialist Party. During the election campaigns of the 1930s, the Nazi Party in Wilhelmshaven used anti-Semitic incitement for political ends, and the Reich presidential election of March 1932 was accompanied by physical violence when, for example, rioters shattered the windows of the Wallheimer garment piecework and tailoring store.

Max Ruda left Wilhelmshaven on 1 October 1929 and Hermann Hartog took his place. While working in Wilhelmshaven, Hermann also remained responsible for the Jewish communities in Jever and its neighbouring villages – as before – as well as teaching music to local children in order to augment his salary. Max Ruda remained a good friend to the Hartogs and others in the Wilhelmshaven Jewish community from his new home in Zurich, and he became a vital point of contact during the 1930s and the early 1940s as that community was forced to disperse.

After 1929, the Nazi movement grew stronger every year in the north-west of Germany – an area that included Wilhelmshaven, Jever and Aurich. The decline of liberal political power, thought and policy was a disastrous time for the Jews and by 1932, the Nazis were the largest political party in the Reichstag and had massive support from the people who lived in and around Wilhelmshaven.

On the evening of Monday 30 January 1933, as the Hartog family sat at their evening meal, they heard over the radio that Adolf Hitler had been appointed as Reich chancellor. Hermann quietly put down his cutlery, and paused for a moment before announcing to his family: 'Well, that is the end of people like us.'

That evening in Jever, Nazi Party members celebrated Hitler's success with a torch-lit procession around the town, accompanied by the noisy singing of anti-Semitic songs. This happened in cities, towns and villages throughout Germany as members of the Nazi Party led similar jubilant parades and assaulted their political rivals.

The appointment of Adolf Hitler as Reich chancellor on that day came as a shock to many European Jews. His politics were driven by racism and eugenics, and his goal was to strengthen the racially defined German people – the *Volk*. And in this view, the Jews were considered to be racially alien and hostile.

Almost immediately, Hitler began dismantling Germany's democratic institutions and imprisoning or murdering his chief opponents. A sense of shock, moderated slightly by the hope that the new government would not last much longer than its predecessors, dominated the early reaction of many German Jews to Hitler's political success. Almost all the opponents of the new government believed that it would soon be politics as usual under what most expected to be a short-lived Hitler government.

But no such mitigation occurred. From the very beginning of 1933, persecution of the Jews became an active Nazi policy with the immediate onset of violent state action. Control of radio broadcasting, which had been under the postmaster general's office, was transferred to the Ministry of Public Enlightenment and Propaganda, with Joseph Goebbels (Reich minister of propaganda) in charge. Radio programmes had to uphold the Nazi ideals of national pride, pride in Hitler and in the Aryan race. The medium was also used for anti-Semitic and militant purposes – and, to ensure that everyone received these messages, special cheap radios called 'People's Receivers' were manufactured.

During the period 1933 to 1939, the non-Jewish population in Jever and the surrounding area soared – sixteen per cent in six years. This was partly due to the building of an airfield in nearby Upjever (as part of the Nazi preparations for war). Three thousand workers were needed to build the airfield, which was to protect the Reich's largest armaments forge. Jever became a garrison town, senior officers moved in, and new office buildings were erected. There were also exciting plans to expand the residential areas of both Jever and Wilhelmshaven into the country area between them. The years of depression seemed to be a thing of the past, and the civic leaders had a new confidence and energy.

Meanwhile, continuing abuse against Jews in Germany triggered calls throughout March 1933 by Jewish leaders around the world for a boycott of German products. The Nazis responded with further bans and boycotts against Jewish doctors, shops, lawyers and stores. The violence of the following few months indicated that the new government was much more dangerous than any previous regime. And there was little support offered to the Jews from other communities.

'Sternly and concerned, the German Jews look into the future,' wrote Ludwig Holländer, the chairman of Germany's Central Jewish Committee. Many of the Jews in Wilhelmshaven – and elsewhere – could identify with Victor Klemperer, who wrote in his diary on 21 February 1933:

> *For something like three weeks now there is the depression of the reactionary government...It is a disgrace, which gets worse with every day that passes. And there's not a sound from anyone and everyone's keeping his head down.*

In Jever, from February 1933, Jewish livestock traders were forbidden access to the public cattle markets. This was a very severe blow to the many Jewish families who relied on this trade for their economic survival. Over the next five years, anti-Jewish boycott measures and propaganda drove Jews out of the cattle trade and forced retailers to sell up and leave.

A few weeks later, in March 1933, Stephen S. Wise, president of the American Jewish Congress, predicted: 'What is happening in Germany today may happen tomorrow in any other land on earth unless it is challenged and rebuked.'

In the same month, Hermann Gröschler was expelled from the city council in Jever and dismissed from all of his civic appointments. One of these was as a board member of the Municipal Savings Bank in Oldenburg, and when he was dismissed from the Board he and his family were also thrown out of the apartment where they lived in Jever, which was owned by the bank.

From 24 March 1933, Jewish ritual slaughter was forbidden by many local governments, so Jews were no longer able to follow their own dietary laws. A few days later, on 29 March, members of the SA (the paramilitary arm of the Nazis) surrounded the synagogue in Aurich and forced the Jews to hand over their ritual knives. These were publicly burned in the market square. On 30 May 1933, Jews were excluded from the slaughter guild in Aurich. Since the guild had been founded in 1911, Jews had always been represented on the Board and had made up most of its members. Acts of violence and breaches of the law against the Jews became commonplace. A degree of hopelessness began to take root amongst some of the Jewish community. And then came the boycotts, with all their aggression, their yellow placards, and guards placed outside shops. All of this happened within a few months of Adolf Hitler coming to power. And everything continued to escalate rapidly.

In the period before the Nazis came to power, the community of Wilhelmshaven-Rüstringen had included about 100 Jewish families, and for most of them their income had been linked to the commercial sector. There was a strong trading tradition in the town, and this alone ensured that they would be a prime target of anti-Semitic activity. Nazi preparations for the general boycott of Jewish commercial enterprises on 1 April 1933 were greatly assisted by the local newspaper which 'helpfully' published a detailed list of Jewish-owned businesses two days prior to the event.

The boycott of Jewish shops on 1 April 1933 – said to be usually one of the best business days of the year, on the Saturday before Easter – was organised by Nazis throughout the Reich. Placards were placed around towns: 'No German buys from a Jew!', 'All traitors!', and uniformed Nazis stationed themselves outside Jewish stores to discourage customers. In Aurich, the boycott began four days earlier than nationally. Members of the SA stood in front of Jewish shops from 28 March, and windows of Jewish shops and businesses were smashed overnight. This state-sponsored boycott of all Jewish professionals and all Jewish-owned businesses left no doubt as to who was especially marked for persecution.

This abuse didn't stop after the end of the April 1933 boycott. Local Nazis in Jever continued to work towards depriving Jews of their economic basis and persuading them to leave the city. There was a noticeable ageing of the local Jewish community as family firms declined under Nazi pressure and young people left the city to try and find work elsewhere. On 1 October 1934, eighteen months later, Nazis displayed banners at the exits of the city:

> *Whoever buys from the Jews is our enemy!*

Anti-Semitic posters were displayed:

> *Don't buy in Jewish shops!*
>
> *The Jews are our misfortune!*

The commercial boycott was not an economic success everywhere. In some areas it generally lacked public enthusiasm, and many Germans found it inconvenient or financially foolish. Nevertheless, it proved to be a psychological success, creating intense fear amongst Jews. The laws that were passed in the same month (April 1933) also limited Jewish participation in the economy. Consequently, unemployment rose amongst the Jews. Fear of the future, continuing intimidation, and escalating anti-Semitism led many Jewish business owners and workers in Wilhelmshaven to try and leave Germany during 1933 and 1934. Until they could do so, many found themselves in poverty. During the winter of 1935/36, the Jewish Winter Relief Agency was helping about twenty per cent of the Jewish population, while others lived as best they could from the proceeds of the sale of their businesses.

A few days after the boycott, the passing of the Civil Service Law on 7 April 1933 shattered any lingering confidence in the fundamental civil rights of German Jews. Jewish legal rights were largely revoked by this law, and it was clear that the era of emancipation for Jews had come to an end. They were now both indirectly and directly dissuaded or banned from privileged and upper-level positions reserved for Aryan Germans, and they were forced to work at more menial positions. In north-west Germany, the Nazis' demolition of democracy was actively encouraged by the unconditional support of the party by significant people in senior positions in education, the protestant church, civic administration, businesses and the media.

In Jever, when Hermann Gröschler was removed from his position at the bank where he worked, and also from his apartment above the bank's building in Albanistraβe, he and his wife, Änne, moved with their children to Blaue Straβe 1, not far from the synagogue.

A national holiday was declared for 1 May 1933 and large rallies were held by the National Socialists throughout the north-west peninsular, after which those people who did not support the Nazis – Social Democrats, communists, trade unionists, etc. – were attacked and arrested, as were other groups close to the opposition parties. It was clear that opposition and dissent would not be tolerated by the new regime. It had been in power for just three months.

In Aurich, Oskar Hartog was the deputy head of the butchers' guild, but after the Nazification of all organisations from 1933, he could no longer hold that office. Members of the guild were informed almost overnight that a new committee would be formed, in which Jewish butchers would no longer be represented or hold public positions. Oskar Hartog bravely asked at one of the next guild meetings in the middle of 1933 if such an action was in accordance with the regulations of the guild.

A further dispute in the Aurich guild assembly concerned the dates of their meetings. Previously, out of consideration for the Jewish members, meetings had never been held on a Friday (the beginning of the Sabbath), but those members who now supported National Socialism bypassed this decision, and also elected new members. Oskar Hartog protested against this to the town council, and there were those who agreed with him. But his protest brought no resolution. However, there were some Christian customers, in spite of all the threats and attempts to deter them from buying from Jews, who continued to buy from the Hartogs for some time. Indeed, in 1934 a police report complained that Butcher Hartog had lost hardly any customers – and, therefore, asked for him to be put into custody.

During the Weimar period (1918 – 1933), Jews in Aurich co-existed with most of the town's population with few problems. But the National Socialists stirred up agitation against the Jews. Most of the anti-Semitic propaganda in Aurich was instigated and led by the protestant pastor Heinrich Meyer. In 1933, the Jewish community in Aurich had had about 400 members – about 6.5% of the city's population. By the end of 1936, not many Jews had left Aurich, and there were still fifty-four students registered at the school in 1937. But this began to change during the autumn of 1937 when Jews were forced to 'Aryanise' their businesses.

The growing persecution of Jews everywhere by the Nazis led to the creation of various Jewish organisations to give help to their communities. The *Reichsvertretung der Deutschen Juden* (the Reich Representation of German Jews) was a Jewish umbrella organisation founded on 17 September 1933 to co-ordinate and represent the activities of Jewish political and religious groups. It had its main office in Berlin but provided a much wider area with legal defence against the escalating persecution. The Berlin rabbi Leo Baeck was elected president of the *Reichsvertretung* and Otto Hirsch was its chairman. The organisation provided administrative information for Jews, and it established central welfare organisations, occupational retraining for dismissed officials, and preparation for emigration. It also supported those schools and institutions, from elementary to higher education, that could be kept open for Jewish students and pupils.

At nine o'clock on the morning of 2 August 1934, the president of Germany, Paul von Hindenburg, died. One hour later it was announced that the offices of the president and the chancellor were now united in Adolf Hitler, who took control as 'Führer'. This declaration, and a government with no opposition parties, subsequently allowed Hitler total control of law-making – and all other decisions. The army also swore an oath of loyalty personally to Hitler, giving him power over the military.

One month later, on 2 September 1934, Hermann Hartog celebrated his jubilee in Jever – twenty-five years since he had first arrived in the town in 1909 as teacher and cantor to a Jewish community of about 200 people. However, by the time of his jubilee service, the Jewish community in Jever had been reduced to less than half that number – ninety-eight people.

A different 'celebratory' service was held eighteen months later, on 15 March 1936, when the Jewish community in Neustadtgödens held its final service, attended by the rabbi of the province, Samuel Blum from Emden. The Jews in Neustadtgödens had previously had strong links with the Jever community for many years. Their synagogue had recently been issued with a closure order by the Nazi authorities, who alleged disrepair. Actually, the building and roof later proved to be stable, but with a reduced community of only a few members by 1936, there was no income for maintenance. In 1924, Jews in Neustadtgödens numbered twenty-eight (with Hermann teaching the four Jewish children there), but by 1933 the entire community had been reduced to twelve members. Liquidation of the Jewish community through emigration had become the goal of the German government by the autumn of 1936, and here it had achieved an early success.

For this final service, Jews visited from far and wide, and the occasion was reported in *Der Israelit*. There are recorded memories of the event from those who knew Rabbi Samuel Blum, and these people remembered it as a glorious and celebratory service – albeit a farewell. The synagogue choir from Jever attended under the direction of Hermann Hartog, and the soloist from Jever, Rudolf Gutentag, sang. For his sermon, Dr Blum chose a verse from Psalm 43 as his text:

> *What are you grieving for, my soul?*
> *And why are you so restless within me?*
> *I shall yet praise him who is my health and my God.*

The synagogue was packed and music and singing filled the building. Two years later, in June 1938, the synagogue was sold to a non-Jewish carpenter from Wilhelmshaven for a reputed 2,500 Reichsmarks.

On 15 September 1935, the 'Nuremberg Laws' were enacted at a special meeting convened during the Nazi Party's annual rally at Nuremberg. They were anti-Semitic and racist laws. The 'Law for the Protection of German Blood and German Honour' forbade marriages and extramarital intercourse between Jews and Germans, as well as the employment of German females under the age of 45 in Jewish households. The 'Reich Citizenship Law' declared that only those people of German or related blood were eligible to be Reich citizens. All others were classed as state subjects without citizenship rights.

The Nuremberg Laws shocked all Jews, and especially the leaders of the *Centralverein deutscher Staatsbürger jüdischen Glaubens* (the Central Association of German Citizens of Jewish Faith), which was now forced to rename itself *Jüdischer Centralverein* (Central Jewish Association) as Jews had ceased to be *Staatsbürger* (citizens). The laws spelt the end of any hope of a civilised life for Jews in Germany. So the association turned to supporting emigration either to Palestine or to other overseas destinations, in an effort to send 100,000 younger Jews out of the country over the next five years.

Throughout the early 1930s, 'Jew-baiting' in the region became more extreme and anti-Jewish sentiment within the local populations never lessened. Jewish children, including Henny and Hermann's daughters, experienced constant anti-Semitic incidents wherever they went, even at school and in the playgrounds.

Between 24 April 1935 and 29 January 1937, Lore (when she was between 10 and 12 years old) attended the Kaiserin Viktoria Luise School in Wilhelmshaven. One of her friends, Gertrud, frequently visited the Hartog family home and remembered Lore's grandfather being there. Gertrud was sometimes in the house when the Friday evening (Sabbath) celebrations took place, and she remembered that Hermann would secretly slip her some of the kosher food that had been prepared. Gertrud was not Jewish and, like many other young girls, had joined the BDM – the *Bund Deutscher Mädel* (the League of German Girls) – the female version of the Hitler Youth. One day, when Gertrud was out on the street, marching with her cohort, Lore saw her and waved cheerfully. Gertrud was appalled, and afterwards said to her: 'Do you not know that you must not do that?'

One of the reasons for Henny and Hermann's move from Jever to Wilhelmshaven had very probably been the opportunity for better education for their daughters. Jewish families placed great importance on the value of education for their children. The (non-Jewish) senior naval officers who lived in the same upper-class area of town as the Hartogs also expected a superior education for their children, and there were good schools available nearby. However, mounting restrictions on all aspects of life for Jews increasingly reduced the educational opportunities for Jewish children. Since April 1933, the proportion of Jewish students enrolled in state schools had been severely restricted, and those Jews who had the financial means looked elsewhere for educational possibilities for their children.

Henny and Hermann decided to try to find a way to send Lore to school in England. Probably responding to an advertisement in the English Jewish newspaper, *Jewish Chronicle*, they got in touch with a Mr and Mrs S.M. Harris (Samuel and Annie) in Westcliff-on-Sea, near Southend in Essex. The Harrises belonged to a similarly orthodox Jewish community as the Hartogs, and since 1929 they had advertised to give accommodation to youngsters 'for long or short periods', and to oversee their education, 'under personal supervision'.

The community around the synagogue in Westcliff-on-Sea had grown fast during the first years of the twentieth century, and in 1930 numbered about 300 families. There was a kosher restaurant in the town, and several Jews owned boarding and guest houses that catered for those Jews looking for a healthy stay by the sea.

At the end of January 1937, Gertrud bought Lore's school books from her, and the following month Lore left Germany to live with the Harrises and to attend school in Westcliff-on-Sea, although she returned home for a few weeks during the school summer holidays later that year, and possibly the following summer. Before Lore left Wilhelmshaven, Henny sewed several items of the family jewellery into her underwear so that she could take some valuables with her but would hopefully avoid detection at customs posts. It was becoming increasingly obvious to Henny and Hermann that a political crisis was brewing and that Lore might need extra resources. She was 12 years old.

The Nuremberg Laws of September 1935 had possibly encouraged Henny and Hermann to take action to send Lore away to a place of safety where she could receive a good education. These laws had revoked Jewish legal equality and declared Jews to be second-class state members, compared with German Reich citizens. Jews had more or less been declared foreigners in their own country. There had already been widespread and increased anti-Semitic activity during the summer of 1935, and this was particularly severe in Wilhelmshaven. As a result, there was a resurgence of Jewish emigration, so that by 1936 there were only 120 Jews living in Wilhelmshaven-Rüstringen – less than two-thirds of the Jewish population of June 1933.

When the Nazis came to power in Germany in 1933, Europe was still facing a refugee problem that it had not known how to handle since 1918, and that had been exacerbated by the Depression. Rampant unemployment in western Europe and in America meant that no one wanted immigrants who would take away jobs or add to the welfare registers. The first wave of emigration from Germany in the early 1930s was defined by the threat of arrest by the Nazis and by the prospect of financial destitution. These emigrants were mostly men who left seeking safety, and who hoped to secure a place for their families. They were generally people from the cities – professional people, politicians, intellectuals, artists, and businessmen who had international contacts who helped them to leave. Most of them expected their asylum to be temporary until the madness passed. They assumed that the violence would pass, and they went away until such time as 'normality' would be restored.

After 1933, expectations changed. Planned emigration overtook panicked flight. Jews looked to sell their property and ship their possessions, and they looked for an asylum that offered them the prospect of earning a living.

In 1936, Jews in Germany were banned from all professional jobs, effectively preventing them from exerting any influence in education, politics, higher education or industry. Jews throughout the country struggled with the dilemma of whether to stay or leave their homeland. For Hermann, who had few transferable skills within his line of work, limited fluency in other languages, and – most importantly – still held a deep commitment to his family and community, it was not easy to consider emigrating. However, as the months passed, he and Henny began communicating with her uncle Max Bodenheimer in Chicago to try to arrange visas for themselves, Lore and Inge to emigrate to the USA.

Jewish friends and colleagues were all struggling with the same dilemma regarding emigration, and it was made even more real for the Hartogs later in 1937 when Hermann travelled to Frankfurt am Main to officiate at the marriage on 5 August of Arthur Bodenheimer (Henny's cousin) and Sitta Siesel at the Pension Rosiner. Less than a year later, on 16 June 1938, Arthur and Sitta sailed from Hamburg, arriving on 24 June in New York, where they went through immigration control at Ellis Island.

Throughout almost six years of Nazi rule after January 1933, Jewish daily life held constant deprivations and humiliations. Jewish people experienced an incremental worsening of their situation and the need to keep adjusting to new circumstances. They were forever navigating a way through the economic hardships, the increasing social isolation and physical threats in order to preserve a sense of sanity and normality in their lives. It was primarily the women within the Jewish communities who had to hold the tension between the normal activities of daily life and the increasingly abnormal situation in which they and their families found themselves.

On 14 April 1937, a new building was opened in Wilhelmshaven, at the address Am Rathausplatz 4/6. It was an employment office, but it was not generally known that the Secret State Police (the Gestapo) had premises there, and that in addition to administrative rooms in this particular building, the Gestapo had several prison rooms in other buildings in Wilhelmshaven. The Gestapo had been created by Hermann Göring in 1933 by amalgamating several different police forces and it became a very powerful presence with a jurisdiction throughout the entire country. One of the main tasks of the Gestapo was harassment of the Jews.

Jewish children needed to continue with their education, even though they faced frequent anti-Semitic behaviour at a personal level from other children and teachers in their schools, as well as restrictions on educational choice at an official level. In Jever, Walter Gröschler and Gert Sternberg (both about 10 years old) were refused admission to the local secondary school in 1933, and Gert's younger brother Rolf (who was just three months older than Inge) experienced his class teacher (who was Hans Förster, also the leader of the local Hitler Youth) once saying to the other children, 'No one touches the filthy Jew,' when they wanted to help Rolf. In 1938, Rolf was expelled from the elementary school on Schlosserplatz in Jever – where Hermann had once taught – and the Sternberg family left Jever to try to emigrate from Bremen. In Wilhelmshaven, Inge and her school friends faced constant taunts, harassment and vicious behaviour from non-Jewish schoolchildren. Even before they were banned from attending the general schools, Jewish children were often banned from events taking place at their schools. Parents dealt with their children's problems at school on a daily basis, and usually lost their battles with the educational establishment.

At the same time, religious and cultural life flourished within the increasingly isolated Jewish communities as Jews struggled to maintain their dignity and their daily survival. In early 1938, the young rabbi in Oldenburg, Leo Trepp, obtained permission to open a Jewish school in a synagogue in Oldenburg for Jewish children who were being persecuted and who were missing out on their education. These children were legally required to go to school, but they had not been allowed to attend the general schools from 1937, so at least here they could have some education and their parents would not be abused for failing to send them to school. Trepp was given permission to form his school along with some funding for school supplies and desks, as well as for the rent for his school space. Inge became one of the pupils at the school in Oldenburg, together with her friends Inge Cohen and Hilde ter Berg. Leo Trepp was just 23 years old when he became the rabbi in Oldenburg in 1936 and he recognised that his dual role included helping the Jewish community not to fragment and also helping those who wished to emigrate.

During the first five years or so of Nazi rule, Jewish women were far less likely to be physically abused, attacked and arrested than Jewish men. It was, therefore, often the women who dealt with school teachers, shopped from stores displaying 'Jews not wanted' signs, organised administrative affairs with local bureaucrats, landlords and the police, went from office to office to collect the necessary emigration papers and pay the taxes, and personally faced the anti-Semitism that had become normalised in these transactions.

Meanwhile, they also kept their households running. After the passing of the Nuremberg Laws, they did so with less paid domestic help as Jews were no longer allowed to employ domestic help from non-Jews under 45 years of age. In the Hartog home, Hermann and Adolf began to help with the cooking. The men were not well-prepared or experienced in this role and Hermann several years later reminisced in a letter to Inge about the time he spoilt their food: 'I can cook better now than I could before in Wilhelmshaven. Dear Inge, do you remember how I left the pea soup to burn? Nowadays I pay more attention.'

It is perhaps not difficult to imagine the bookish Hermann burning the soup.

Within just a few years of taking power, the Nazis had very successfully deepened the gap between Jews and non-Jews in Germany. The belief that Jews were another race was generally widespread by the mid-1930s and many Jews found themselves increasingly rejected by their non-Jewish friends and forced to turn to, and rely on, each other for solace and comfort as they continued to keep the Jewish laws and celebrate Jewish holy days. Those who felt that emigration was the only way forward shared their knowledge and experiences of the process and procedures, and many spent time learning a language that could be useful, and even a trade or a livelihood that might help them to survive the move.

But increasingly there were greater barriers to emigration. Countries restricted immigration as the worldwide economic depression of the 1930s deepened. In July 1938, delegates from thirty-two nations attended a conference at Evian, and they all regretted that they could not take any more Jews.

It was not only difficult to gain entry into a country, it was also difficult to get out of Germany. The *Reichsfluchtsteuer* (Reich Flight Tax) was a stringent tax to limit the amount of currency and property that Jews could take out of the country with them. In 1937, when Henny's cousin, Arthur Bodenheimer, emigrated from Frankfurt to America, his father, Louis Bodenheimer, paid 5,000 Reichsmarks in *Reichsfluchtsteuer*. In order to find the money to do this, he had to sell one of his properties. And then, on 24 January 1938, Louis Bodenheimer was forced to close his business. For many others, the tax was such a prohibitive restriction that it actually made emigration impossible.

Raiding the assets of Jewish people was partly an action by the state to ward off the threat of bankruptcy as the country re-armed. However, those Jews who found the taxes and financial limitations for emigration impossible were inevitably left behind in Germany, so the state was still left with Jews who were penniless – the poor, the elderly, the single, and even those amongst the wealthy whose savings had already been confiscated in some way or another or had been spent enabling a younger relative to flee.

The change in the way that Jewish people were perceived and treated in the north-west region of Germany is strikingly illustrated by the life stories of two brothers who lived in Jever – August and Moses Schwabe. Their other brother Julius had been one of the three leaders of the Jever synagogue during the late 1920s and early 1930s, and August and Moses had both been leading members of the Jewish community there.

August – watchmaker, poet, and lottery-collector – died in Jever at the age of 85 on 29 March 1932. He was given an honourable obituary in the *Jeversches Wochenblatt,* where he was described as a 'quiet, pleasant person' who was welcome 'in all circles of the citizenry' – at a time when aggressive anti-Semitic attitudes were strong in the locality.

Moses was ten years younger than August and his death ten years after his brother's (in 1942) was not recorded in their home town. Forced to give up the family business of shoe-making that he had continued after his father, Moses was 'evacuated' from Jever by the Nazis, obliged to live in a 'Jew house' when he arrived in Dortmund, and then deported to Riga, where he died in January 1942. Within the space of a few years, the situation had changed so dramatically for Jewish people – from integration into bourgeois society to racist exclusion and murder.

Julius Schwabe and his wife Henny moved from Jever to Hamburg in April 1937 and Julius was able to set up a business trading in office supplies. But his business was liquidated in 1938 when all Jewish businesses had to be either 'Aryanised' or liquidated.

During 1938, Hitler began to enact his strategy of extending the country's national boundaries. From the beginning of that year, the Nazis seemed to feel more confident that their regime was secure, the economy was strong, and they could, therefore, pursue even more ambitious goals.

On 13 March 1938, Austria was annexed to Germany and on that day the German Army marched triumphantly into Vienna. Popular euphoria for Hitler, National Socialism, and unification with Germany brought an immediate wave of ferocious hatred for and violence against Jews. There were about 185,000 Jews living in Austria, and this display of Germany's power brought even more terror and disorientation to their communities, while politicians in France and England seemed unable or unwilling to confront Germany's increasing power.

As the American journalist Dorothy Thompson recognised in an article a few weeks later, the idea that anti-Semitic persecution in either Germany or Austria could remain merely a domestic problem would have to be abandoned. This was now a 'world problem' and would require concerted international efforts to address it.

A month later, the Christian festival of Easter fell on Sunday 17 April, and coincided with the Jewish festival of Pesach (Passover), which was celebrated between 15 and 23 April. Lore sent Passover greetings from England to the Aunts Cohn in Jever, who responded warmly to her on a postcard showing a picture of the town and its castle. They'd had a 'beautiful Easter' and asked after Lore and her younger friend, Hans Weinstein, who had emigrated from Jever to England with his parents in November 1937.

During the 1930s, German Jews needed to turn ever more frequently to the aid services of their communities. Thirty years earlier, they had set up the *Hilfsverein der deutschen Juden* (The Aid Society for German Jews) with its main office in Berlin, partly to help Jews in Eastern Europe who were fleeing westwards. In the intervening years, the society had lost some impact within the community, but during the 1930s it once again became an important advisory and supporting service – this time for Jews wanting to emigrate from Nazi Germany. Energy and resources were especially directed at helping young people to escape, and by 1939, eighty-three per cent of Jews under the age of 24 had been able to do so.

Throughout 1938, Jews in Germany were subjected to increasingly severe laws that gradually stripped them of their German nationality – to the extent that the aid society was forced to change its name to *Hilfsverein der Juden in Deutschland* (The Aid Society for Jews in Germany), since there were no longer deemed to be any 'German Jews'. This stripping of nationality alarmed politicians in other countries, who envisaged hordes of migrants trying to find a place of refuge elsewhere. In May 1938, new visa regulations for anyone with a German or Austrian passport came into effect in Britain to discourage them from seeking even temporary asylum. There was a real fear, relayed from Whitehall to consuls and passport officers, that refugees would apply to enter Britain on a temporary visa and then try to remain indefinitely.

By the summer of 1938, Jewish families in Germany were required to complete forms for an inventory of 'Assets of Jews'. To many of them, there seemed little point to this exercise as they no longer had any assets to declare. But they had long been accustomed to living without any rights, and to being ritually humiliated – and so they filled in the forms. By August 1938, it was clear to most of them that political change in Germany was unlikely and also that politicians in other countries were equally unlikely to intervene. Tension increased amongst the Jews, and everywhere there was fear of war.

But trying to escape was not for the faint-hearted. If you wanted to be interviewed by the US consulate, and present your paperwork for emigration, you needed to register to do so – and you also needed to join the waiting list. By 1938, you could expect to wait two years for a visa. In the meantime, there were documents – many of them – that you needed to collect. To obtain these, you had to go to many different government offices, and you had to be prepared to pay often quite hefty fees to acquire these documents. Many documents also had an expiry date, so would often need to be renewed more than once. The document list included – amongst others – a birth certificate, at least one tax document, medical clearance, a police certificate, and a military discharge (if appropriate).

By mid-October 1938, Henny had managed to finalise the emigration papers for Lore and Inge and on 14 October these were registered in Hamburg with the numbers 'Hamburg 8635 and 8636'. It is unclear whether or not papers were registered for Hermann and herself at the same time, but it is likely. Henny had been working hard at this for some time, and attempting to obtain an affidavit from her uncle, Max Bodenheimer, who had been living in America since 1890.

In most of their letters, Henny and Hermann – and their friends – pleaded with Lore to find a way for them to emigrate to England as soon as possible. Kurt de Taube, a member of the Board of the Jewish community in Wilhelmshaven, was visiting Hermann one day in 1938, and wrote this to Lore (in English):

> *Your father is just handing me this writing paper and asks me to write you some lines. Here it goes. How do you do, dear Lore? I hope rather good. Here all is quite the same. We all are waiting for news from you...Perhaps you have found there in the meantime a friend who will let us come. My best regards to him and you.*

Lore was 13 years old.

In Aurich, in September 1938, Dr Manfred Louis Hoffmann had his licence to practice medicine revoked. He was a Jewish doctor who lived at Wallstraβe 20 – a few doors away from the Hartogs – with his wife, Rosi. By then, he had already lost many of his non-Jewish patients who no longer came to see him for fear of being denounced. To see his Jewish patients, he often had to make long journeys into the surrounding countryside.

At the end of that month, on 30 September 1938, German troops invaded Czechoslovakia and Hitler followed them in triumph.

Yom Kippur, the holiest day of the year for Jews, began at sundown four days later, on Tuesday 4 October 1938, and lasted until nightfall the following day. There was fasting, and long prayer services were held, led by Hermann Hartog in Jever as the Jewish community there celebrated this festival of repentance and atonement. Afterwards, the Aunts Cohn sent another postcard to Lore – this time showing a picture of the Jever railway station and pleasant square outside it, that had once been so near Lore's home in Bahnhofstraβe. They wrote:

> *Dear Lore, we thank you warmly for the card for the feast days, and we were really happy that your dear Dad held the service here. It was very festive and beautiful again.*

By then, there were only about fifty Jews living in Jever. Dwindling numbers, the advanced age of many in the remaining community, and the deteriorating financial situation of the Jews and their synagogue had meant not only that they were unable to support their own teacher, but also that they could now no longer continue to maintain the synagogue building. Repeated anti-Semitic attacks over recent years had left broken windows in the synagogue that the small community was unable to mend or replace.

Even before it was burned down in 1938, the synagogue in Jever was a frequent target of anti-Semitic attacks, which the police never solved – if they investigated at all. In addition to swastika graffiti, 'unknown perpetrators' smashed window panes. In 1935, Martin Folkerts, who had been a member of the National Socialist Party since 1929, became the mayor of Jever. The following year he wrote to Hermann Gröschler about the unsightly state of the synagogue, noting the smashed window panes that had been covered in wood and cardboard, and regretting that the building had become an eyesore in the otherwise beautiful city. He had called on the Jewish community to restore the synagogue windows to a proper condition as soon as possible. The Jewish community had always been forced to make repairs at its own expense, thereby further impoverishing itself.

So, while the Yom Kippur service was no doubt a beautiful occasion for those who celebrated, the building itself was probably less beautiful than on previous occasions. It was, however, possibly the last service to be held in the synagogue as shocking events a few weeks later would almost totally destroy this once glorious building.

CHAPTER 5

The Hour of the Women: November 1938

Just four weeks after these celebrations for Yom Kippur, on the night of Wednesday 9 and Thursday 10 November 1938, Nazi activists set light to the synagogue in Jever. During the following day, the SA seized all Jewish dwellings and commercial buildings – often with violence and looting. Meanwhile, fourteen Jewish men aged between 16 and 70 were taken from Jever to the concentration camp at Sachsenhausen, near Berlin. (Only the 81-year-old Moses Schwabe was allowed home.) There they joined other Jewish men from the surrounding Oldenburg area.

In the evening, members of the SA and the Hitler Youth, together with other civilians, looted all the Jewish property in Jever – causing great distress to the women and children who remained.

One of the men taken to Sachsenhausen from Jever was Hermann Gröschler who, as the leader of the synagogue community, felt enormous responsibility for his members. That night, he and his wife Änne were woken by the telephone ringing at about 2.30 a.m.

'The synagogue is on fire!'

They lived quite near to the synagogue and from their apartment in Blaue Straβe, Hermann and Änne could see the flames from where they stood in their upstairs bedroom window. They watched as the brightness lit up the sky and crowds gathered in the streets. Hermann wanted to find out what was going on and what had caused the fire. He could not be dissuaded. He ran outside, half-dressed. Änne watched from the window as shortly afterwards an SA man in uniform tapped him on the shoulder, and both men disappeared from view. Her husband did not return, and a friend told her that he had been arrested. The women then discovered that all the Jewish men had been arrested and taken to the town prison.

It was a chaotic night.

Later that same night, members of the SA and the Hitler Youth arrived at the Gröschler home. They forced entry and stamped noisily up the stairs to the apartment where Änne was in bed. Feeling threatened, she stood by and watched as they took her fine linen, which had been carefully wrapped and laid out in a cupboard, helped themselves to her husband's cigars (and smoked them in front of her), and stole valuable items – works of art, items of silver, Hermann's suits, and money that she had saved. All the while the men were arrogant and offensive towards her.

When they had gone, the policeman on watch outside the house ordered her to dress and accompany him to the prison. He stood guard over her while she dressed, the flat was locked behind her, and she walked the short distance with him. At the prison, she encountered the other women from the Jewish community in Jever.

They were guarded constantly by women prison warders, even when going to the toilet, and although they were offered some coffee and bread, most of the women were too distraught to eat anything. After several hours, they were gradually allowed back to their homes, which most of them found had been ransacked. Their menfolk did not return home.

During the next day, the women got word from the men that they were to be moved, and some of them asked for items of clothing and toiletries to be brought quickly to the prison. The women rushed to gather a few things together and ran with them through the streets to the prison, where they found the men herded together outside waiting for transport to take them elsewhere. They were taken with other Jewish men from neighbouring towns and villages in the area to Sachsenhausen concentration camp, where they remained for several weeks.

On 11 November, *the Jeversches Wochenblatt* reported that the torching of the synagogue was a result of the 'justified indignation of the population over the assassination of von Rath'. (See below.) It claimed that 'all measures were taken, in the best discipline' and congratulated the SA and the Hitler Youth for 'their commitment' and for carrying out 'the necessary surveillance and arrests':

> *Voluntarily and with commendable sacrifice, everyone fulfilled their tasks, which had proved to be absolutely necessary. To the just retaliation of the outrageous machinations of internationally filthy Judaism. In this context, it was also necessary to take the Jews of Jever into protective custody.*

Ten days later, on 22 November, the *Jeversches Wochenblatt* printed another opinion:

> *Every down-to-earth inhabitant has always turned away with distaste from the disgusting, and internally and externally alien and repulsive activities, of the Jews...Perhaps it won't be long before the last Jew has finally turned his back on our homeland. Then a 250-year-old inglorious "guest performance" will have finally come to an end.*

For Hermann Gröschler, the main reason he had remained in Jever was that he did not want to let the local Jewish community down, even though by 1938 there were only about fifty Jewish people living there. This was a sentiment shared by many of the leaders of Jewish communities throughout Germany and partly explains their reluctance to leave Germany, when it might have personally served them well to do so. Once released from Sachsenhausen, having signed the required agreement to leave Germany, these community leaders remained conflicted. It was not easy for them to see when was the right time to leave their country, and it was even less easy to know how they might survive in a country where they had no language skills and little to offer professionally.

Similar events to those in Jever took place all over Germany. The ninth of November had for several years been an important date for the National Socialist Party as on that evening they celebrated the failed Hitler *putsch* (rebellion) of 1923. So, in 1938, members and officials of the party were already in uniform and celebrating, mainly with food and drink. During their celebrations, word came through that the German diplomat Ernst von Rath had died in Paris after an assassination attempt on him by a young Polish Jew, Herschel Grünspan. The news was an immediate excuse for Nazis throughout Germany to enact retaliation, revenge and aggression against the entire Jewish population, and to seize their property and assets. Local Nazi leaders were instructed to burn down all synagogues and to make the ensuing mayhem appear to be the result of 'popular anger'.

In Jever, 44-year-old Hans Flügel, district leader of the National Socialists in the area, led the attack on the synagogue. Even knowing that the punishment for 'arson endangering human beings' was twelve years in prison, he set in train the orders that he received from his superior, the Nazi leader in Oldenburg. He changed out of his Nazi uniform that he had been wearing for the evening's *putsch* celebrations and, wearing plain clothes, drove from neighbouring Varel to Jever to give orders to the Nazis there – Fritz Husmann, Theodor Wilken, and Hans Förster. Before he left Varel to go to Jever, he reported the planned arson to the police, and also contacted the local fire services. The fire brigade was informed that it was required to protect the neighbouring houses, not the synagogue. The Nazi mayor of Jever, Martin Folkerts, was informed of the night's planned attack.

Paul Liebenow joined in the action. He was the head of the municipal waste collection point, which had previously been confiscated from the Gröschler family's business interests, and he also seems to have managed to get hold of the synagogue keys. Well after midnight, the men gathered together waste oil, petrol and waste paper from the municipal waste collection point, and from Husmann's garage drove it to the synagogue in Husmann's car and attempted to get into the building. This proved more difficult than expected as the synagogue was kept well-secured after previous break-in attempts and they had difficulties with the keys. Eventually, with the use of tools, the men broke in through the vestibule leading to the women's gallery and the schoolroom. Local wisdom has always asserted that the synagogue was looted before it was burned, and no artefacts and Jewish religious treasures have ever since come to light. Presumably unbeknown to the intruders, Rosalie Grünberg, who was 60 years old, was living in the schoolroom (since it could no longer be used for its original purpose) and had barricaded herself in. She was terrified when, in the middle of the night, she heard people breaking in nearby, and she screamed for help. At the last minute, as the other men prepared to torch the building, Liebenow managed to drag her forcibly by her hair through a window.

The fire took hold quickly and flames soon engulfed the synagogue. At about three o'clock in the morning, the fire brigade intervened to protect the neighbouring buildings. Just a few metres away, three elderly women – the Aunts Cohn – living in the synagogue community centre, woke to flames, heat and noisy chaos. Later that night, all three of them (aged 76, 69 and 66) were taken into custody with the other Jewish women.

Towards morning, the perpetrators of the arson went home, changed back into their Nazi uniforms, and returned to inspect the scene of the fire. Some of them were also involved in taking Jewish people into custody, which began at about five o'clock in the morning, and in plundering their homes. The following evening there were riots in the city as Jewish homes were ransacked and the Nazis and their supporting mob created mayhem on the streets.

There were similar actions, arson and brutalities wherever there were Jewish communities in Germany. The Sternberg family from Jever had moved to Bremen by November 1938, in their efforts to emigrate. When the SA stormed their apartment to arrest Philipp Sternberg, 12-year-old Rolf opened the door to them and announced that his father was at the cinema. The young boy was threatened with death.

Der Israelit reported that in Wilhelmshaven:

> *...at 3 o'clock in the morning the synagogue was set on fire – probably by a large amount of petrol being poured over it. The fire department was present and secured the surrounding buildings. The fire was rekindled a few hours later until around 10.30 am the roof space was burning. Later the surrounding walls were blown up. Ritual items from the synagogue were displayed on the street.*

This sparse, controlled and unemotional account tells us little of an event that would change the Jewish community for ever.

The fire that had been deliberately started by Nazi activists resulted in the complete destruction of the whole building. After several attempts at rekindling the fire, during the course of the following morning the gable roof collapsed over the vestibule and the rear room. The front gable then came adrift from the dome and unidentified perpetrators tried to tear it down with a rope. The dome eventually collapsed later that afternoon. The local paper, the *Wilhelmshavener Zeitung*, which had long actively encouraged anti-Semitic activity in the city, reported on 11 November 1938 on the 'spontaneous anti-Jewish rallies in the city' and 'excited demonstrations in front of Jewish shops.'

During the night of 9/10 November 1938, those Jewish shops in Wilhelmshaven that still existed and many of the houses that were occupied by Jews were devastated, destroyed and looted. Most of the Jewish inhabitants were taken from their apartments, abused and marched through the streets to the Jahnhalle (a large hall for local events), some forced to wear cardboard signs round their necks saying things like 'I am a Jewish pig'. Spectators threw stones at the group and spat on them.

Hermann Hartog was detained in Wilhelmshaven during that night, along with thirty-three others. The following morning they were all marched from the Jahnhalle, past the burnt-out synagogue and the shattered Jewish business premises, to the railway station, where they were put on a special train that took them to Sachsenhausen concentration camp. On the way, the train picked up other Jewish men – including those from Jever and Aurich – who had been detained. More than 6,000 Jews from the larger surrounding area were taken to Sachsenhausen. They were subjected to much harsher treatment than other prisoners in a brutal and frightening experience that was designed to bring home the reality of Nazi intentions to every Jewish prisoner.

Four Jewish businesses in Wilhelmshaven were plundered and destroyed during the night of 10 November: the pawnbrokers' businesses of Reisner and of Silbermann, the Gartina shoe shop, and the Pfeffer clothes shop. The Jewish inn belonging to the Gerhards was robbed of wine and spirits, which were taken to be drunk by the Gestapo at the SA headquarters to celebrate the success of the pogrom. The goods seized from the shops were taken to a classroom in the Angari school where items stolen from the pawn shops were sorted and given back to the owners who had pledged them.

Hermann was imprisoned for over four weeks at Sachsenhausen between Thursday 10 November 1938 and Monday 12 December 1938 (although he did not know his release date until the day itself). Henny and Inge were not taken to a concentration camp, but they were taken into custody overnight on 9/10 November, as was Henny's father, Adolf Scheuer. Adolf was spared imprisonment in a concentration camp because he was over 60 years old. The three of them were allowed to go home at about 6.30 a.m. Later that day, Hermann's eldest sister Berta arrived from Aurich to be with Henny for a few hours before returning on the bus in time for Shabbat. She told Henny what had happened back home in Aurich.

The riots on that same night were triggered in Aurich by the leader of the local SA, Georg Eltze, who lived in Emden. He was alerted for action between 11 p.m. and midnight – probably receiving his orders from the Oldenburg SA district leader.

Eltze then phoned the local Nazi leader, Heinrich Bohnens, to order him to go to Aurich with other SA men to take part in the action against the Jews. Eltze got hold of petrol in Emden and Bohnens informed the fire brigade in Aurich that an exercise would take place, so the fire alarm system should be shut down. Bohnens and Eltze met with the Aurich and Emden SA troops on the market square to finalise arrangements.

The SA cordoned off the area and Eltze and the other SA men set fire to the synagogue in the early hours of the morning. The fire brigade was only allowed to move in to protect a neighbouring private house and also the Jewish school, above which lived Moritz Lachmann and his wife Friederike, from the spreading flames. The synagogue burned down completely. That night, the synagogues of the neighbouring towns and villages of Emden. Esens, Leer, Norden and Weener were also burnt down.

While the synagogue burned, SA guards blocked both the exit roads and the streets where many Jewish citizens lived, and the Jews were rounded up. Wolff Wolffs was woken with his brother Benno and their father, the master painter Abraham Wolffs, in the middle of the night. The door of their house at Wallstraβe 14 was smashed and they were driven through the streets in only makeshift clothing and taken to the agricultural auction hall known as the Bullenhalle, where they were joined by many other Jewish men and some women, all of whom were assaulted.

SA men stormed into the apartment of the Jewish doctor Manfred Louis Hoffmann and his wife Rosi at Wallstraβe 20, just a few doors away from the Hartogs' house. They destroyed not only his personal possessions but also his doctor's practice furnishings. A bullet was said to have been fired into the wall above his bed, and his car, bicycle and expensive camera were confiscated, as well as his cash. When he was taken to the Bullenhalle, a guard kicked him.

Teacher Moritz Lachmann was arrested from his apartment above the Jewish school and taken to the Bullenhalle. Wolff Wolffs witnessed that the guards gave the 64-year-old teacher a prayer book, opened it at the first page, and ordered him to read it out in German. When Lachmann began to read 'Great is the Living God…', the guards hit him, and he fell. He was then mocked and abused all night.

The elderly Samson brothers, who lived with their housekeeper at Zingelstraβe 3, were woken that night when the SA broke into their building. Bendit Samson, aged 78, opened the door to them in his pyjamas. All three men were taken to the Bullenhalle and the younger two (Herz, aged 75, and Ruben, aged 70) were kept there until the following evening. Bendit was allowed home, but an SA squad followed him to search their entire house and take away furniture and linen.

In the Bullenhalle, Abraham Wolffs – who was the leader of the Jewish community, and nearly 65 years old – was beaten and verbally abused until a senior SA officer intervened to prevent worse things from happening, saying, 'We don't want any corpses yet.'

Several houses belonging to Jews were violently broken into. Windows, doors and furniture were smashed, shots were fired, and business premises were looted. SS men (the Schutzstaffel, a major paramilitary organisation of the Nazi Party) and members of the National Socialist Motor Vehicle Corps (NSKK) as well as SA troops from the neighbouring villages of Holtrop and Westerende were also involved. The elderly, the infirm, women and children were soon released from the Bullenhalle and sent home, but the men who had to stay behind had to wait until the following day without any food or drink. The man in charge was the former head of the Aurich SA, an Austrian by the name of Haas, who made sure that the Jewish men were humiliated, harassed and tortured with sports and other drill exercises. The sports manager of the Aurich SA, Wilhelm Bock, ruled over proceedings, making the men do leapfrogs, run laps, and jump over obstacles.

Around noon on 10 November, those men who had not already been released (about forty to fifty of them) were then driven on foot from the Bullenhalle through the streets to the Ellernfeld, a sports field that was being drained by the city at the time. Here – with curious spectators from the town watching what was going on – they were subjected to further harassment. They had to play 'sports', dig trenches, carry drainage pipes backwards and forwards, and drive sand in wheelbarrows. Werner Hoffman was forced to shout, 'I am a racial molester.' Benno Wolffs, who was 28 years old, later said that he expected to be shot on the spot, especially since there were large piles of sand from the drainage works nearby. A few local people wanted to help and tried to give water to the men who were being humiliated, but eventually, in the late afternoon, the Jewish men were led back to the Bullenhalle.

The police had meanwhile received instructions from Gestapo headquarters in Wilhelmshaven to take the Jews into 'protective custody' and to bring them to the court prison. Some older men were released home, but at around 6 p.m., forty-two were taken to the prison. The next morning, 11 November, these men were taken by bus to Oldenburg and from there by train to Sachsenhausen. In January 1939, the last of them was allowed to return to Aurich. After the night of the pogrom, it was the task of the Gestapo to search for, seize and deport all Jews to concentration or extermination camps.

Harri Hoffmann was a cabinet maker who ran a furniture and carpentry store with his father Louis from their home at Wallstraβe 20. The Hoffmanns' business was one of those destroyed on the night of the November pogrom. Harri was arrested, but on the train journey to Sachsenhausen, he pretended to have advanced and open tuberculosis, so he was allowed off the train to return to Aurich.

For the Jewish community in Neustadtgödens, the night's events were slightly different. The synagogue was not burned down because a few years earlier it had been sold to a non-Jewish owner. To have destroyed the property of an Aryan would have resulted in claims for damages. But the order for action made by the SA in Emden was to arrest all the Jews in the area, and to take their funds and valuables. Just 2km away from Neustadtgödens was Horster Grashaus, a large agricultural estate owned by the respected Jewish de Taube family, where agricultural training was given to those hoping to emigrate to Palestine. Seven Jews from Neustadtgödens, plus another eleven from the de Taube estate (including the 83-year-old owner Samuel de Taube), were arrested and taken to the town centre where they were held in the open before being taken to the office of the SA, where their money and valuables were confiscated. Later that night, the women were released and the men were led under guard to the 'Hotel zur Deutschen Eiche', diagonally opposite the old synagogue, where they tried to sleep on the floor of a hall on the upper floor.

During the next day, the men were taken in a cattle truck to nearby Sande, from where they were taken by train to Oldenburg. As they left the village in the truck, many of their neighbours were sympathetic towards the men, but the schoolchildren and their two teachers are said to have stood in the street and sung an anti-Semitic song:

Throw the whole gang
of Jews out of our Fatherland.

At Oldenburg, the arrested men joined other Jews from the locality, and they were all taken by train to Sachsenhausen, although by then Samuel de Taube and his elderly brother had been allowed to return to Neustadtgödens. When Robert de Taube was released from Sachsenhausen four weeks later (on 9 December 1938), he was not allowed to return to his agricultural property, which had been redistributed to twenty-five farmers in the neighbourhood. Instead, he was required to stay in Wilhelmshaven and report to the Gestapo every day. An intimidating experience as the gate was always locked behind him when he reported there.

Erich Levy, who was arrested in Jever, remembered that they had to wait in the cold for hours for the train at Oldenburg, and then they were herded through the street to the station like cattle. All the while, young people insulted them and threw stones at them. The Jewish men travelled in a 'special train' via Bremen to Sachsenhausen. One of the men arrested and taken to Sachsenhausen was their rabbi Leo Trepp, from Oldenburg, who remembered all the prisoners being called for a roll-call at four o'clock in the morning, and in the bitter cold being threatened by guards with machine-guns and being told: 'You are the dregs of humanity. I don't see why you should live.'

To the Jewish people in the north-west of Germany who had endured more than a decade of anti-Semitic abuse, the words 'concentration camp' meant death. For one Jewish citizen from Jever, this proved to be true. Joseph Haas, who was 56 years old, was a tobacco dealer in Jever with a shop in Grosser Burgstraβe. He moved to Hamburg in 1937 to escape the anti-Semitic pressure of small-town Jever and from there he was rounded up with others on the night of the pogrom and taken to Sachsenhausen, where he died from the abuse he received in the concentration camp. The camp was completely overcrowded, it was bitterly cold, with the winter temperature falling many degrees below freezing, and every day the deaths of several inmates were recorded. The surviving men were controlled by whips and dogs in a brutal regime.

With Hermann arrested and taken to Sachsenhausen with no known date of release, Henny Hartog returned to her home with her father and Inge. She had a great deal to think about and a lot to do very quickly. She was very grateful for Berta's visit from Aurich, and the two women started to organise and re-establish their households without the men. Henny found Berta 'very melancholy' and it is clear that Henny felt the same.

It was indeed 'the hour of the women' in all Jewish communities throughout Germany. Where the men had been taken away, their homes and businesses had been effectively destroyed, but children and old people still needed to be cared for, and decisions had to be made for the future. Only the women could do this, and they engaged with each other to find such safety, hope and practical solutions as the occasion allowed. They had no money, very little food, and were carrying great sorrow. But they worked for solutions.

In Jever, Änne Gröschler found that former non-Jewish 'friends' were no longer willing to be friendly or helpful. Administrators who had once worked with her husband were no longer available on the telephone – or were themselves too frightened to be seen or heard being sympathetic or helpful to a Jewish person. How on earth was she going to get Hermann released from the concentration camp?

With the help of a Dutch friend of her brother-in-law, Änne drove to the intimidating Gestapo building at Am Rathausplatz in Wilhelmshaven where they were both admitted and Änne was able to place her papers showing her and Hermann's eligibility for emigration to the Netherlands. With great courage, she recounted what had happened to the Jewish community in Jever – the burning of the synagogue, the arrest of the Jewish men, the theft of their valuable belongings, and the ransacking of businesses.

Änne Gröschler was successful. Their emigration was granted, and her husband and his brother were freed within the next few days.

In Wilhelmshaven, Henny acted on the decisions that she had no doubt discussed with Berta on the day after Hermann's arrest.

The day after Berta left, Saturday 12 November 1938, Henny sat down to write an urgent letter to Lore. She was still exhausted and very emotional after the experiences of the previous forty-eight hours: 'Today my head cannot write, and I would rather cry my eyes out!' But she steeled herself to be focused and to organise what needed to be done.

Her priorities were clear: she needed to get Hermann out of Sachsenhausen; she needed to get Inge to a place of safety; and she needed to expedite the emigration of Hermann, herself and Inge. For that, she enlisted the help of her elder daughter in England and tried to give her clear and sound advice and direction. But first she needed to reassure Lore – as best she could – about the situation back home in Wilhelmshaven:

> *Vati cannot write to you. You will probably not hear from him. Don't be too sad; we must be brave and hope that he will soon be here again. I think of him all the time, and also of you. Inge is alright again and Opa is well. Hilda ter Berg and Ingrid [Cohen] are also here and so Inge has some company.*

Henny also acknowledged her sadness as she shared with Lore the loss of something small but of special value that she had treasured because it had once been given to her by her sister Cilly for a special occasion and then been deliberately and thuggishly stolen or ruined in the looting by the Nazis: 'Do you remember the white pillows that dear Aunt Cilly made for the day that you were born? They used to lie on my place – but they are there no longer.'

Indeed, an abiding memory of 9/10 November 1938 for many Jewish women was that of feathers flying as the Nazis and their supporters brutally slashed through the pillows, quilts and duvets of their homes.

Henny then gave concise instructions to Lore, who was just a few days short of her fourteenth birthday. Lore was to explain to Mr and Mrs Harris, and to her school, the details around the pogrom of the past few days and thus excuse the possible late payment of school and accommodation fees. She was also to 'do everything that you can, so that we can come to England. I know that this is dreadfully difficult, but it is not impossible.'

She explained to Lore that, 'it is only people who have something special to achieve who can come to England,' and suggested that for Hermann this might be his skills as a cantor, or some aspect of his singing. For herself, 'I would straight away and happily begin as a cook for the Harrises, but if I cannot get any entry approval to England for Vati, then Inge and I also cannot go.'

Henny had recently been in touch again with the American Consulate about their application for emigration to the USA, but 'because of the enormous crowd, we could wait about one year to be called – and until everything is ready it could take two years.'

She was also impatient for some international recognition of what the Jewish community in Germany was enduring: 'We know everything that the foreign newspapers write, and there should be not so much talk but more action.'

Henny was very aware that she was asking a great deal of her young daughter. 'You are still so young, my dear, and I must already require so much of you.'

Nevertheless, she forged ahead with her requests. 'Go soon to London and call Philip Hartog, and if you can see him personally you should. Then get in touch with the Marks in London. A way must be found.'

Hermann had earlier made a recording on vinyl of his singing – in one of the shops in Wilhelmshaven where this was possible – and Henny had already sent this to Lore.

> *Take the record with you to London. Let the men advise you who know about these decisions. For this you must stay in London for several days. Write to me about this immediately afterwards. Only influential men can really help. You must do everything as soon as half term or earlier. This question at the moment is for me more important than you can understand, my dear Lore.*
>
> *I close with many kisses, your Mutti.*
>
> *And write in the next few days.*

Lore did indeed carry out the wishes of her mother. She made contact again with Sir Philip and Lady Mabel Hartog and took the recording of her father singing to the chief rabbi in London. She was accompanied by someone, probably Lady Hartog, as she tried to make the case for her father to be given entry to Britain.

She was bitterly disappointed by his dismissive response: 'My dear, there are thousands of people like him.'

Henny remained very busy in Wilhelmshaven. On 15 November 1938, five days after the devastation of the pogrom in Germany and Austria, a delegation of British Jewish and Quaker leaders appealed in person to the prime minister of the United Kingdom, Neville Chamberlain. Newspaper reports of the violence of the November pogrom had elicited public sympathy in Britain, and, among other requests, the members of the delegation had asked that the British government permit the temporary admission to Britain of unaccompanied Jewish children, without their parents. This was debated in the House of Commons the following day, and subsequently a Bill to waive certain immigration requirements was quickly presented to Parliament. On 21 November, the British government agreed to permit the temporary admission of Jewish children under 17 years of age without their parents, and without the requirement of a visa. The Anglo-Jewish community would be responsible for the funding, and it was initially expected that 5,000 children would travel in groups of 200 to 500. On arrival in England, the children would be housed in holiday camps that were empty during the winter season. This transportation of children became known as the Kindertransport.

In Germany, Henny watched carefully, and followed the debate keenly. As soon as the decision was agreed, she began making arrangements for Inge to be taken on a Kindertransport to England. Clearly, not all children whose parents wanted them to go to England would be able to do so. Henny worked fast to secure a place for her younger daughter within the necessary selection process. It was an extremely stressful time for all the women who were hoping for and planning a place on the Kindertransport for their children. In just a few days and hours, they tried to cram a lifetime of care and advice into very few moments – while also trying to reassure both themselves and their children that this was merely a temporary parting.

Funding for the scheme was secured by the Central British Fund for German Jewry, and monetary, housing and other aid was promised by Jewish and other communities. None of the refugees should become a financial burden on the public, and so every child had to have a guarantee of £50 sterling to finance their eventual re-emigration. It was expected that the children would stay only temporarily in England, which perhaps made such heartbreaking arrangements possible for parents to contemplate.

In the early days after the November pogrom, places were offered to children based solely on the urgency of their situation. This included those children – like Inge – with a parent who had been arrested. If a child had some connections – through family, business, friends, or a school – to enable them to ask a British person to stand as guarantor, that was viewed favourably. (A private guarantor could be a sign that a child was from a middle-class, and therefore well-connected, family with international friends. It might also suggest an ability to write in English.) Henny was able to call on the Harrises – who were already caring for Lore – and the Jewish community in Westcliff, as well as Lord and Lady Hartog, as possible guarantors for Inge.

She worked as fast as she could to apply for a place on the Kindertransport for Inge. She had very little – if any – communication with Hermann at this time, but very possibly this was a scenario that they had frequently discussed together. After all, they had jointly arranged for Lore to be educated in England a few years previously, and all their correspondence suggests that they worked together in family decision-making and shared very similar ideas and values. So, Henny began on the paperwork on her own.

She needed to complete a questionnaire concerning Inge's character and background and enclose a photograph of her that were both sent to the local Jewish social worker's office. This office sent the documents to Berlin – to the *Reichsvertretung der Juden in Deutschland* (the Federal Representation of Jews in Germany), together with Inge's health certificate – in order to receive permission to leave the country. Henny also had to sign a statement allowing the committee in Britain to look after Inge, and another statement that declared the religion that Inge had been brought up in. All the documentation was sent to London for review by the Refugee Children's Movement. After that, if the application was accepted, an entry permit would be sent back to Germany and submitted to the police.

All went well, and Henny was swiftly issued with a travel date and departure details for Inge, who was allowed to take a small, sealed suitcase with her – but no valuables, and only 10 Marks in money. She was included, with almost 200 other children, on the first Kindertransport, which left Germany on Thursday 1 December 1938. Inge was three days short of her twelfth birthday.

Parents said farewell to their children at the train stations in Berlin and Hamburg. It was a tightly controlled situation, with Nazi police forbidding emotional farewells on the station platforms. Special trains took the children to their meeting point on the German/Dutch border crossing at Bad Bentheim. Nazi guards then boarded the train and ransacked the luggage but did not harm the terrified children – who were accompanied by social workers as far as the north coast of Holland.

Those who wished the Kindertransport success kept strictly to the rules so that future transports would not be compromised. At the coast, the social workers returned to Germany to allay any fears that they might flee Germany themselves.

As she waited for the ship to leave, Inge wrote a few lines on a postcard to her mother and grandfather back in Wilhelmshaven:

> *Dear Mutti and Opa, now it is evening and many children are writing. We were wonderfully received in Holland. We received quite a lot. First there was meat, then lemonade, chocolate. In an hour we are going by ship to England. I will write all about it in a letter to you. My writing is very bad. Much love and kisses, your Inge.*

Inge was not alone in describing the delights of the warm reception as their train travelled through Holland – the unexpected kindness, warm food, soda and snacks that greeted them along the way. She remembered it with gratitude for the rest of her life. Inge and the other children sailed on *Die Prague*, arriving in Harwich, England, in the early hours of 2 December 1938.

For the parents who waved goodbye to their children as they left on the Kindertransport, there were many emotions. Some mothers – and there were generally only mothers, aunts or grandmothers, because the fathers had all been arrested – have spoken of returning to a house full of silence. Silence, fear, regret, and heartbreak.

Henny has not left a record of what life was like for her after Inge left on 1 December 1938, but she returned home on her own to great uncertainty. Hermann was still in Sachsenhausen and may not even have known that their younger daughter had left for England. From later correspondence, it is clear that none of them anticipated that this was, in fact, their final farewell. Henny had always been the person who made a joyful celebration for family birthdays – and she continued to try to do so over the following years, even when their family was split and there was no money for festivities. In those first few days of December, after Inge had left, there was nobody with whom to celebrate Inge's twelfth birthday, and all that Henny and Hermann had been able to send Lore for her birthday in November was a loving letter. Having arranged safety for Inge, Henny now had to dissolve her home and find a way for herself and Hermann to get away and to be reunited with their daughters.

November 1938, after the pogrom, was a terrible time for all Jews in Germany. Just two days afterwards, on 12 November, a fine of one billion Reichsmarks was imposed on the entire community of Jews, which was blamed for the conflagrations and destruction of the pogrom. On the same day it was announced that Jews were no longer allowed to visit cinemas, theatres, concerts or exhibitions. Since they were already not allowed to run a business, Jews were excluded from all commercial and cultural life in the country. Their isolation was almost complete.

On 15 November, Jewish children were expelled from all German schools and on the same day, in Frankfurt, Louis Bodenheimer was forced to 'sell' his second-hand dealer business at Klostergasse 34 – 36 (probably to Alois Gassner – and probably at a very low price). By the end of the month, all Jewish companies that had not been sold were confiscated. Jewish people were subject to restrictions that only allowed them to move around at certain times and in certain areas, and Jewish lawyers were no longer allowed to practise.

In the first few days of December 1938, Jews were no longer allowed to own cars and were deprived of their driving licences and registration papers for motor vehicles. They were also required to hand over any securities and jewellery that they owned. On 5 December, Jews had all their financial assets frozen. It was increasingly difficult for them to afford to emigrate, even though this was the stated wish of the Nazis.

During these weeks, while Hermann was still trying to survive in Sachsenhausen, Henny arranged for a load of what was left of their furniture and household goods from their flat in Bismarckstraße to be stored in the warehouse of F.W. Neukirch in the freeport of Bremen. This was a common activity for Jews who were hoping and planning to emigrate, and the large containers for storage were often seen outside the apartments of those families, waiting to be filled. The containers were called 'Lifts' and the Hartog Lift was numbered 1109. Henny paid 1,320 Reichsmarks for storage and arranged for its anticipated eventual freight to New York. The Neukirch business, with its warehouses and offices near the railway station in Bremen, was both an official carrier for the German railways and also a popular company with Jews who wanted to emigrate to North and South America. Business boomed for them in the 1930s.

Henny tried everything to find a way to escape from Germany with Hermann. Increasingly, at this time, she considered England to be more likely than America to be able to provide them with a place of safety quickly, while all the time continuing with her long-term plan of emigration to the USA. She searched through her belongings and found the autograph book that her friends at the finishing school in Lausanne had signed more than twenty years earlier. She looked for the message from Nathalie Laurence, scribbled over the Lausanne address to avoid confusion, tore out the page and sent the useful half to Lore – with instructions for her to ask Lady Hartog to locate Nathalie and her family so that the two women could reconnect and maybe Nathalie could help Henny. Lore did as she was asked but the search took time and was ultimately not successful. Nathalie and her family had moved away and could not be found.

Hoping that their plans to emigrate would move forward, Henny needed to know that her father, Adolf Scheuer, would still be cared for and safe back in Germany. He had no desire to emigrate and neither did Hermann's siblings in Aurich (and none of them had the money to pay to escape), so plans were made for Adolf to join the Hartog household in Wallstraβe in Aurich, and he went to live there in December 1938. He had been living happily with Henny and Hermann in Wilhelmshaven for almost ten years, but much had changed, and he also felt the absence of his granddaughters very keenly.

What is abundantly clear is that this was an exhausting time for Henny, who had worked hard to ensure the best for her family. While the November pogrom was indeed a turning point in the Nazis' persecution of the Jewish people, it was also a turning point in Henny's personal life. Especially during the three weeks between the pogrom of 9/10 November and Inge's departure on 1 December, Henny showed the strength of her character – her tenacity, her empathy, and her organisational skills – as she fought for the safety and security of her family. Meanwhile, she also managed everything about her household entirely on her own. The pogrom had struck like lightning, shattering everything it touched and shocking those who suffered it. With synagogues and businesses destroyed, and private home spaces violated, it was left to the women to free their men, repair their homes, and help their families to flee to safety. Traditionally, men had guarded the safety and honour of their community. With all the men imprisoned, it was left to the women to guard themselves, their families and homes, and their Jewish way of life.

The assault of the widespread Nazi violence and the pressure of their now legalised plundering led to even more intensive efforts from Jews to flee Germany. This was rarely possible immediately because emigration, even assuming that a host country could be found, encountered high hurdles that had to be overcome in Germany itself. That is one reason why many parents decided to respond quickly to the offer of international aid organisations and to send their children forward in the Kindertransport. By the end of 1938, six young people from Jever had escaped from Germany by means of the Kindertransport.

But the events of 9/10 November 1938 also showed the Nazi regime that they could broadly count on nationwide support of anti-Semitism from the general public in Germany, and this emboldened them to move forward with their plans – knowing that they could do so without much opposition. For the Jews, it was clear that they needed to leave Germany in order to breathe freely – or even at all.

In the concentration camp at Sachsenhausen, the Jewish men endured horrific conditions, trauma, abuse, and uncertainty about the future. After several weeks, many of them were gradually released. They'd had a taste of what the Nazis intended to inflict on them and their families, and it had been intended as a warning to them. Their experience was expected to encourage them to emigrate – to leave the country and thus allow it to be 'Jew-free'.

On Monday 12 December 1938, Hermann was released from Sachsenhausen, along with other men over the age of 50. He was 51. Like other Jews who were released from a concentration camp at this time, he was only allowed to leave because he signed a document stating his intention to emigrate – as well as other statements that claimed he was in good health and would not talk about what he had seen and experienced. On his return to Wilhelmshaven, he was required to report to the state police.

At the end of that week, on the Saturday after Hermann's release, members of the Jewish community lit their first candles for Hanukkah – the Festival of Lights. By then, Henny and Hermann were no longer allowed to live in their flat in Bismarckstraβe because it was not owned by a Jew. They were obliged to live in a 'Jew House', and therefore in January 1939 they had to move to Tonndeichstraβe 4 – the home of Samuel Mordechai Reisner, whose pawnbroker business had been ransacked and destroyed on 9 November.

Between 7 and 12 November 1938, Nazi officials and the mobs on the streets had destroyed 1,500 synagogues throughout Germany, devastated 7,000 shops, robbed tens of thousands of homes, and killed 400 people during these riots. The state then deported 30,000 Jews to the concentration camps. Another 1,000 were murdered or became victims of brutal conditions in the camps. Thousands more were seriously injured and traumatised. Most accounts of a returning prisoner after even a short period in a concentration camp speak only of trauma and of a thoroughly weakened, changed, silenced and dehumanised person.

On 26 November 1938, the board of the state fire insurance company approved a reward of 100 Reichsmarks to the volunteer fire brigade in Jever for its prudent behaviour in the fire of the synagogue since they had 'proceeded very carefully in the firefighting and especially in the protection of the neighbouring houses.' Every firefighting brigade in the country had done exactly the same that night to ensure that no synagogue would remain standing.

November 1938 marked a real turning point for German Jews. Until then, they had been increasingly humiliated, deprived of their rights as German citizens, and driven into poverty, but after 9 November 1938 the politics of disenfranchisement had been replaced by the politics of expulsion – which was enforced against a community of people who had nowhere left to go. It finally became unmistakably clear that Jewish people could no longer even take their lives for granted, and the number of Jews trying to emigrate skyrocketed. The November pogroms had made a mockery of civilised norms and afterwards, Jews could only think in terms of death or life. Until then they had told themselves that even though they might be outcasts, they would still be tolerated. Now they were desperate. The pogrom swelled the number of Jews seeking asylum. There was no longer a place in Germany for Jews – not in the country's religious, nor in its cultural or economic, life.

On 5 December 1938, shortly after his return to Jever from the concentration camp at Sachsenhausen, Hermann Gröschler received a letter informing him that he and the Jewish community were required to remove the remaining standing walls of the synagogue at their own expense. Less than a fortnight later, the mayor, Martin Folkerts, reported to his superiors that the synagogue and the community centre had been sold by the Jewish community to a building contractor, I. Giesenberg (and this transaction was validated in March 1939). The ruins of the synagogue were demolished above ground between January and March 1939.

Hermann Gröschler, his brother Julius, and their families had to sell everything they possessed in order to leave Germany. They were obliged to accept a very poor price for their belongings, and then they set about leaving. Every piece of paper required money; everything was subject to control; so many offices had to be visited to acquire the right paperwork. Most of the men who returned from Sachsenhausen were in no fit state (physically or mentally) to do any of this, so all over Germany the work of obtaining exit visas, paying tax, arranging furniture removal – and everything else – became the experience of so many Jewish women during the last weeks of 1938 (and beyond).

By the end of 1938, Henny and Hermann were a reduced family, but at least the two of them were together again. There was no work for Hermann anywhere in the country, and no longer much of a Jewish community to guide, help, encourage or protect. Much of what had identified him as a person seemed to have been destroyed. He was required by the Nazis to leave, and he had signed papers to that effect. What he and Henny wanted more than anything else was to leave the country and to live with their daughters, even though it meant leaving others behind. They were both absolutely clear in their resolve: they had to get out – together.

CHAPTER 6

Leaving Germany: 1939

As civil society disintegrated in Germany, Jews looked to their family networks in order to make emigration possible. American immigration laws and policies increasingly made immigration very difficult, and only those Jews with family members or friends who were able and willing to vouch for their maintenance had any chance of success. Anyone wishing to emigrate to America needed to have an affidavit from someone already resident in the country. Henny and Hermann were relying on Henny's Uncle Max – Max Bodenheimer, her mother's brother, who had lived in America for the past forty-six years, since 1892 – to provide these guarantees for them. The affidavit was a sworn assurance of financial means to care for the would-be immigrant. Arranging for these important papers through written communication across the continents, with people they hardly knew proved to be a stressful, difficult, and ultimately unsuccessful negotiation.

From the time a few years before, when Henny and Hermann had first recognised the need to leave Germany, America had been their expected destination. But circumstances had changed, and both their daughters were now in England. More than anything else, Henny and Hermann wanted to be reunited with their daughters as quickly as possible, and England now seemed to offer that possibility. So they worked on several fronts: getting out of Germany as quickly as possible; hoping to obtain an affidavit from Uncle Max to facilitate entry to America; joining Lore and Inge in England if a way could be found. Although Hermann had some professional contacts in England within the Jewish communities of Westcliff and Leeds, their main personal contact in the country was their daughter, 14-year-old Lore, and they relied heavily on her to help them to find a solution.

Every few days it became increasingly difficult for Jews to leave Germany, and by 1 January 1939 they were obliged to have a large red 'J' stamped on their identity cards and passports, together with their fingerprints. 'Israel' and 'Sarah' also needed to be added to identity cards of Jews. It was absolutely clear that Jews were no longer tolerated in German society.

On 22 January 1939, Lady Hartog wrote to Lore to update her on Henny's request for information about her friend, Nathalie Laurence, from her time at finishing school in Lausanne twenty-five years earlier:

> *I am trying to trace the address of the Lawrences [sic] who lived at 33 Greville Road for your mother, but I am afraid it may not be easy. The people who are living there now did not take the house direct from Mrs Lawrence, but they are trying to find out where she went...I have written to the Chief Rabbi's Religious Emergency Fund about your parents' case.*

In that same month, January 1939, Änne and Hermann Gröschler left Jever for the Netherlands. They went with great sorrow as well as much relief, and Änne's detailed account of their experience is probably not very different from what so many emigrating Jewish people felt at the time. People who had built a home, created a family, enjoyed fulfilling work and professional relationships, and encouraged and inspired their community had so much that they valued and cherished that they had to leave behind. It was a heartbreaking and exhausting process to say farewell to precious friends and family members and to walk away from what had once been a vibrant and joyous lifestyle and look ahead to a future that could only be seen as bleak, uncertain and unpredictable. It was not easy to leave one's place of birth, turn one's back on those who must remain and feel forced from one's homeland. It was difficult for anyone to comprehend the chaos into which they had been thrown.

At the end of that month, in his speech in the Reichstag on 30 January – six years after being made chancellor – Hitler threatened annihilation of the Jews in Europe if they were to bring about war against Germany. He declared himself to be a man of peace, and yet a few days later there was a government announcement of the expansion of the country's submarine fleet and its air force.

From Aurich, Benno Wolffs went to Hamburg in February 1939, while his brother Wolff Wolffs stayed in Aurich to help in his father's painting and decorating business. After the synagogue was destroyed, Jewish services took place in the apartment of Amalie Wolff, the widow of the Jewish teacher Benjamin Wolff. Since the Jewish school had been confiscated by the SA, classes now took place in the private rooms of the last head of the synagogue, Abraham Wolff. The previous teacher, Moritz Lachmann, and his wife Friederike (who had lived in the apartment above the school) had to live temporarily with Friederike's older brother, the merchant Joseph Hess, at Marktplatz 15. The Lachmanns left Aurich on 23 February 1939 and moved to the Jewish retirement home in Emden. Their sons, Henry, Jakob and Siegbert, had already left Aurich in the early 1930s and had been able to emigrate to the USA in good time.

The Jews in Germany were not without friends on the international stage who fought for their cause, but they were perhaps unlikely to appreciate whether or not this concern made much difference in practice to their individual fates. In February 1939, the Bishop of Chichester, George Bell, delivered a lecture in London entitled *Humanity and the Refugees* as part of an annual series of lectures that had been instituted by the Jewish Historical Society of England. In an introduction, the chief rabbi spoke of the 'inferno of misery and suffering' that Jews in Europe were currently experiencing as they tried to escape the terror. As he explained, 'Against them, all doors are barred and bolted. They are, as it were, trapped on a burning ship, and yet are refused landing.'

In his lecture, George Bell cited the Nuremberg Laws and decried the 'denial of civic rights, the exclusion from public office and employment' and all the other persecution that stemmed from them:

> *It is a terrible catalogue of crimes, of unspeakable damage to both oppressor and victim; for the degradation of the persecutor is no less terrible than the humiliation of the persecuted people.*

But he asserted:

> *An end will come; justice, mercy, liberty will re-assert their sway. The oppression will cease, as it has ceased before. Belief in God, and the lessons of history, forbid us to despair.*

He was not, however, expecting mere faith in events to mitigate the outcome:

> *We must do everything we can to help the victims, of all classes, occupations and creeds. And this "everything we can" means more than a philanthropy or private charity. The refugee problem is a problem which the state itself cannot escape...The problem of the refugee is a political and an economic problem, which cannot be solved unless the governments are determined that it shall be. It is a task which requires generosity and courage and insight in the Heads of governments and their advisers in the New World and in the Old.*

In a vote of thanks after the lecture, it was noted (with prescience):

> *This thousand-year-old pain may still not satisfy the lust of our persecutors; yet I am confident that Jewish courage and Jewish faith will triumph over cruelty and ignorance.*

As Henny had earlier noticed and commented, the words were fine, but more action was needed.

In the spring of 1939, the synagogue ruins in both Jever and Wilhelmshaven were flattened. In Jever, the ruins were demolished in the period between January and March, the gap was closed with a board fence, and the land was sold on 7 March 1939. The school annexe – where Hermann had taught – was permanently damaged on the roof truss and the schoolroom remained in its demolished state. There were plans for a commercial building on the site, but these were not immediately realised because of the imminent war.

By now, there was no place for Jews in the religious or economic life of Germany. Their property, synagogues and businesses had been totally destroyed. Increasingly, Jews tried to leave but it became much harder to do so. Ever larger numbers of people camped outside consular offices in order to be near the head of the queue when the doors opened early in the day. Everyday life became a nightmare of not knowing, of uncertainty, with all the depressing and enervating feelings that permeated every minute of every day. As Victor Klemperer noted in his diary:

> *The terrible thing about the last few weeks is that they have been at once empty and overcrowded. No possibility of concentrating on any work. Waiting for terrible news, which always comes. Being kept busy. Writing to government offices... We continue in this simultaneously crushing and stupefying chaos, this empty and breathless busyness... But I do not want to assert prematurely that we have reached the last circle of hell, for uncertainty is not the worst thing, because in uncertainty there is still hope.*

In Aurich, in March 1939, Herta Hoffmann left her home at Osterstraβe 13 to go to Hamburg, and then on to Milwaukee in America with her husband, Harri Hoffmann, her parents, Sally and Meta Goldschmidt, and Harri's parents, Louis and Lina Hoffmann. Harri's brother, Doctor Manfred Louis Hoffmann, went with them, together with his wife Rosi.

On 1 April 1939, Hitler visited Wilhelmshaven for the launch of the battleship *Tirpitz*. The date chosen was Bismarck's birthday and Hitler addressed a crowd of 80,000 at the town hall. The main purpose of his speech was to prepare the ground for the expected termination of the naval agreement with Britain, and also to signal to the world that Germany was readying herself for war. Wilhelmshaven was essentially a huge construction site with expansion of the building of ships for the Reich's navy, the creation of extra port facilities, the production of armaments, as well as increased facilities for air defence and air-raid protection, and also residential accommodation. The warship *Tirpitz* – the largest of its era – was a demonstration of that strength and power.

On 10 April 1939, Henny's aunt, Henrietta, died in Frankfurt, and soon afterwards Henny travelled to Frankfurt, in part to say her farewells to her family there. She was delayed from leaving Aurich as news arrived from London that her documents requesting work and refuge in Britain had been refused. It was a disappointing start to her journey, but she remained positive and enjoyed both the journey in the spring weather, and the sight of the hills and forests as she approached Frankfurt.

'It is always a great pleasure for me to see the mountains and forests again,' she wrote to her daughters.

She arrived on 27 April 1939 and stayed for two weeks. The day after her arrival, she wrote to Lore and Inge:

> *I arrived here yesterday at about half past eight in the evening and I want to say how very pleased I am to see the people here again. Uncle Louis and Aunt Hedwig seem just the same, although Aunt Hener has become a lot thinner, and because they are not as young as they used to be they also have a number of health complaints.*

As well as enjoying a 'holiday' in the place where she grew up, Henny worked hard to care for her elderly relatives while she was there, and to prepare a place in her uncle's home for her father. Meanwhile, Hermann took care of Adolf in Aurich, and began to take over some of the teaching duties in the Jewish community, where he was pleased to be received enthusiastically. He also looked after his sister Berta, who had been unwell in bed for several weeks.

On her return journey from Frankfurt, Henny passed through Cologne, where she visited Hermann's sister Henny and the Polak family. She was pleased to find Aunt Henny well and cheerful, and when she arrived back in Aurich on 14 May 1939, she was surprised and delighted to find Hermann waiting for her at the train station. As he told Lore and Inge:

> *I collected Mutti from Emden, and she had no idea that I was waiting for her at the train station. Suddenly I was standing in front of her, and I saw her amazed expression!*

In Aurich, Henny immediately busied herself with a long letter to Lore and Inge with detailed instructions about their summer clothes, and her plans to send them whatever they needed. Since Hermann had little work to do at the school and within the Jewish community, he was planning 'lots of walks' with Henny on Saturdays and Sundays and that very day (14 May) the two of them went for a walk by the Ems-Jade-Canal in Aurich.

> *Mutti had a good rest in Frankfurt, even though she had a lot of work to do, and hopefully she will continue to rest here. Our beloved Mutti, I am happy that she is here again.*

In the same letter on 14 May 1939, Hermann agreed with a suggestion from Lore that they should write on particular days of each week so that they could receive each other's letters before replying. At that time, a letter posted from England on a Saturday evening was arriving in Germany by the following Tuesday, so an immediate reply would arrive in England by the end of the week, on the Sabbath. Both Henny and Hermann were thrilled with photos that Lore and Inge had sent of themselves.

'You don't know how terribly pleased I am with your photos! I have looked at you for so long!' wrote Henny.

A week later, after six months living with Hermann's siblings, Adolf Scheuer left Aurich to live in Frankfurt at the home of his brother-in-law, Louis Bodenheimer, at Scheffelstraβe 26. After nine years living with Hermann, Henny, Lore and Inge in Wilhelmshaven, and a similar length of time previously in Berlin with Cilly and her husband, Adolf was returning to Frankfurt to be part of a city with many memories, and to be with his wife's family. Everybody tried to make the best of the situation.

'Opa is pleased to be going to Frankfurt. It will be lovely for him there,' Henny wrote optimistically.

On the same day Adolf left Aurich, 21 May 1939, teacher Max Moses also left Aurich, for Hamburg, from where he planned to leave by ship for America. Hermann replaced him as the teacher within the Jewish community in Aurich, for the few months until he was able to leave Germany. Meanwhile, Henny found a small job that paid her a little, but the Hartog family no longer had much money and during that May Hermann cautioned Lore and Inge:

> *About the question of your clothes, we will deal with everything from here. You should not spend anything on clothes. The money that hopefully you still have should only be for small things that you buy for school or to eat, because it is now very difficult to get you anything from* Hilfe und Aufbau *[a Jewish aid agency].*

That week, Hermann planned to write to contacts in the Jewish communities in Westcliff and in Leeds to see if anyone had any suggestions to help them to emigrate. Meanwhile, Henny was making a cheesecake to send to her daughters in England.

Rieka Peiser, who had once been a near neighbour of the Hartogs in Jever, emigrated on 8 June and went to live in London. She made contact with Lore when she arrived and offered help and advice to her over the coming years.

In Aurich, there had been seventy-seven houses in Jewish ownership in 1933. In June 1939, there were only twenty-eight houses.

A few weeks later, yet further restrictions were placed on the daily lives of Jews in Germany. From July 1939, they were only allowed to shop with a few merchants – up to twice a week for a few fixed minutes – and, even then, some merchants refused to serve them. It was very difficult for most Jews either to afford or to acquire an adequate diet, and their health suffered, with malnutrition becoming normal, and with diseases normally associated with deprivation (such as rickets) re-appearing in previously well-off and healthy individuals.

Meanwhile, Hermann used the contacts provided by his sister Henny's employers to link up with other Jewish emigrés in Brussels. On 6 July 1939, he was given a police certificate of good conduct, which was valid for three months for emigration purposes. He had to pay 1 Reichsmark for the certificate. He was also issued with a clearance certificate from the tax office that confirmed he had paid the Reich Flight Tax and that he did not owe the state any money. This was a prerequisite for legal permanent departure from Germany. Three weeks later, he was issued with a passport (no. 451) at Wilhelmshaven, as was Henny (no. 452). Both passports were valid for one year, and exactly a month later, on 27 August 1939, Hermann and Henny became official residents of Aurich.

Political tensions throughout the country continued to rise during the summer months, and without any mobilisation actually being announced, mobilisation was taking place. There were noticeable troop movements, cars were requisitioned, horses disappeared from the streets as they were taken away to be used by the forces. On the night of 23/24 August, Germany and Russia signed a pact that they would not attack each other, and they secretly divided up the countries that lay between them.

In Wilhelmshaven, Rosa de Taube managed to emigrate with her husband, Samuel, from Horster Grashaus near Neustadtgödens, on 25 August 1939. (Their son, Robert, who had been in charge of the estate at Horster Grashaus with his father since 1919, eventually survived the war in Berlin, where he went once he was released from Sachsenhausen.)

On 28 August, food rationing was imposed on all Germans and ration cards were distributed. An American journalist visiting Berlin found it to be 'a city of short rations and straightened friendships'.

That month, German troops mustered at Aurich train station prior to a war posting. Hermann's brother, Oskar Hartog, decided to visit the station and was recorded as being 'offensive' as he 'in a particularly noticeable way, went repeatedly up and down the platform alongside the train, displaying a strikingly provoking behaviour for show.' It was said in a report from Aurich to the Gestapo in Wilhelmshaven that 'the Jew Hartog accompanied the moving scenes of farewell with malicious smiles.' In addition, 'he was not in possession of a ticket.' This was not behaviour from a Jew that would go unpunished, and on 30 August Oskar Hartog was taken into custody. The district administrator asked the Gestapo to imprison him in a concentration camp if possible.

Just a week after their pact with the Soviets, at dawn on Friday 1 September 1939, Germany invaded Poland with a mighty advance force of tanks, bombers and fighter planes. This provoked the anticipated response from others and on Sunday 3 September, in accordance with their guarantees of Poland's border, Britain and France declared war on Germany. All over Europe, including in Britain, the weather was fine and calm. Henny and Hermann were still in Aurich and this announcement brought extreme urgency to their plans.

Immediately, the situation for Jews in Germany became far more serious and difficult. The German government placed a curfew on all Jews; 8pm in winter and 9pm in summer. Although Jews rarely ventured out after dark anyway, this was another coercive and isolating stricture. Jews were already limited in when and where they were allowed to shop (usually restricted to one hour's shopping per day), and often they were charged higher prices than non-Jews. Their food rations were also cut, and they received less meat and butter than Aryans, resulting in even more malnutrition and disease.

On 17 September, the Soviet Union invaded eastern Poland, and the Polish government fled the country that same day, going into exile in Paris. The Polish Army had mobilised late and lacked modern arms and equipment. It was defeated within weeks. Warsaw officially surrendered to the Germans on 28 September 1939, and the last Polish resistance ended on 6 October.

For those Jews, such as Henny and Hermann, who were still in Germany, emigration suddenly became vastly more difficult.

Jews who had already moved to the Netherlands (like the Gröschler-Löwenbergs with their relatives from Jever) lived in constant anxiety that the Germans would turn in the other direction and occupy the Netherlands.

The cattle trader Philipp Sternberg, the Hartogs' former neighbour from Schlosserstraβe in Jever, with his wife, Anna Maria, and their sons, Gert and Rolf, emigrated from Bremen to Argentina after war was declared – just in time.

On Friday and Saturday 22/23 September 1939, Jews in Germany prepared to observe Yom Kippur, maybe the most sacred day in the Jewish calendar. The Nazis chose that day to confiscate radios owned by Jews, so observant Jews were obliged to miss their prayer services and disregard Jewish laws about working on the holidays as they hauled their bulky, heavy radios to government offices and waited to deposit them. It was just another day of cruelty, and of contempt for their religion.

A few days later, on 4 October 1939, Hermann Hartog at last managed to leave Aurich and get to Belgium. He used contacts provided by his sister Henny's employers to link up with other Jewish emigrés and reached Brussels via Aachen. He hoped desperately that Henny would manage to follow him.

A dilemma that plagued all refugees was that they left family members behind, and they worried that running away from danger meant running from their responsibilities. Like so many other emigrants, they left behind a great deal that they cherished – not only their physical belongings, but also their sense of community and identity. It cannot have been at all easy for Hermann to leave Aurich – his birthplace and the familiar community of friends and kinspeople, which had once seemed so solid and stable. 'Freedom' brought its heartbreak for all who were forced to leave. Perhaps it was those very bonds of community and kinship that had made them delay their leave of Germany until it was almost too late. In order to leave, there were so many practical details to deal with: papers to collect together, and every document cost a lot of money. Every item that would be taken out of the country was subject to control, taxes had to be paid, and there was a huge amount of work required to travel the distance to the relevant office at the required time and queue with others in the same predicament. Breaking the ties that bound people to their families, their friends, their work, their communities, and their country – everything that defined their identity – was a bleak and agonising experience. It was an absolutely exhausting and heart-wrenching business – physically, mentally and emotionally. Until they had finally crossed the border, no Jew could believe that they would truly manage to leave Germany.

In a list from 10 October 1939, the city recorded 155 Jews registered with the police in Aurich and seventeen in the vicinity. Hardly any of the Jewish men still practised their former occupation. Twenty-five were now employed as workers in road construction or in agriculture, thirty-three were described as unemployed, and there was no information on fifteen. Fifty-two women were referred to as housewives or domestic servants. In addition, a painter, two cultural officials, a teacher, two on private incomes, nineteen schoolchildren and five small children lived in the city.

In Jever at the end of 1939, thirty-six Jews still lived in the city, in houses that were for forced sale, or with other Jews for rent, because non-Jews were not allowed to rent to Jews. The Aunts Cohn lived in the retirement home of the community on the Mönchwarf overlooking the ruins of the synagogue. By restricting the Jews' housing and freedom of movement, the Nazis created a ghetto. In Jever, this was concentrated on only a few addresses where Jews were allowed to live in Jew Houses, such as the one at Mühlenstraße 4. From these addresses the remaining members of the Jewish community in Jever would later be evicted to similar ghettos in bigger cities such as Hamburg and Bremen.

Henny joined Hermann in Brussels after an agonising few weeks. She travelled via Cologne but was unable to say how and where she had entered Belgium. By then, the border between Germany and Belgium had been closed.

CHAPTER 7

Brussels: Winter 1939 to Spring 1940

I have been here since midday today. I arrived safely, thank God, and I hope that Mutti can come soon. Please write to me immediately at the address below without my name, because I don't have an apartment yet. I am still very nervous and can't write much yet, but everything at home is fine. I am just feeling very bad at the moment. I have no money and I don't know what to do to get any help. Do you still have some money? And would you be able to send me a small amount? But only if it is possible.

This was a message Hermann wrote on a postcard to Lore and Inge as soon as he arrived in Brussels on 4 October 1939. He was, as he said, 'feeling very bad', and completely disorientated – he had no idea where to turn for the very basics of life. 'The address below' to which he refers was that of a younger couple – Karl and Anneliese Elsberg – who had themselves also just arrived from Germany and who were living in an apartment at 22 rue de l'Hotel des Monnaies. They invited him to use their address for post until he had an approved residential address of his own. Hermann knew of them through his sister Henny in Cologne, but we do not know exactly how much of their meeting in Brussels was a chance encounter within the Jewish community and how much might be attributed to family connections. Hermann's sister worked as a housekeeper for the Polak family – Emmy and Benjamin, with their son Helmuth – in Cologne. Emmy Polak's maiden name was Elsberg, and it might be this connection that gave Hermann his contact with Karl and Anneliese soon after he arrived in Brussels. They were able to help Hermann to navigate his way around the necessary bureaucracy and access immediate help and support from the Jewish aid agencies. Karl and Anneliese remained cherished friends to both Hermann and Henny until their ways diverged a few years later.

Karl (later Charles) Elsberg (born in 1904) was nearly twenty years younger than Hermann and had qualified as a lawyer. Before leaving for Brussels, he lived in his Jewish family's home in Warendorf (about 200km south of Aurich) and in 1933, aged 29, he was banned from following his profession by the Nazis, just eight weeks after qualifying. He married Anneliese Marx in January 1939 and shortly afterwards they both fled Germany. Their first attempts to emigrate to Paraguay failed at the last moment, and so they were late in organising an escape to Brussels. They arrived there on 14 September, just three weeks before Hermann.

But it was a day or two after his arrival before Hermann made contact with the Elsbergs. When he first arrived, Hermann took shelter with someone with the name of De Wolf at 171a rue van der Kindere in the wooded southern outskirts of Brussels where many affluent French immigrants lived – maybe because that is where the people who helped him across the border sent him. As soon as he was able, he sought help from the Jewish Committee for Assistance to Jewish Refugees, which had its headquarters an hour's walk away in the centre of the city, at rue Roger van der Weyden 25 – 27. This was a welfare committee that was set up with private funds in 1933 and had Professor Max Gottschalk as its Chair. There were about seventy volunteers who worked at the committee, and they did their best to help and advise Jewish refugees who arrived in the city. They particularly gave assistance with finding accommodation, and with financial, social, medical and legal support.

On 10 October 1939, within a week of his arrival and his postcard to Lore and Inge, Hermann presented himself to the Belgian authorities to apply for refugee status and residency papers. He was given a questionnaire to complete. After factual questions about his name, place and date of birth and his passport details, he also answered the following questions:

Why did you flee your country?	*My brother has been in custody since 30 August. I also was threatened. In November/December 1938 I was in a concentration camp in Sachsenhausen, from 9 November until 13 December.*
Have you been arrested or interned?	*Yes, in Sachsenhausen*
Why?	*The November action.*
Were you mistreated?	*Yes*
Do you have a criminal record?	*No*
(i) political?	*No*
(ii) criminal?	*No*
Do you have a copy of the judgement or any other legal document?	*No. The release certificate from the concentration camp had to be handed in when registering with the Gestapo.*

When did you arrive in Belgium?	*4 October 1939*
Across which border?	*Aachen or Eupen*
Why did you choose Belgium?	*That was the least of my concerns.*
Did you come voluntarily to Belgium?	*Yes*
Under what circumstances?	*Further emigration to the USA*
Have you been brought across the border by a foreign agent?	*No*
To which Belgian supporting authority can you appeal?	*Comité d'Assistance aux Refugiés Juifs*
Do you have relatives in Belgium?	*No*
Do you have funds? Which?	*Yes, small*
What work do you have in Belgium?	*None*

Hermann gave the references that were required, and he chose to give the names of Lore's guarantor in England, Mr Harris, and of Lord Philip Hartog in London. The clerk in the Ministry of Justice – after noting that Hermann was not engaged in any political activities – immediately gave him the refugee status of 'model B'.

However, the validation could not be completed until confirmation of Hermann's financial status could be received from Wilhelmshaven, and this arrived two days later on 12 October 1939. Hermann was already amassing an impressive quantity of paperwork – the fate of all refugees.

Ten days later, he had found a room to live in at 144, Avenue Rogier in the Schaerbeek area of Brussels. Schaerbeek was an area that housed a large number of Jewish families who had moved to Belgium from Germany and Eastern Europe. They had set up a prayer room in a house in rue des Coteaux, which was just a seven-minute walk for Hermann on the Sabbath. Avenue Rogier is a wide and busy thoroughfare in Brussels, and Hermann's room at number 144 was one of several in a tall, narrow, old-style building. And it was quite possibly a noisy place from both the road and the nearby railway.

By the end of 1939, there were tens of thousands of refugees living in Belgium. While the numbers of refugees arriving from the German Third Reich had increased during the 1930s, the Belgian authorities had been very unwilling to recognise 'political refugees'. They were afraid of a massive influx of impoverished people at a time when Belgium – like other countries – was experiencing an economic crisis. Refugee camps had been set up at the beginning of the previous year, and the Belgian government had theoretically closed its borders on 30 April 1939. But many 'illegal' refugees who had managed to make their way to Belgium were tolerated as long as private organisations took care of them. Jewish communities in Brussels were mainly centred on Schaerbeek and Anderlecht, close to the main railway stations. Unfortunately, those efficient railway networks later became a deadly disadvantage to the Jews when Nazi authorities decided to deport them.

The *Comité d'Assistance aux Refugiés Juifs* (Committee for Assistance to Jewish Refugees) that helped Hermann – and later Henny – had been set up in Belgium in 1933 to welcome Jews who were fleeing Nazism from Germany, Austria and Czechoslovakia. It helped them with their most urgent needs – not only shelter, but also financial, social, medical and legal assistance. It helped them with the complicated paperwork of residence certificates, transit visas for other countries, emigration papers and formalities, and it kept an eye on the latest emigration quota allowances for different countries. The committee also took a great pastoral care for the refugees who passed through its doors and tried to alert them to the cultural differences and expectations of living in another country in a state of war. For this reason, various behaviours were admonished or advised – and some of the committee's exhortations were painted (in German) as a warning onto the wall of the entrance courtyard to the committee's premises. They can still be seen today – 2023:

> *Earn the hospitality that you receive in Belgium!*
> *Always conduct yourself in an exemplary manner!*
> *Respect the customs of the country.*
> *Don't get noticed.*
> *Avoid speaking out loudly on the streets and in public spaces.*
> *Practise discipline.*
> *It is in your own interest.*

While Belgium was taking a neutral position in the war, those responsible for refugees in the country recognised that anything could spark a major confrontation, and so Jewish welfare organisations were anxious that their clients should show themselves worthy of the welcome they had received – if only in their own self-interest. Apart from the recommendations painted on the committee's walls, Jews were discouraged from conversations in German in the street or on the tram, from meandering (or loitering) around the town centre, from frequenting public spaces such as cafés, restaurants and cinemas, and even from visiting the committee's premises, except in an extreme emergency.

Clients received a message warning them:

> *...non-observance could lead to the most serious consequences. Those refugees whom we take care of who do not observe these prescriptions also expose themselves to being removed from our lists, with all the consequences that this removal entails. We expect that each refugee will support us and ensure that those measures are observed by everyone around them.*

In 1939, the German-Jewish Surrealist painter Felix Nussbaum painted *The Refugee*. Nussbaum, like Hermann, and later Henny, lived in Brussels as a refugee and the painting expresses his isolation as well as his constant and great fear. In it, a man is slumped in a chair in apparent despair, with his head in his hands. He is alone in a room devoid of any marks of humanity. There is just one large table, upon which is an over-emphasised globe, and his own meagre belongings of a walking stick and a small bundle lie on the floor at his feet. Bare trees can be seen through an arched doorway, and a flock of black birds circles overhead. The painting depicts the painful and desolate bleakness of life for so many Jewish refugees at the time, with the circling horrors from which there was no escape, in a world where no country on the globe would offer refuge.

Fear, desperation and helplessness were what people like Hermann and Henny Hartog felt as they fled their home, family and earlier way of life. As Hermann wrote on his postcard, he was 'feeling very bad' and he was clearly very shaken by his experiences. He was exhausted from the physical and emotional stresses of leaving Aurich and from the difficult journey across the closed border. He felt utterly bereft without Henny – and terrified that she might not be able to join him – but he was relieved to be alive and free.

Without any official residency papers, any money, or a settled place to live, Hermann felt absolutely lost. He didn't speak the language and had never before been to Brussels. It was early October, and he hadn't heard from Lore and Inge since August. In tiny writing on the postcard (to make best use of the space), Hermann urged his daughters:

> *We wait every day, my dear children, for a sign of writing from you. I would be terribly happy to have a few lines from you, and then I will write to you in detail.*
>
> *Much love, loving kisses, your Vati.*

Immediately upon receiving the postcard, Lore and Inge replied – but (to Hermann's frustration) their letter didn't arrive until more than two weeks later, on 22 October 1939. 'You must write "Lang: German", then it goes faster. But I was very happy.'

In the meantime, Hermann sorted out his residency papers, found the room at Avenue Rogier, made friends with the Elsbergs and began to breathe a little more freely. However, Henny was still in Cologne – and there were other worries. He was very concerned about their ability to survive with no money or assets, no job, and no prospect of being able to work in Belgium. It was important for him to know that the small amount of money they had initially sent with Lore was still safe.

'Do you still have the money?' he asked her.

'The money and the jewellery are with Mr and Mrs Braunsberg, 60 St Paul's Churchyard, London EC1. I want to decide with Mutti what will happen to it.'

A few years later, most of the property around St Paul's Cathedral in London would be burnt to the ground, Lore and Inge would be evacuated to Wales, and nobody knows about Mr and Mrs Braunsberg, but these things were difficult to organise from afar. Hermann seems to have been in touch with Henny throughout these weeks, although he was not able to share with her some of the contents of Lore and Inge's letters. Apparently, in one of their letters they had mentioned the existence of some money (outside Germany) and also made reference to Hermann's time in the concentration camp. Either of those comments could have caused trouble if they had been intercepted and read by the Gestapo and – at the very least – hindered any chance of Henny leaving.

But Hermann was still confident that their belongings would arrive from Germany. 'I don't need my blue shirt yet. I expect my things out from Germany soon.' He also tried to sound confident that Henny would be able to leave.

> *You, dear Inge, write very lovely wishes, which will happen with God's help and fulfilment. When Mutti arrives, you will get a message immediately. Stay well, both of my beloved. Many kisses from your loving Vati.*

A week after writing this, Henny arrived – on Sunday 29 October 1939. Both Hermann and Henny were overjoyed.

'Our beloved Mutti has just arrived, and we are both very happy that she is finally here,' wrote Hermann, and Henny wrote to her daughters:

> *Dear precious ones,*
> *After many long weeks, I can finally write to you. After an adventurous journey, I at last arrived with Vati today and you will feel our great joy. But my head is still so dazed after all the exertion that I cannot write much. I will write about everything that I experienced later. Greetings to the Harrises. Mutti.*

Henny joined Hermann at new lodgings he had found at 127 rue Royale Ste Marie. In a quiet, wide road these were possibly more suitable for the two of them than his previous room. While they were glad of a new sense of liberation, they were still able to do very little except exist and write to their daughters. But they had escaped the discrimination, humiliation and persecution by the Nazis in Germany – and they were grateful for that. Looking for any paid employment was impossible, given their refugees status, and they were both worn out with anxiety for the future and with the exertions of the past few months and years. They were also constantly trying to find new ways to move their plans forward for emigration to America, but they were unable to control any of the procedures and felt helpless in the hands of other people.

Both Henny and Hermann recognised that they needed to refresh and relearn languages other than German, and in their next joint letter to Lore and Inge, Henny wrote her share in English, as well as referring to her time at finishing school in Lausanne in 1914.

> *Since 25 years I didn't speak French and I have forgotten much, so Daddy and I must begin to learn. It's a beautiful language and soon I hope to speak it again.*

In the same letter, they wrote that 'we are hoping to go to the USA in nine months' – but even as they wrote the words, the waiting times were lengthening, and further restrictions were being implemented to make this difficult.

Henny and Hermann's letter at the end of November was a long and chatty birthday gift, since they were unable to send any parcels in the post. Both girls celebrated their birthdays within a fortnight of each other at the end of November and the beginning of December and these had always been joyous occasions for the whole family.

'How I would like to set a birthday table for you with all the lovely things that you would like for yourself!' wrote Henny. 'I wish everything that is good for you both, but you know also that wishes are not always fulfilled, and that often in life we must exert ourselves to achieve something.'

Parenting from a distance was not easy, and Hermann reflected on his enforced absence the previous year (when he was in Sachsenhausen) when writing to Inge:

> *This is already the second birthday that I have not been able to wish you a happy birthday in person, and it is already more than one year since you have been separated from your parents. I wish you everything good for your new year, for good health, and I only wish that it will not be long before we can all be together again. May God grant that.*

There was some practical information as well. The money Lore had sent when Hermann asked her, after he first arrived in Brussels, had still not arrived, and Hermann was unable to access anything from the Post Office since his identity card and residency papers had not yet been processed. He was frustrated that he had asked for the money to be sent to the Elsbergs' address, but Lore had sent it to the Post Office. 'You see again that it is better if you do as I wish, then we don't have any difficulties.'

Both Henny and Hermann were also discouraged that they were not allowed work permits and so could not apply for any jobs.

> *For that reason, we hope that we will soon be able to go from here to the USA. But it will now take perhaps a year. That is life. Perhaps if the war ends sooner, then everything would be quicker for us.*

Henny regretted that they were not able to write as frequently as they would like, but. 'For the price of a stamp to England, we can buy a small loaf of bread. You know how much we must economise.'

She gave a few more details about the house where they were living, where they had one room to themselves:

> *Here in the house, there are only other immigrants, and our landlady is a good elderly Belgian woman. Vati can communicate well because French and Flemish are both spoken here, and Flemish is similar to Dutch and Low German. We have a big cooking stove in our room and a big couch. I am doing the cooking myself. Usually, Vati does the shopping and I cook, and we both find it tasty. Be very thrifty with all your things, dear children, because we cannot buy any more. We are well, although Vati and I have lost some weight, but hopefully you have gained some.*

They told Lore and Inge that they had received good news from the relatives in Aurich, as well as from Opa in Frankfurt, and from Max Ruda in Zurich. They enclosed letters for the Harrises, as well as a letter from Aunt Henny to Lore and Inge.

A few days later, at 10 o'clock on the morning of Tuesday 5 December 1939, there was a knock on the door and Henny Hartog was arrested. The police record states that they took into custody 'the foreigner Scheuer, Henny, wife of Hartog, Hermann, no profession.'

She was taken by car and appeared in front of the local magistrate at 1 o'clock that afternoon, charged with violating an article of the aliens police. She had failed to report her arrival in Brussels several weeks previously and thus had failed to be accorded any residency permit. Given her recent knowledge and understanding of the Nazis in Germany, this was probably a very frightening experience, and she never told her daughters what had happened. In fact, her case was dismissed, and she was granted the same status as Hermann – 'model B'. Hermann's status was valid until 28 May 1940, and Henny's until 19 August 1940.

On the police notes that still exist in the Brussels archives, the officer writing the final report to the submitting officer, who was the deputy senior official for the day, handwrote:

> *(Relax! Isn't this sabotaging the law? It is obvious that Public Security would be willing to put the wife in the same situation as her husband, even though there was still a violation of AL of 28 September 1939!)*

And typed into the report, his final decision is: 'I think that there is nothing left for us to do but to deliver to Scheuer the certificate model B registration of foreigners while waiting for emigration.'

Even so, Henny seems to have given the police a revised version of when she had arrived in Belgium, giving them the date of 6 November 1939, rather than the date a week earlier when both she and Hermann wrote to Lore and Inge to say that she had arrived. She also had no idea through which point on the border she had crossed. When asked why she had chosen to flee to Belgium, she answered, 'I had no choice but to be with my husband.'

The letter Henny and Hermann sent to Lore and Inge a few weeks after this event sounds a little less confident and certain – or maybe they were just tired and a little sadder. It was mid-December, and – as Henny said – 'The weather is very cold, and if it's not cold here it's raining.'

They both just wanted the family to be reunited.

> *Often Vati and I speak about you, and about how nice it will be once we are all together again. Both of us are quite well. Don't be afraid; we are not hungry and that's the main point.*

Henny described how she and Hermann had recently found some work to do. It must have been an informal arrangement within the Jewish community, and it might not have been paid work, but it gave them both pleasure. It came through friendly contacts between the refugees (and the grapevine always seemed to work extraordinarily efficiently). Relatives of the wealthy Knurr family from Aurich were in Brussels awaiting emigration to America, and Henny and Hermann gave them the domestic help that they needed.

'There are three children – a very lovely baby of 6 months called Susette, the little blond Rosanne 4 years, and the dark-haired intelligent boy Richard, who is 5 years old. While Vati is teaching and playing with Rosanne and Richard, I am sewing or ironing,' explained Henny.

Practical issues of daily living were always to the fore – and some family members already in the USA had sent some money to help Henny and Hermann. They were still in contact with many members of the Aurich, Jever and Wilhelmshaven communities and sent news on to Lore and Inge from there. And they kept up a strong correspondence with people in America and elsewhere who might be able to help with their emigration. Letters went constantly back and forth as they tried to find a way, any loophole, that might make leaving possible.

But a shift – and perhaps a problem – was showing in communication between the girls and the people they knew in Germany – and, to some extent, with their parents. Lore and Inge had been immersed in the English language since the day that they had each landed in England and they were finding it increasingly difficult to write in German. They still sometimes spoke German to refugee friends in England, and occasionally to each other, but more frequently they spoke English to everyone. Henny and Hermann understandably found this very difficult, and other members of the family found it impossible.

'We have had letters from Aurich and from Opa. Your letters that are written in German are sent to Aurich and then they are later sent to Frankfurt.'

This was a development – and a problem – that would only intensify over time.

On 26 January 1940, Wolff Benjamin Wolffs was forced by the SS and the Wilhelmshaven Gestapo to arrange to evacuate all Jews from Aurich. His father, the leader of the Jewish community in Aurich, was too sick to undertake the task. There were then 150 Jews still remaining in Aurich but they all had to expect and make plans to leave.

The background to this expulsion was the imminent invasion of the Netherlands by the armed forces of the Wehrmacht. Plans had been made for the invasion to take place in January 1940, but on 10 January a German courier aircraft on its way to Cologne became lost in fog and crashed in Belgium. The courier, Major Helmuth Reubriger of the German 7th Airborne Division, ran from the wreckage, carrying the detailed plans for the western offensive with him – setting fire to his briefcase as he ran. The fire was spotted by some Belgian soldiers who retrieved such papers as they could. When Reubriger was taken to military headquarters nearby, he again tried to destroy remaining papers in a stove, but a Belgian soldier snatched them from the flames.

Officials at Luftwaffe headquarters in Berlin were very concerned when they heard about the incident and on 13 January the planned troop movements were cancelled. When the invasion actually took place four months later, the details of the attack had all been drastically changed.

That same month, January 1940, (in Brussels) Henny and Hermann moved with their belongings to different accommodation at rue Seutin 58, where their landlord was a Monsieur Friedrichs. They had a fair amount of luggage to take with them – 'one large overseas trunk, one leather suitcase, one brown and one grey (new) suitcase and a black hat box, everything packed full of things,' as Hermann wrote a few months later to Lore and Inge. Their new rooms were in the same area of Brussels as they had been living – a ten-minute walk from their previous place, and in a similar style of house.

The following month, the district administrator in Aurich sent a reply to the administrator of Public Security in Brussels:

> *Concerning the arrival of Hermann Israel Hartog: the statements made by Hartog correspond to the facts. He has no criminal record. Nothing else that is detrimental to him has become known.*

On 6 February 1940, Henny and Hermann wrote a short postcard to Lore and Inge from their new address, grateful that a letter from their daughters had arrived the previous day. Henny wrote chattily about the pullover she was knitting for Lore, expecting that she would be able to put it in the post within a few days. It was very cold in Brussels that winter and Henny also reported that Hermann had recently slipped down two flights of icy steps and hurt himself. He had managed to see a doctor who had diagnosed a broken or bruised rib and advised that Hermann 'keep quiet' but also stay moderately active. She fretted that it would soon be Hermann's birthday but that 'again I have nothing to prepare to make him happy'. With typical optimism, she asserted, 'We must always keep our courage and believe that better times will come to us again.'

Hermann's share of the postcard was more business-like:

> *A letter came yesterday from Aurich, but there was nothing much in it. I have still had no answer from the American Consulate. We are hoping that we will hear that we can go together with you to the USA in about half a year. Until then we must endure things here, where it is very difficult. Many loving, loving kisses from your Vati.*

He was concerned at the uncharacteristic lack of news from his sisters and brother. In the previous fourteen days he had received only two small postcards, and he and Henny were aware that the political news from the region was not good. But four days later, on 11 February 1940, there was indeed news from Aurich: Hermann's siblings, Berta, Sara and Oskar, had been forced to leave their home in Wallstraße to live in an 'old people's home' in Emden, 27km away to the south-west. At the end of that month, the Gestapo also ordered that all Jews in Aurich must leave the area of Ostfriesland by 1 April 1940.

This forcible removal included 82-year-old Lipmann Knurr and his sister-in-law Henny Knurr, who was 75. Their younger relatives who had managed to get to America pressed them to marry each other so that they could emigrate on a married persons' visa (since there were no visas available for single people by this date). But Henny Knurr was a very religious woman, and Jewish laws forbade in-law marriage, so she and Lipmann stayed in Germany and went to live with relatives in Bremen.

The Jewish communities Henny and Hermann Hartog had known in Germany were fragmenting.

'The aunts and Uncle Oskar are now in an old people's home in Emden. Jakob is in Vegesack near Bremen, and Martha has gone to Cologne. I don't know where Hosi is. In general, I don't know where most of them are,' wrote Hermann at the end of February 1940.

That same month, the postal service between England and Belgium – which had been running fairly smoothly until then – suddenly started to become 'topsy-turvy', as Henny Hartog described it. This was particularly unfortunate since it had become apparent from the letters, postcards and school reports that arrived in an odd sequence in Brussels that Lore's attitude and performance at school had also become 'topsy-turvy'. It was perhaps unsurprising that the 15-year-old girl was unable to give her best at school, but Henny recognised that 'apparently you have fallen back into your old mistakes and have become somewhat careless.'

In the reply that Henny wrote to both girls on 10 February 1940, she tried her best to give the counsel she would have given if they had both been at her side:

> *Dear Lore, I do not want at all to reproach you about it; I think that you are clever enough to recognise your own mistakes and steady enough in character to soon lose them. Also, dear child, today I give you – not for the first time – good motherly and also friendly advice: work hard and make your work tidy, get used to it and carry out even the smallest thing neatly. Believe me, that brings for all good work – also later in life – its own reward.*
>
> *'I ask you next time to write in detail in German why you had slackened, and how you have now changed your position. We know English quite well but when the words are often written illegibly and wrong, I cannot translate it, and sometimes we do not know what it should mean. Report in detail about yourself. Who understands you, my dear child, better than your parents? So, my dear, take note.*
>
> *And also, you, dear Inge: people often make mistakes, and from them they should be better, and prove that they are a worthy person.*
>
> *Here it is very cold. Hopefully, you have enough warm clothes to wear. With many warm kisses, your Mutti.*

Hermann fully endorsed Henny's message:

> *Dear children, your mother has already written everything that we thought from the receipt of Mr Harris's letter. In addition, I state that nowadays we really must expect that you both do your best to work hard and respectably in everything. We are having a hard time here and must begin to build a completely new life. So, we expect from you that in your school and in later life, you prepare yourself well. You and we can be glad that we are out of Germany because it must have become very bad there. Much love and many kisses, your Vati.*

Meanwhile, Henny and Hermann were glad of the warm room in their new accommodation as the weather had turned bitterly cold. They were also appreciative of some money Uncle Max had been able to send them from America.

Despite Henny's sadness that Hermann's birthday would not be adequately celebrated, he was happy to receive a letter with greetings from Lore and Inge in time for his birthday. In response, he stated very simply – as he would time and time again – 'we just hope that the good God will grant that we can be together again soon.'

Meanwhile, he and Henny were cheerfully preparing a parcel of goodies to send to their daughters, despite acknowledging that 'everything becomes difficult'.

They were both concerned, towards the end of February, that they had not had any news 'from Aurich' – which had become a sort of shorthand for any of the Jews who had previously lived there, and particularly for Hermann's family. They both knew (and told Lore and Inge) that all the Jews would need to leave the entire area of Ostfresia within a few weeks, even though the elderly people in their own family had only recently been shifted from Aurich to Emden.

'It is terrible that these old people have to leave their home, and the Jews are met with ever new tortures. We are happy to be here. The children from Aurich are all in a children's home away from their parents, and we are glad, dear Inge, that you came to England in good time. You both, dear children, are a thousand times better off in England,' wrote Hermann.

And he reminded them again of the numbers and date on their emigration papers, which had been lodged in Hamburg.

That evening, Hermann's fifty-third birthday, on 22 February, Henny's share of the letter to their daughters described their new way of living. It was a very different picture from their previous life together in Wilhelmshaven. It was 10.30 in the evening when she wrote, and she was very tired. She had recently found some new work where she gave domestic help to another Jewish family.

> *I leave at eight in the morning, and I come back dead tired to our beloved Vati at nine in the evening. Just think: Vati has to keep the room clean, cook, wash, iron – and even darn his own socks! And it is a great joy that when I come back to him in the evening everything is so beautifully tidy. I am so busy, but I will find time to write to you. Don't be sad that I can write so little.*

Hermann added that if they needed money, he would try to send some, and a week later he sent them £1 – although he commented that they did not seem to be very thrifty. As well as his domestic chores while Henny was working, Hermann taught pupils for a few hours each week, 'but it pays hardly anything'. Henny's progress with knitting the pullover had slowed down considerably since she started her new job, and in the evenings, she was too tired either to complete her knitting or to make arrangements to get it sent to Lore.

Both Henny and Hermann tried so hard to keep a balance between the new demands of wartime living, their own anxieties about being refugees, and the desire to parent their daughters in these strange times.

> *If you enclose a small letter for Opa or for the people in Aurich, do not give the name of any town (I mean Westcliff). Do you understand me on that? If it is not too expensive, get yourselves photographed together – just the heads. We long so much for a photo. In addition, we would also like to know what size you are and ask you to send us your measurements. Soon we will no longer know what you look like.*

A week later, on 4 March 1940, Henny was feeling less exhausted as she had decided to quit her job. After a few days' rest, she felt refreshed and better able to organise her life. She shared her experiences and thoughts with her young daughters:

> *I have stayed away from the people for whom I worked because they were so demanding and outrageous. But they have already been twice to ask me to go back again. Now, instead of going from eight in the morning until nine in the evening, I will go from one at lunchtime until eight in the evening.*

She was pleased with the pullover, which had embroidered flowers on it – worked by a fellow refugee living in their house who turned out to be a friend of one of Henny's aunts. There was considerable correspondence about the parcel that included the pullover, and eventually Hermann was able to report that:

> *After all sorts of difficulties and much money I got rid of the parcel. We have to send the parcel by freight on the railway. Hopefully, it will now go well and have no difficulties at the customs because there are only old things in it. The chocolate will taste good. The blue material is handmade. You must share the things between you, as you know is necessary. The hat is of first-class quality and if you don't need it send it back.*

This is probably the last gift we know that Henny and Hermann were able to send to their daughters.

At the same time, there was an update from Henny on emigration plans and possibilities:

> *God willing, we will go together to the USA. If the American Consulate has not yet answered, write to Bloomsbury House and*

explain everything – perhaps they have the form there for the Consulate. I have written to Uncle Max about the affidavits. In order for things to work out, he must issue your affidavit independently from ours. That means that the Consul in London and the Consul in Belgium should not know that an independent affidavit has been issued for you, and the Consul in London need not know that your parents have also been issued an affidavit by Max Bodenheimer, because that affidavit for four people is not sufficient. So, when you have filled in the form, you do not know who issued an affidavit to your parents. Have you understood? I will explain it again. We calculate that it will be July.

Under wartime conditions, preparations for emigration were now vastly more difficult than they had been a few years previously. In fact, both Henny and Hermann knew that completing the necessary paperwork was just the first hurdle – the main problem was going to be finances. They had none.

Naturally, the biggest worry is who will give us the foreign exchange for the travel money, because the aid organisations can no longer work as they did earlier, because they have given a lot of money to Poland where the need of the Jews is enormous.

On 9 March 1940, Hermann's cousin, Rosa Wolffs – who once lived just across the road from the Hartogs in Aurich, at Wallstraβe 25 – departed from Antwerp with her daughter Else to join Rosa's sons (Meinhard and Siegbert), who were already in Chicago. Hermann passed this news to Lore and Inge, as well as telling them that the elderly Aunts Cohn in Jever had been forced to move to Hamburg. 'They always ask after you in every letter.'

The following day, on 10 March, Henny and Hermann celebrated their nineteenth wedding anniversary. 'For the first time in a foreign country,' wrote Hermann to his daughters. 'Your beloved Mutti, with whom I have been together for nineteen years.'

Hermann noted and celebrated the Jewish festivals, even as a refugee, and later that month, on 23 March, was the festival of Purim. This commemorates the saving of the Jewish people in the fifth century BCE from annihilation and it celebrates the actions of Queen Esther. It is a day of rejoicing and feasting for Jewish people and Hermann wondered whether or not his daughters still followed the customs.

Were you in the synagogue at Purim to hear the story of Esther? Do you still know the story of Purim? Today is Purim and I have

> *come straight from the morning service. It is the first time in over thirty years that I have not chanted the Megillah. This afternoon Mutti and I have been invited for Purim celebrations by the chief here.*

The Megillah is the scroll of the Book of Esther, which is chanted in the synagogue on the eve of Purim, and hitherto it had been Hermann's role to do this. It was a hard road for him, being denied the outward expression of his faith, and unable to lead the community's celebrations, as he had once done. Like many other middle-aged refugees, his confidence was shattered by his inability to provide for his family, and he suffered keenly from a loss of identity and dignity as he remained unable to continue his professional work. It was a significant event for Hermann that he was unable to sing the Megillah, and he felt it with great heaviness.

For Henny, the celebrations were mainly about how they affected her within the family and at home. She was hoping to enjoy the festival with Hermann, since her employer had gone to Ostend for a few days.

> *Today is Purim. Hopefully, not many more festivals will pass before we are together again. Soon it will be Pesach, and this year I have had a huge house clean.*

Henny's work outside the home did not give her much pleasure. Her boss was a singer who allegedly had 'dreadful moods' and was 'very demanding'. Henny was not sorry when she went to Ostend for two days over the Easter weekend to perform at a concert.

> *Dear Lore, you ask what my work is: cooking, washing, ironing, keeping the room clean. The people live in a lavishly furnished apartment on the eleventh floor of a skyscraper with a lovely roof garden. From the window you can see the whole of Brussels laid out.*

During April, Henny and Hermann received Lore's school report. She had now reached school-leaving age in England, and there was no money available to fund the higher education or university studies that everyone (including Lore) had wanted and hoped for her to pursue.

'I would have thought that after Easter there should be trainee placements. Is nothing like that happening?' asked Hermann.

Both Henny and Hermann were feeling increasingly excluded from their daughters' lives. They didn't fully understand the educational processes in England, nor how they affected Lore and Inge. They were astonished to learn from Lore that she had sold some of her own gold jewellery to meet her expenses. They had given her explicit instructions about the sale of the family jewellery without being at all appreciative of the market value of any of it in England. And the rules of social etiquette that had applied to Henny and Hermann as they navigated their young adult years amongst their Jewish communities in Germany in the early years of the twentieth century no longer held any resonance amongst the youngsters of a refugee community in England in the 1940s. This dissonance could only magnify over the next few years as they all lived their different lives.

News from Emden during April 1940 was that Sara had written to say that they 'were not bad'. Although it had been a most difficult and traumatic move from Aurich, she said they had settled down – although it is difficult to tell how much of what they wrote down was knowing that the Gestapo was taking note. Eighty elderly people were being accommodated in the old people's home.

That month, from 22 to 30 April, Jewish people celebrated Pesach, or the Passover – a major religious festival that celebrates the Israelites' ancient escape from slavery in Egypt. Part of the ritual celebrations include the Seder when the story of the exodus of the Jewish people is retold, and when symbolic foods are eaten, including unleavened bread – matzos. Henny and Hermann ordered the matzos and planned to stay at home for the celebrations, with perhaps two or three guests. They sent some matzos to Opa in Frankfurt.

And Henny wrote to Lore and Inge, 'On Seder evening, we will think a lot about you and hope to spend next Seder with you. May the matzos taste good! Many heartfelt kisses, your Mutti.'

Meanwhile, Hermann arranged to take English lessons as part of his emigration preparations. 'I am learning so that I will not disgrace myself in front of you later. So far, people laugh at my accent, but hopefully not for much longer.'

He and Henny were not particularly pleased when Uncle Max wrote to say he would delay sending the affidavit until certain conditions were in place, but there was nothing they could do about it. Both Henny and Hermann were realistic about the problems associated with emigration and wanted to share those realities with Lore and Inge.

'Dear children, it is better that you do not count the days until we can be together once again,' wrote Henny. 'Instead of July, it could be the autumn, and you know that at the present time we cannot predict very well. What should we write to you? We know nothing ourselves about the future. If the Lift with everything in it were to come here, there is nobody to pay the freight to the USA. Truly, it would cost one year of German currency to send it to New York. The dispatch expenditure would be huge.'

By the beginning of April, they decided to have their Lift – the container with their belongings that had been held in Bremen – sent to them in Brussels. They recognised that they could no longer afford its freight to America, and there was nobody else in the family who had the resources to help with this expenditure. They hoped to sell much of the Lift's contents, but they were fearful that in the current circumstances they would get very little money in return for their goods.

> *We will only keep the linen. Maybe it will be useful later. Hopefully the parcels of glass will not get broken on the way because it is still worth a lot if we can sell it. We paid the freight in Germany before the war, because we all thought otherwise. Now the money is more or less completely lost, like all the rest. But we can't do much about that. There was nothing else we could do, and with God's help better times will come for everyone.*

It was difficult for them to explain how much their lives had changed, but they sometimes chose differences in everyday domestic life to illustrate their predicament. Lore had expressed some astonishment and concern that her mother was working so hard physically and stated that she really needed a maid – as in the days when Lore had last been at home in Wilhelmshaven.

> *God grant, dear Lore, that you are right if you think that later I should again have a maid. There is very little prospect of that. We must stop everything for a time and work capably. Vati has just gone to wash the laundry. What do you think of that? That is how it is now. So, dear good children, your mother is dog-tired and going to bed to think of you. A thousand kisses, Mutti.*

The work Henny was given at the end of April 1940 required that she live in at her employer's house, and this meant that she was not with Hermann. While it was important for them to earn some money, they both found this extremely difficult.

'Mutti has taken up a new position and I think that she has struck lucky,' wrote Hermann on 26 April 1940. 'But I am now alone all day and night and visit Mutti only a couple of times a week. Then it is a long way from our flat. If I could find a cheap room nearby, I would like to move there soon.'

They were both comforted that it was a short-term assignment for just four weeks, so they could consider other plans afterwards. The comment he made about the Aunts Cohn in Hamburg and the Hartog siblings in Aurich applied just as much to him and Henny. 'They are finding it difficult to get used to the new circumstances, but they have to.'

Nevertheless, Henny was finding the physical demands of this new life quite difficult. ('You well know that I am not so strong, but I must work a lot.') She and Hermann were also considering what skills they could present for a positive immigration application and began to think that their background and experiences with the Aurich and Jever cattle businesses might give them an entry into working in leather or hide concerns. Another entrepreneurial activity suggested itself:

> *Dear Lore, we are* **very** *interested to know if there is in Westcliff or Southend a workshop or a business that deals in leather goods – such as shoes, handbags, or suitcases. It would be a huge chance for us, dear Lore, if you could learn something about this.*

This idea was not successful. Ideas that might have improved their chances of obtaining a visa to Britain for employment in industry, commerce or artistic fields were no longer valid. Trying to obtain a visa remained extremely difficult – if not impossible – and nerve-wracking.

At the end of April 1940, with great jubilation from the Nazis, the area of Ostfriesland (which included Aurich) was declared 'Jew Free'.

On 6 May 1940, Henny wrote to Lore and Inge to tell them that she had given up her job. She regretted that she simply was not strong enough to do the work, and she also worried about Hermann being on his own, and only seeing him twice a week. She had heard from the Antwerp Consulate that she and Hermann could expect to be summoned for emigration some time in August – a mere three months away.

And then Belgium was invaded by the Germans.

Early in the morning of a fine spring day, 10 May 1940, air-raid sirens sounded in Brussels as the forces of Germany's Third Reich launched an attack. Bombs fell on several areas of the city – including Schaerbeek, where Henny and Hermann were living.

German diplomats had explained, in a pre-dawn meeting in Berlin with their counterparts from the Low Countries, that German troops were coming to protect them from imminent attacks from the British and French. They were also told that any opposition would be crushed. In Brussels, the Belgian foreign minister was unimpressed by the German ambassador's message and observed that – without any warning other than the attack itself – Germany had violated the promises that it had undertaken to acknowledge Belgium's neutrality. The calm of the phoney war that had existed for the past eight months was over.

On 15 May, Holland surrendered to the Germans, and on 28 May the king of Belgium also surrendered. By then, the Belgian fort Eben Emael had fallen (on 11 May), the Germans had crossed the Albert Canal, and the Allied troops were in retreat towards the English Channel. The speed with which all this was achieved was unbelievable to observers. British troops moved into Belgium to try to stop the German advance, but disaster came more swiftly to the French than anyone could comprehend.

We do not have an account from either Henny or Hermann about what happened to them, but others who lived in the vicinity have left their records. The massive assault came almost as a complete surprise. It was a swift offensive by the Germans, and neither the Belgian nor the Dutch forces could withstand the attack.

On the very day of the invasion, Henny wrote a hurried postcard to her daughters:

> *My dearest children, I am in a great hurry to say to you that Vati and I are quite well. Please don't worry about the war, and if you don't get letters from us don't be sad. Because it is [Shabbat], Vati cannot write any more to you. All our love for you both, Mutti.*
>
> *P.S. We don't know long we will be here in Brussels but write just the same as usual. If you do not have much to tell us, please only use postcards.*

Within hours of the German invasion, on that same day, 10 May 1940, the radio announced that all Germans living in Belgium faced internment and had to report to the nearest police station. The Belgian state security service wished to protect the territory from subversive activities by Germans and their sympathisers. From the police station, crowds of men, women and children were directed to large halls locally. The women and children were then told that they could leave. Most of those detained were, in fact, German Jewish refugees who had themselves fled from Nazi aggression. It was, as Henny had noted, the Jewish Shabbat.

By 12 May, Brussels was largely deserted and in chaos. Only a few trams were running, the schools were closed, and many of the city's inhabitants had fled to the south and west. The Belgian government was overwhelmed by the turn of events and ideas for a controlled evacuation were abandoned. The need to organise a serious defence was hampered by the need to deal with the mass of refugees who thronged the roads going west – away from the advancing army.

It was a swift assault and events moved too rapidly and dramatically for the various news outlets to keep up to date. When the Netherlands surrendered, all hopes that Jewish refugees had of escaping to England were shattered.

On 15 May, Henny and Hermann left Brussels, and on the evening of Sunday 19 May, they arrived in Paris. About two million refugees fled Belgium and descended on Paris. The French were not prepared for this number of displaced people to arrive in their capital city. During that time, both Antwerp and Brussels fell to the German invaders (on 17 and 18 May) and the military governor of Paris ordered the internment of 'Greater German subjects between 17 and 55'. During these chaotic days, reliable news of events was in short supply and most people could only operate on what they heard as rumour.

The Belgians had prepared files on those whom they deemed to be dangerous and knew the whereabouts of all Jewish refugees in their country. They acted quickly and arrested and interned all those they suspected might be part of a 'fifth column'. The 'deportees' of 1940 included pro-German Belgians and activists – but the vast majority were Jewish refugees from the Third Reich. The Belgian government made no attempt to distinguish between the different groups.

We have no record of Henny and Hermann's journey, although Hermann suggests in a letter that they travelled together, and Henny wrote to their daughters the day after they arrived in Paris:

> *It is not possible to say or to tell you about all that has happened. All our clothes and wardrobe have stayed in Brussels, and we have almost nothing here. I think that all our things have been lost.*

Their friend, Karl Elsberg, had been interned in a barracks in Brussels and then sent to the south of France. Karl's wife, Anneliese, remained in Brussels for the time being.

But Henny and Hermann were still alive. For the moment they were still together – and together they would face whatever the future would hold.

CHAPTER 8

Paris: May 1940

It was difficult to convey quite how different everyday life had become. Henny's message to Lore and Inge was written in French – not her customary German – on a postcard and, as she explained to them:

> *We are only allowed to write in French, so please get this card translated and if you write it is better if you can get something written in French. I don't know if Vati is able to write in French.*

Judging from rough pencil jottings on the card in Lore's handwriting, she had managed to translate this herself with the aid of a dictionary.

As Henny wrote that day, Monday 20 May, she had no idea of the whereabouts of Hermann. On their arrival in Paris the previous evening, they had been separated and sent to different internment camps. Henny went to the women's holding centre at the indoor cycling stadium, Vélodrome d'Hiver, near the Eiffel Tower and close to the River Seine.

This enormous glass-roofed racing track and sports stadium was where Henny waited on one of the stone benches with thousands of other women. They were divided into groups of four in order to prevent any mass action of protest. She recognised some held there and met up with others she had known in Germany. None of them knew what would happen to them, and as the days passed the collective nervousness grew. Every time an aeroplane flew over the glass roof the women feared a bombardment. Remembering 'Kristallnacht', they apprehensively expected the roof to shatter over their heads.

The weather was warm during that May and the stadium became hot. The women were given water and were adequately fed but they remained very uneasy about their situation and mistrustful of their future. It was, however, a slight consolation that they were guarded by the French rather than German SS men. Henny remained there for three days until she was transported elsewhere.

Meanwhile, Hermann had joined other men who were interned at another cycling and sports complex at Stade Buffalo, in Montrouge, about 3km from Henny.

As Henny explained on her postcard:

> *Vati is not with me. He is in another camp, because we are interned with thousands of people in a very big velodrome. We have been able to escape [from the German invasion] and I am sure that you are very happy that your parents are alive. I think about you very often my children! But I do not think that I can write often. I kiss you a thousand times!*

Just three days later, on 23 May 1940, Hermann also wrote to his daughters – in German – from the internment camp at Stade Buffalo:

> *Dear children, since Sunday evening, Mutti and I have been brought separately to these camps. We have no idea what will happen next. We will soon have another address. We have not heard from Emden for weeks so I have written to the Red Cross in Geneva, and I hope that we will soon receive news. Please write to this address and I will write to you. Write also if you get news from Mutti. Stay brave in life and if the dear God wills, he will bring us together again. Beloved Lore and beloved Inge, always stay close together in life. Much love, loving kisses, from your Vati.*

Everything had indeed changed dramatically, and the physical manifestations of war had now entered their lives. For perhaps the first time, both Henny and Hermann faltered in their optimism as the suggestion now enters their correspondence with Lore and Inge that the future might not be one that they can all count on being able to share together, and that maybe 'being alive' should not be taken for granted.

Henny and Hermann had escaped just in time. On the same day they arrived in Paris, seven armoured tank divisions of the German Army had driven relentlessly towards the English Channel, arriving by the sea at Abbeville just as Henny and Hermann were being sent to their internment camps. The French authorities – like the Belgian – feared a fifth column and so required all men between 15 and 55 years of age, and all unmarried or childless women of German nationality, or who had come from Germany, to report to collection camps. At that time, Hermann was 53 years old, and their children were not with them.

As the German troops, guns and following motorised infantry smashed their way westwards across national borders, hurtling along the roads at great speed, the citizens of northern France and Paris fled in panic from their homes in droves. The roads became jammed with German soldiers and their equipment, and also with thousands of refugees fleeing in panic from France, Belgium and the Netherlands.

Three weeks later, this continuing flood of people walking, driving, cycling towards the west and south of France increased dramatically as it became apparent that Paris would soon fall. German troops entered Paris on 14 June 1940 and soon the Nazi swastika flag flew from the Eiffel Tower and other public buildings and monuments. French troops had withdrawn from the city the previous day and Paris was declared an 'Open City'. Under international law, this meant that Paris would not be defended and that the Germans would be expected to occupy the city peacefully, rather than destroy it. So, German soldiers entered an eerily silent city as most people had already fled, and all shops and businesses had been closed.

A week earlier, on 8 June, distant artillery fire had been heard in Paris and the last few trains to leave the city from the Gare d'Austerlitz for destinations in the south of France were packed. People also took to the road with whatever transport they could find – cars, trucks, lorries, tourist buses, bicycles. The numbers involved meant that no one moved very fast – if at all – and further blockages were created by vehicles that broke down, ran out of petrol, or were abandoned. Many of those fleeing found that walking was quicker and more reliable. Prams and carts were used not only for pushing babies, but also for transporting belongings, children and elderly people.

And all the time the Germans were behind and above them, roaring overhead and strafing this slowly moving column of refugees. The journey south from Paris crossed the big rivers that ran east-west across France, whose bridges were sometimes found to have been hit or destroyed. These hundreds of thousands of people on the move had little to eat, and nowhere comfortable to sleep. Local people shared their barns and their food as far as they could but there was never enough to go round, even when those fleeing came across deserted and abandoned villages. All the while, there was no accurate idea of what was happening elsewhere, and terrifying rumours spread around.

Further chaos was introduced as the refugees became mixed up with members of the retreating French Army, some of whom arrived with their mechanised units and others who presented as apparent civilians, having taken off their uniforms or insignia and merged into the crowds.

Meanwhile, the evacuation from France of Allied troops in the face of the German advance took place at Dunkirk. The last troops were evacuated during the night of Monday 3 June 1940.

On Sunday 9 June, the French government fled Paris and two days later installed itself in Tours – 240km south-west of the capital – before re-assembling in the port city of Bordeaux. On Friday 14 June, the Germans entered Paris unopposed and two days later, Philippe Pétain became prime minister of France. French leaders were keen to avoid another war being fought on French terrain and so sought an armistice quickly. Peace negotiations with Germany commenced and Pétain announced a ceasefire at 12.30 p.m. on Monday 17 June.

The negotiations took place in the Forest of Compiègne, in the same railway coach of Marshal Foch in which the armistice of 11 November 1918 had been signed. This armistice between France and Germany was announced on Saturday 22 June 1940. It established a German occupation zone in the north and west of France, but the remainder of the country was left 'free' to be governed by the French.

After six weeks of fighting, most French people viewed the armistice with relief. They were glad to be spared the horrific death and destruction that had been the country's experience during the Great War, and they hoped for a speedy return to 'normal life'.

Henny and Hermann were not caught up in this chaos on the roads. By then, both of them had left Paris, where they had stayed in uncomfortable conditions in their respective camps for three or four days and nights. On Thursday 23 May, they were taken with other internees – probably by cattle carts on trains – to different internment camps further south, arriving later the same day or the following morning.

Hermann found himself at a camp at Bassens, in the Gironde – near the Atlantic coast and about 12km north of Bordeaux. The camp was in the 18th Military Area and had been set up about two months previously in an old disused gunpowder factory that had been built in the First World War and closed down in 1921. It was now being used to house foreigners who were seen as 'Undesirables' in France. There were about 1,100 internees from the Paris region in the camp, including German anti-fascists, Czech communists and intellectuals, and about 750 Jews. During their time at the camp, the healthy internees were required to unload ships in the port for long hours and low wages.

On 30 May, a week after his arrival at Bassens, Hermann sent a postcard to Lore and Inge, giving his new address and saying:

> *My beloved children, I now have my correct address and should immediately let you have news. Hopefully I will soon find out where Mutti is. I have heard nothing at all from her for 12 days. Also, I am waiting for an immediate answer from you. Thank God Mutti and I were in time coming away from Brussels. Afterwards I will write more to you. You will definitely get at least a page of news from me once a month. If you already have news from Mutti send me her address so that I can write to her. Greetings to Mr and Mrs Harris. God keep you well. Your Vati.*

Two days after Hermann wrote his postcard from the internment camp at Bassens, F.W. Neukirch raised an invoice that they sent to his address in Brussels, requesting payment for three month's storage of the Lift and its contents – 72 Reichsmarks for the period 1 June to 30 September 1940. The invoice eventually turned up in the family letters over thirty years later – and has probably never been paid. The Lift, on the other hand, has never been found.

As the German military advance continued during June, there was considerable anguish in Hermann's camp at Bassens amongst the internees who feared being captured by the Germans and delivered to the Gestapo on account of their political views or racial origins. The men could hear the approaching guns from within their camp.

One of the German-Jewish prisoners in the camp was Georg Bernhard, a prominent left-wing political economist and journalist who was active against National Socialism. On 18 June 1940, he led a deputation to the commandant of the camp to try to convince him to release those prisoners who were most at risk from the advancing army. The following day, 19 June, the commandant allowed the release of those internees with families in France, and all those who who had been persecuted for political reasons. There was enormous confusion within the camp as the criteria for release changed several times during the day, but by the evening most of those who desired release were given a certificate of liberation. They were to go south.

This sudden release was welcome but also terrifying. The terms of the armistice were still not known. The released prisoners had scarcely any money, and generally no idea where their wives and family were. The aid agencies for refugees were overwhelmed. Affidavits and visas for emigration had suddenly become worthless. Postal communication had almost broken down, and the grapevine had become the best hope for information about the whereabouts of family members. Along with all the other refugees fleeing the oncoming German Army, they crowded into what was designated the non-occupied area of France after the signing of the armistice.

Hermann was among these released prisoners, and – after his internment of four weeks – he immediately went in search of Henny.

CHAPTER 9

Camp de Gurs: Summer 1940

Hermann found Henny at an internment camp at Gurs, about 250km south of the camp he had left at Bassens.

Separation from family members and loved ones was a common experience in the dramatic exodus of such large numbers of displaced people from the north of France during the summer of 1940. The trauma of separation, and the difficulty and uncertainty of ever meeting up again, heightened the stress of the circumstances. There was not much reliable formal information to be found – just rumours, anxiety, intense hunger and exhaustion, desperation, and panic.

We do not know how Hermann had any idea of Henny's whereabouts in order to go to find her – nor how he travelled the 250km. But the grapevine and informal communication networks seem to have been extraordinarily successful. For those refugees on the road, there were chalked messages and notes left at official buildings or at points along the way by those trying to reconnect with family members. But Henny had been sent by train with other foreign Jewish women who had been held in the same place as her in Paris. She'd had few opportunities to let Hermann know when and where she was.

Hermann arrived at Camp de Gurs on the very day that the armistice between France and Germany was signed – 22 June 1940 – and on that day a line of demarcation was drawn across France, defining the 'occupied' area of France that was occupied by the Germans, and the 'non-occupied' parts of the country. It went through the heart of the Basques-Pyrénées department. There was also a further 'Forbidden zone' in the north and east of the country to prevent the return of displaced persons who had left during the exodus. In all, it extended through seventeen departments all the way to the Swiss border. The terms of the treaty would take effect from 25 June 1940. By then, some of the refugees who had fled from their homes in Paris had started to return to them.

The demarcation line ran just north of the camp at Bassens, from which Hermann had been released three days previously, so when he went to search for Henny he was already in the non-occupied – or 'free' – zone – as was the Camp de Gurs.

Shortly after Henny and Hermann had first arrived together in Paris a few weeks previously, the authorities there had become increasingly concerned about the rising tension and paranoia in the population about a possible fifth column and so had quickly made arrangements to transport the refugees out of the city – away from the Stade Buffalo and the Vélodrome d'Hiver – to departments in the south and west of the country. So Hermann had been sent with other men to Bassens and Henny with other women to Gurs.

The new and prevailing atmosphere in Paris and the rest of the country meant that whereas the foreign refugees had quite recently provoked sympathy, they were now seen as potential spies and many of them have recorded the overt hostility they experienced as they made the journey south.

One account describes a journey of nine days by rail from Brussels to Gurs in May 1940, in which the foreign Jewish women who were being evacuated from the city to the internment camp travelled in well-guarded cattle trucks that were closed and locked. There were about fifty people in each windowless carriage and they had nothing to eat or drink, although after a few hours of travelling a guard opened the door to the very hot wagon and distributed some water.

Most of the women were young and very stressed about their situation and upset about the inability to change their clothes or to wash at any time during the long journey. The train was frequently bombed by the Germans and some of the passengers became injured or were killed. There were frequent stops on this slow journey to avoid damaged railway tracks, and that was when the refugees were subjected to stones being thrown at the train by local French people, who also screamed abuse at them loudly.

The author of this account arrived at Gurs on the same day as Henny, and writes of one suffering ending and another beginning. Henny had experienced a shorter and possibly less traumatic journey, although she too was probably transported to the south-west of France in a closed cattle wagon in the heat of a day in May. Hannah Arendt, a German-Jewish historian and political theorist who had been living in Paris, had also been interned in the Vélodrome d'Hiver and has described how, on 23 May (maybe a day or so before Henny), she and other women were taken by bus across Paris to the Gare de Lyon. As they travelled along the banks of the Seine, suspecting that this might be their last view of Paris for a long time, many of the French women wept with fear and sorrow as they were taken away from their home city. All the women who took this journey from Paris to the south-west of France shared an experience where uncertainty, fear of bombing, and their squalid circumstances were probably much the same for them all.

The train from Gare de Lyon arrived at the railway station in the small town of Oloron-Sainte-Marie. Today, the same journey would take about seven hours in a fast train, but in the summer of 1940 the women would have been much longer in transit – in terrible conditions. From Oloron-Sainte-Marie, the women were transported by lorry to the camp 15km away.

The demarcation line separating the occupied and non-occupied zones was a mere 8km away from the camp. German officials made frequent visits to the camp to make enquiries and to give instructions, but the camp was under the administration of the French military authorities. In the summer of 1940, it was under the control of the French general commandant of the 18th Division but was actually administered by the commandant of the *Corps des Gardes Mobiles* – who held something between police and soldier status. The prefect of the Basses-Pyrénées in 1940 was Angelo Chiappe, whose base was in the regional capital at Pau. He was involved with far-right politics and became a strong supporter of the Vichy regime and an active collaborator with the Germans. He had oversight of Camp de Gurs.

The internment camp at Gurs had originally been established in 1939 to receive Republican refugees from the Spanish civil war, and it served this purpose from 2 April 1939 until 10 May 1940, holding in total more than 27,000 people – all Spanish men. At the start of the Second World War, the French government decided to use the camp to house ordinary prisoners as well as any citizens of enemy countries.

The first contingent of foreign Jewish women arrived there on 21 May 1940. Henny arrived two days later.

The camp was very large – 1.5km long and 200m wide – with one street running its length. On either side of the road were plots called 'îlots'. Each îlot was really a separate world, and they were separated from the street and from each other by barbed wire fences, which were doubled behind the îlots to allow for a walkway where the French guards circulated. There were about thirty cabins in each îlot and about 382 cabins in the entire camp. The camp was deemed able to 'receive' 22,000 people. That May, 2,364 interned women from Paris and other parts of France were added to the camp population, which had reached 6,356 people by the end of June.

The cabins where the women had to live had been made from thin planks of wood and covered with a tarred fabric – much of which had by then deteriorated. They measured about 30m x 6m and were expected to accommodate sixty people. There were no windows apart from a few small openings in the wooden wall. The women slept on sacks of straw that were small and lined up close together on the floor – and were often home to lice and bugs. As Henny soon wrote to her daughters, 'Mrs Katz is with me and sleeps beside me.' But Lore and Inge could hardly have imagined the reality of her situation. There were not enough blankets and the women were cold at night. There were no seats in the barracks and so the women could only sit on their beds on the floor.

Toilet facilities were rudimentary communal latrines situated in a central area. There was no sanitation, running water or plumbing. When Henny arrived in May, the ground was possibly fairly dry, but the area receives a great deal of rain and then the whole camp became a sea of mud where it was difficult to keep upright when walking around. The whole situation was particularly difficult for the elderly women amongst the refugees.

When they arrived, the women were given a plate, a spoon and a glass but it was a long time before they had any food because the kitchen had not yet been adequately set up. In any case, food was very scarce – and very bad. Many goods, such as butter, milk, cheese and soap were completely absent and most of the internees could hardly believe the lack of nutrition. In May 1940, the women had coffee and a piece of bread in the morning, and around noon they were given a lentil soup that was more water than lentils. On some days they had what was called a 'meat paste' that seemed to contain no meat. Vegetables and fruit were extremely rare. The medical section of the camp became busy with the many cases of bowel disease and dysentery, and the women starved. They queued in the open for their food and they queued again for the toilet.

One refugee recorded how an order came down to the internees from the French authorities instructing them to keep their huts clean. But how were they to do this without a broom, a bucket, or any other equipment? She remembered that at the Vélodrome d'Hiver they had at least been given straw brooms to sweep the floors, and so she cut rush grass to make some kind of a broom, but it didn't last long, and the grass supply soon became exhausted. From time to time, the women formed a human chain and passed their eating bowls, wash bowls, and mugs containing water in an attempt to wash the barrack floor and reduce the likelihood of fleas and bugs. It was a primitive existence and internees required initial good health and vitality to survive.

Gurs was not a labour camp, but the women chose to work not only to keep their surroundings as sanitary as possible, but also as an antidote to the despair that so many of them felt. Keeping some routine such as shaking out the straw bedding each morning, emptying the latrines regularly, cleaning the cooking pots kept both their hands and minds busy. Conditions in Camp de Gurs were atrocious. In their haste to keep Jews and foreigners under surveillance in cheap and convenient accommodation, the French authorities had created an overcrowded, insanitary and unsafe environment.

The women who had fled their homes only a few days previously and who now found themselves in this grim situation had left in such circumstances that they had been able to bring hardly anything with them. And they now found themselves more or less destitute. As Henny wrote to her daughters: 'All our clothes etc are in Brussels and I think that all is lost.'

These were women who had fled from one country to another – and then fled again. They had packed up so many homes during their lives, and now they had been forced to leave what little they still owned. They were in Gurs penniless, without clothes or belongings, exhausted and discouraged. So many Jewish women had been forced from their homes, thrown away the key to the door, and been forced to do so again and again. Added to which, they were now known (and labelled) as 'Undesirables'.

Henny arrived at this camp on 23 May – the same day Hermann arrived at Bassens. Three days later, on 26 May, she wrote to her daughters from the hut where she was then living – 'barrack 5, îlot J'. Her postcard was this time written in English:

> *My dearest children, have you got my card from Paris? Don't worry about us. God will help. On 23rd we arrived here in this big camp. Daddy is in another camp, but I can't yet give you the exact address. Perhaps he has written to you. Surely you are very interested about our trip. Please don't ask much. I can't tell you all about me. Mrs Katz is with me and sleeps beside me. All our clothes etc are in Brussels and I think that all is lost: it's a shame! If Lady Hartog asks for us, please tell the truth; perhaps she is able to do something for us. If you are writing to Uncle Max, ask him to send our papers for immigration to the American Consulate to Bordeaux, naturally only for Daddy and myself. The affidavit has to be excellent and correctly in order to be in time, that's very much important for us. Daddy and myself are in a hurry to get out. We think that you dearest Lore and Inge are not evacuated and that you and Mr and Mrs Harris are well. I have nothing to work and I think much of you. All my love for you, Mummy.*

It is not clear who 'Mrs Katz' refers to, but there had been a Katz family in Aurich, and often refugees met up by chance with people they knew when they were herded into the refugee centres. Henny might have included this information as a reassuring point of reference for her daughters in an otherwise unrelatable account.

During the month that Henny was at Camp de Gurs, Paris fell, and the terms of an armistice were agreed between France and Germany. News of this filtered through to all the internment camps where foreign Jews were imprisoned and there was extreme alarm amongst those who had escaped from the Reich. In his readiness to deal with the Germans, Pétain had agreed to allow the Nazis to extradite all those they wished to repatriate from both the occupied and the non-occupied zones. This betrayal of the principle of asylum alarmed many German Jews, who feared being handed over to the Germans, and there was a wave of suicides in the camps.

Internment in camps such as Gurs was not initially intended as a punishment, nor as a prelude to further deportation. It was, rather, a holding camp – a solution to the perceived social and economic problem of unwelcome Jewish refugees. So, in the early days of May and June 1940, it was not impossible to find one's way out of an internment camp. Henny was not the only person to leave when her husband (or it could be some other relative) presented themselves at the gate with some identification papers. Also, at that particular time, a woman who could produce proof of an address, or had sufficient funds to support herself, was allowed to leave and was provided with the necessary papers.

Release from the camps seems to have been granted to internees based on one of three things: ill health, proof of sufficient money to support themselves outside of the camp, or proof of the ability to emigrate in the near future. In the case of having sufficient money to support themselves, it was also necessary to obtain permission from some department to live there, and to get a lodging certificate.

For those internees who were released from the camps, the logical step after locating other members of their family was to try to get out of France – whether you were a French or a foreign Jew. Refugees wanting to leave the country needed to be persistent, have good contacts, and – most importantly – be extremely wealthy.

As ever, it was time-consuming and costly to acquire the necessary documentation and visas that allowed access to a departing ship or permission to cross the frontier into Spain. Until 15 June, it had been relatively easy to get to Lisbon, but just days before the armistice, the Portuguese authorities decided that their country was saturated and would only admit those refugees with visas. By this time, Spain had also become more hostile to the never-ending stream of hopeful refugees.

But the Nazi government had also seen that occupied France would serve as a fine dumping ground for the Jews they wished to lose. The Nazis' forced expulsion of Jews was both opportunistic and part of a larger plan to transport all of Europe's Jews to Madagascar. With the collapse of France this idea – which had been rumoured in Berlin since the 1930s – appeared possible and it was revived in the summer of 1940. Parking Jews in the non-occupied zone brought them nearer to a departure point. (This plan ultimately failed.)

Many of the refugees who were sent to Gurs had once obtained quota numbers for the United States. Now they would have to obtain new affidavits and visas. But, imprisoned in internment camps, the refugees could not queue up at consulate offices and police stations in pursuit of entry and exit papers. Emigration had suddenly become an increasingly hopeless expectation.

Back in February 1939, when more than 300,000 Spanish refugees had streamed over the Pyrénées and into concentration camps like Gurs, there had been a massive humanitarian response from several denominational and non-governmental organisations. The Quakers had been present then in internment camps, and so they were already active in the south of France, and they rose quickly to the new challenges.

In 1940, as refugees descended on this area in the south-west from the north of France, the Quakers quickly re-established a connection with this new influx of wartime refugees. The American Friends Service Committee (AFSC), a relief organisation administered by the Quakers, provided aid to ordinary French people as well as to refugees and concentration camp prisoners. They were one of the organisations that were allowed to establish themselves in Camp de Gurs. They were also the only organisation that had official permission to receive monetary donations from private citizens abroad for their relatives in the camps. As regular banks were not allowed to do business with foreign refugees, the AFSC provided a vital service in this respect and millions of francs passed through their hands. With any money that refugees received from their relatives abroad, they could more easily support themselves outside the internment camps. Those people who were helped by the Quakers at this time remembered not only the practical assistance but the manner in which it was given.

'The Quakers not only bring us food but give it in a spirit of friendship which, especially at this time of hatred, we appreciate more than anything else.'

It might well have been during her stay at Camp de Gurs in June 1940 that Henny came into contact with the Quakers who subsequently helped her and Hermann at different times over the next two years.

In the late summer of 1940, AFSC opened an office at 29, Boulevard d'Athenes in Marseille and refugees immediately arrived at their door, begging for advice and assistance. Even so, the workers with AFSC found that 'most of the people in the camps are more miserable than those who are not' and had greater need of moral and material help. British Quakers had been forced to leave France at the outbreak of war, so the office in Marseille was staffed by a small number of American, Dutch, Norwegian and Irish workers – not all of whom were Quakers.

Women joined the AFSC in order to assist refugees interned in French camps and to provide aid to Jewish as well as non-Jewish French children. When war broke out, many of the women who were not French stayed in France anyway. Those unable to return to their home countries had little choice, but all who remained felt morally that they were unable to stand by as they saw people suffering as a result of the German occupation.

When Hermann presented himself at Camp de Gurs and discovered that Henny really was resident there, he must have needed to have fulfilled one of the criteria for her release. Was that sufficient money to support themselves? Or proof of emigration, perhaps with letters from Uncle Max in support? Or ill health? Any of these are possibilities, but at least they were successful in procuring Henny's release.

The next time we hear from them, they are in the small town of Orthez, 35km north of Camp de Gurs, in the direction of Bordeaux. Orthez was on the demarcation line between the occupied and non-occupied zones and was the central point where the road and railway crossed the line. Over the next few weeks, the crossing points would be surrounded by movable barriers with guard houses and rest stations, and surveillance of pedestrians, road traffic, trains and merchandise continued throughout twenty-four hours a day, with meticulous control of identity cards by both the German Army and the French police. All traffic was forbidden between 1 a.m. and 5 a.m., except for urgent medical, military and police vehicles. Clandestine crossing was harshly repressed.

Nowadays, it lies in peaceful scenery and its ancient bridge with its four arches still crosses the Gave de Pau. Fourteenth-century buildings still exist and in the picturesque town there are the remains of the later spinning and weaving industries, and the milling that once brought prosperity to this old capital of Béarn.

What brought Henny and Hermann here? Were they aiming for Bordeaux, and the opportunity to emigrate with the papers they had asked Lore to instruct Uncle Max to send to the office there? After all, they were, as Henny had said, 'in a hurry to get out'.

Whilst in Orthez, they sent a quick postcard to Lore and Inge. In the tiniest of writing (in order to get everything on to the card) they wrote in French. Hermann's contribution was short:

> *My dear daughters, Lore and Inge,*
> *I received a card from you yesterday and I am with Mutti again, so I am happier. Mutti has not received my letters, and nothing from you. I hope that you are well. God will help us. I think of you and kiss you. Vati.*

Henny wrote:

> *Vati and I have our liberty and we are no longer in a camp. Vati came to find me yesterday and I was happy to see him. He is very well. Now we hope to stay together but we do not know if we shall stay here and we cannot give you our address. I was in Camp de Gurs for 4½ weeks. I wrote to you often, but I doubt that you received my cards. Have you received my registered letter? I hope that you have understood everything. In that letter I have asked you to send me a parcel with some very important things, which unfortunately we do not have. But at the moment please do not send anything. I hope that you are both well. Many good wishes to Mr and Mrs Harris, and a thousand kisses for you both. Mutti.*

They wrote this on 23 June 1940, and we have no record of the registered letter that Henny had sent whilst in Camp de Gurs.

Their next communication comes a week later, from the small hamlet of Montory, 60km south of Orthez and close to the Spanish border.

What were they doing there? What had happened?

CHAPTER 10

Montory: Autumn 1940

'Now we are in a little village in the mountains, near the Spanish border and it is magnificent here. We are together with other refugees, and we are in good health,' wrote Henny to Lore and Inge on 30 June 1940.

'It is very good here and the high mountains are very beautiful. We do not know how long we will be here,' Hermann added to Henny's postcard on the same day.

Henny and Hermann Hartog were given a cautious but generous welcome by the people of the village of Montory in the Basse-Pyrénées department of France (now known as the Pyrénées-Atlantiques department). This area, lying at the foothills of the Pyrénées, is in the far south-west corner of France and covers French Basque country and the Béarn. The mountain ranges – steeper on the French side than the Spanish – have long been a barrier to invading armies and are a natural physical frontier. The mountains are steep, wild and windy, and, during the 1940s, it could be expected that the mountaintops would be covered in snow between about October and May or June. There are deep valleys, and the area is home to brown bears, chamois, deer and wild boar.

Montory is part of the province of Soule, which is one of the seven territories that make up the Basque country. Local people consider themselves to be 'French Basques' with their own language, traditions and music. It is a pastoral region and in the 1940s relied mainly on the agricultural life that centred around the transhumance – the trek of farmers and their livestock (cattle or sheep) from the winter shelter in the valley to the pastures in the higher parts of the mountains where the grass was lusher. At that time there was very little industry in the area.

Basque (or Xiberoan) customary law requires its citizens to protect both its community and its hearth (or house) from outside danger. In the summer of 1940, the arrival into the area of hundreds of refugees from elsewhere in France, and from other countries and different faiths, certainly constituted a perceived threat to the inhabitants of these isolated and rural villages. But the area has long been a land of passage and refuge – often to or from the other side of the neighbouring mountains – and the people hold on to their traditions of freedom, independence, and a careful welcome to a safe haven.

Montory still has its twelfth-century church, sixteenth-century public fountain, and the old communal stone troughs that were once used by the women for washing laundry. A small river – Le Gastou – runs through the valley area of the village and in the past powered a mill there.

There had been refugees living in Montory and the surrounding villages since the end of 1939. When war was first declared at the beginning of September that year, national plans for evacuation from targeted places were drawn up. It was expected that the most likely places to be affected by bombing and fighting would be the Paris region and possibly Alsace and Lorraine, and many civilians from those areas were evacuated to the south of the country. Montory and neighbouring villages received evacuees from the departments of Seine, Seine-et-Oise, and Seine-et-Marne.

When Henny and Hermann lived there, it was an agricultural area with old houses and farms. The community was small, and everyone knew everyone else – including any newly arrived residents. It was a pastoral community and most of the people living in Montory cultivated small farms along the valley. Many of the men were shepherds and their lives involved caring for their numerous sheep pastured in the lush, steep mountain fields. This included the period during the summer when they took their sheep along the rough, narrow trails through the dense forests to the higher pastures and whilst they were there they made sheep's cheese from the abundant supplies of milk, storing it in their huts on the mountain where they lived during this period. These same trails had been used for centuries by smugglers and were later used by refugees and other fugitives wishing to escape from the Germans to find their way over the Pyrénées into Spain.

In the village, the women were responsible for their residences in the traditionally built stone houses where the kitchen was the social centre of the home. These kitchens were generally dominated by the wide, deep hearth with its carved mantelpiece, where food was cooked in a pot hanging over an open fire. In September and October, the women gathered apples, walnuts, hazelnuts and chestnuts. And during those months in 1940, Henny was pleased to join them and to benefit from their occasional gifts of gathered produce.

The Basque language (one of the most ancient languages in Europe) was spoken by most people in the villages, and the fluent French that Henny had learnt at her Swiss finishing school was hardly sufficient to enable her to understand her neighbours. She was frequently frustrated with being unable to communicate with them adequately.

Neighbours were important in this community. One of the main tenets of rural Basque life remains that of 'first neighbour', in which every person responds to give aid when needed by those living nearest to them – regardless of kinship ties. And so the villagers in this area of France were generally respectful of their Jewish refugee neighbours and happy to help those who came to live amongst them. Both Henny and Hermann remained very grateful and appreciative of the ancient Basque traditions of trust, mutual aid and hospitality that were extended towards them. With government help, all kinds of committees were organised locally to make food and housing – and other facilities – available to the new refugee neighbours. These values accorded well with those that Henny and Hermann themselves had always lived by.

The Spanish government had decided to be officially neutral during this conflict that came so soon after its own civil war, although it leaned towards giving support to Germany, which had been an ally during the previous years of conflict in Spain. There were some pro-German inhabitants of Montory during the early 1940s, who might have felt less well disposed to give assistance to Jews, but Henny and Hermann appear not to have been affected by them. At the time, Pétain was seen not only as a leader but (by many French people) almost as a redeeming Messiah who would lead France to national renewal through these confusing and chaotic times. His prestige and policies were accepted by almost all sectors of French society, and he enjoyed firm political support from most political quarters where he was viewed as the one man who could save France.

By the middle of May 1940, the first refugees from the north arrived in the Basque country, especially in the coastal towns in the hope of escaping from the country by boat. Hotels had quickly filled up in towns such as Bayonne, where a reception centre was set up in the railway station. An unknown number of confused people were flooding into the town and looking for anywhere they could to rest – outside in the public squares, the gardens, and along the quays. As the town had become overwhelmed by the numbers of refugees arriving, coaches were requisitioned to take them further inland. A hundred kilometres away, in Montory and its neighbouring villages, the authorities were urgently requesting details from local people about any further available places where refugees could be lodged, and asking for material aid – such as mattresses, kitchen utensils, furniture and clothes – to be loaned or donated.

On 21 June 1940, several thousand people (probably about 5,000) were able to get away from the French coast by ship for England or for north Africa. The following day, the armistice between France and Germany was signed. On 27 June, German troops entered Bayonne in force, displaying their power before a stunned populace that had never expected events to move so fast. For several hours, there were military parades in the streets, Nazi flags flying throughout the town, and the sound of marching boots reverberating through the streets.

By 1940, in some of the villages in the Basses-Pyrénées, young people had already left the countryside in search of work in the cities. There was also a shortage of manpower caused by the slaughter of a generation of young men during the First World War, during which some 20,000 Béarnais and Basque soldiers had been killed in action. Agriculture no longer seemed an attractive occupation in a time of substantial change and modernisation and the population of the village of Montory had fallen from just over 1,000 people at the end of the nineteenth century to about 600 in the 1940s. There were, therefore, empty houses in many of the villages in the region and these became available to the refugees, who could also qualify for state benefits that were available to anyone who was displaced from their residence. However, unlike refugees with French nationality (who were given cash), foreign refugees were only able to access help in the form of food and accommodation 'in kind'. In June 1940, the council that governed Montory voted 10,000 francs for the payment of allowances to refugees – and noted that it had been obliged to receive a large number of evacuees 'from the east'. Populations of towns and villages doubled within a few weeks.

Once refugees had been registered in a certain village or commune, they were required to stay in the same place until they were informed otherwise. They could only move to another area if they obtained permission from the appropriate authorities. Local papers carried this information, and posters from the mayor's office were pinned up advising every one of the situation.

Contrary to what she had earlier requested, Henny now urged her daughters to stop Uncle Max from sending emigration papers to Bordeaux.

'He should not send the affidavit to Bordeaux because Bordeaux is occupied. The papers for Vati and me should stay in America until I know of a consulate in a town which is not occupied,' explained Henny – adding for reassurance, 'I am not worried about us. A thousand kisses, Mutti.'

There was no reply from England. A few weeks later, on 25 July 1940, they wrote to their daughters again, giving as their address, Poste restante, Montory, Basses-Pyrénées. Despite their 'many worries', they sound relieved and glad to be in the place where they had now been settled for the past four weeks. They wrote a long letter, with Henny taking the first part:

> *The countryside here on the Spanish border is very beautiful. Like most of the refugees, we are here with a little money that we must use to buy the bare essentials to eat. We do not know when and if we can return to Brussels, or whether our American immigration will really happen – God grant that it will. Dear children, I know that you often think about us – as we do you – and I know that you greeted me in spirit on my birthday.*

Henny was feeling very cut off from any news about what was happening, but she had been reading some French newspapers and was concerned about current travel to America:

> *The newspapers say that all children in England are going to the USA or Canada, and I don't know what will happen to you. We also do not know here whether there is still a connection by ship between the French territories and the USA. Please inform us if possible.*

She urged the girls to write to them through the Red Cross, and also to keep Uncle Max informed. By then, Rosa Wolffs had arrived in Chicago from Aurich with her daughter (Else), joining her sons (Meinhard and Siegbert), and Henny reminded Lore and Inge that they might now be in a position to be able to help. Finally:

> *Are you dear children well? How often we speak about you! Hopefully the day will come when we can meet again. Stay brave and do not worry about us. We are well.*

In his part of the letter, Hermann repeated the information that Lore and Inge might need in the future about the whereabouts of their belongings in Brussels – names of landlords, various useful addresses, numbers of trunks, suitcases and hat boxes, etc. – and the details for the Lift in Bremen. He was pleased to pass on news about members of the family, which they had received via Max Ruda in Zurich:

> *The Aunts and Uncle Oskar are well. This is the first news that we have had of them since the beginning of May [almost three months previously]. We have no news from Opa, but we know from others that he has received news from us. You have your holidays now, so I hope that you rest well. We always think about you and speak warmly about you. Now, my two dear children, stay well and be heartily kissed by your Vati.*

Whilst at Camp de Gurs, Henny had written to many relatives and friends, without ever knowing whether or not her letters and postcards were received, but gradually some responses came through.

Her cousin, Arthur Bodenheimer, wrote to her from Brooklyn on 7 July 1940:

> *We were very happy to receive your airmail of 18 June from Camp de Gurs – finally, a direct sign of life. I will send the letter to Frankfurt with mine today. We had received your address through Frankfurt the previous week.*

Henny's airmail letter had arrived in America on 5 July – more than two weeks after being sent – and Arthur had immediately tried to send money to Henny.

> *But the post will not send money to France, and no bank is accepting transfers at the moment because the government side of this payment is blocked. It is still possible to send packages under certain circumstances. As soon as I have your wish list, I will send you what you want.*

He had been busy on their behalf chasing further administrative matters.

> *Last Thursday was a public holiday so I was free to pursue your cause and worked on it from 9 until 6. So, everything concerning your papers will be issued by Uncle Max, but only once he has received the request.*
>
> *As far as Lore and Inge are concerned, I have contacted the British consulate, as well as two Jewish organisations, so that they come with the children transports. I have also written all of this to Lore. Uncle Max had a letter from Lore a few weeks ago and he sent her five dollars.*
>
> *Keep up your spirits and be brave. This day will pass. All good wishes and kisses, your cousin, Arthur.*

Henny and Hermann wrote again to Lore four weeks later, on 22 August 1940, although they had heard nothing from her in the meantime. They wrote their letter in English, perhaps in an attempt to simplify restrictions around the censor – or simply to reach more directly to their English-speaking daughters. Henny described their day-to-day existence:

> *As you know, we have been here for eight weeks, in a very little village near the Spanish border. We are quite well and are living alone in a very old farmhouse. I cook for Vati and me, and people give us the absolute basics for living. Often, my dearest children, we are very worried about everything. God knows what will happen to us, and when we can see you again. Perhaps we will stay here for some months, but perhaps we will set off for the American Consulate in Marseille, concerning our immigration – but I expect there will be many difficulties!*

She again encouraged them to contact Max Bodenheimer about their affidavits, and to write to them as soon as possible – sending the letter via Max Ruda in Zurich.

Henny was keen for the girls to send a photo of themselves, but Hermann thought that photos might slow down a letter, and so advised against sending any. They were both becoming slightly frustrated by the lack of news and post in their little village, and the lack of progress with emigration possibilities. As Hermann wrote: 'When we set off from Brussels, we did not think that it would take a long way like this!'

In their next letter, a month later in September, Hermann started with a serious opening:

> *In the last few months, since I have again been with Mutti, we have often written to you, but we have received no answer. We have written to you through Herr Ruda, but we do not know if that letter has arrived with you. We also do not know if you are still in England, or somewhere in America – while we are sitting here on the Spanish border.*

That month, on 27 September, a new law in France authorised prefects to intern male immigrants between the ages of 18 and 55 who were regarded as 'superfluous in the French economy'. Alternatively, male immigrants in those age brackets who could work could be forced into *Groupements de Travailleurs Etrangers* (GTE). These were essentially civilian labour groups made out of immigrant men. Hermann – then aged 53 – would shortly find himself a member of one of these groups.

During September, Howard Kershner was appointed to direct the American Quakers who were working in France. His office was in Marseille, and from there he and his co-workers acted as a link between the Quaker delegations in France and their headquarters in Philadelphia. Kershner also acted as a key contact between the Quakers and the American embassy in Marseille.

Henny and Hermann had received reassuring news via Max Ruda about relatives in Emden and Frankfurt, but they were also hearing reports about German bombing over southern England, and they became increasingly concerned about Lore and Inge (who had actually been evacuated to Wales a few weeks earlier in July, but whose letters with this news had failed to arrive with Henny and Hermann).

Hermann was already aware of the major difficulty concerning their hoped-for emigration – a lack of sufficient funds for their onward journey. They simply had no money themselves for the cost of the tickets for their travel by ship from France to America.

> *We have written twice to the American Consulate in Marseille but we have had no answer, and* ***we have no money to buy tickets for the USA****. Perhaps there are Jewish organisations in Marseille who can help. Here we are able to help each other quite well, but we do not know what it will be like in Marseille.*

Henny added the explanation that since they were foreigners, they were not allowed to travel out of their area to go to Marseille – and Marseille was the only place that dealt with emigration.

She gave more details of their life in Montory, which she described as 'a tiny village, which is very isolated and secluded'. They were now living a life that any Basque villager could recognise. Cooking over an open fire, or placing wrapped food in the embers, did not come easily to this sophisticated woman who had been raised in the Frankfurt metropolis and completed her education at a Lausanne finishing school. In their house in Montory, there was no running water and no modern toilet facilities. It was very difficult for her to find a way to provide a comfortable home for herself and Hermann. They were almost destitute, with none of their clothes and belongings around them, but Henny remained realistic, optimistic – and hopeful.

> *We are sitting in a large old farm kitchen. Up until now, it was warm but in the last few days it has become cool. We have neither oven nor stove but an open fire (with wood) on which we cook our food. The food tastes rather of smoke but it tastes very good, and we are thankful not to go hungry, which in these times can happen. Every day, Vati searches for blackberries and hazelnuts – of which there are many – and the farmers, whom we occasionally help, often give us vegetables etc.*

She had a host of questions to ask them – about how they were and where they were, their school studies and results, whether or not they were in touch with Lady Hartog, what they had heard from America about the affidavit. How frustrating it was to be so out of touch with her daughters' lives in this beautiful, 'isolated and secluded' village where they were cut off from everyone and everywhere by war.

> *Soon it will be Rosh Hashana and by the time this letter reaches you it will already be past. I wish for you what I will wish as long as I am in this world, that you stay in good health and that you should have good fortune in life. May God protect you and lead us together again soon. With thousands of kisses, Mutti.*

During the last few months of 1940, the postal service between England and the south-west of France became increasingly erratic. Anyone trying to communicate with family members, or attempting to trace relatives, struggled with communication difficulties. Some Post Office officials actually fled their posts during the chaotic summer exodus, leaving telecommunications networks unattended. Sending letters, parcels or money orders across the demarcation line between occupied and non-occupied France was strictly forbidden. This line was intended to be used to introduce harsh border controls, with checkpoints on both the roads and the railways. Lists of those categories of people forbidden from crossing the demarcation line (which included Jews and stateless people) were sent by the German to the French authorities in September 1940.

Henny and Hermann continued to write once a month to their daughters and waited anxiously for replies that never came. They suggested new routes for the post, apart from via Max Ruda in Zurich. The International Red Cross helped with some postal arrangements, but this didn't seem to work from Montory, and there were suggestions about sending letters with a reply slip via organisations in Lisbon, but it was a rare occasion when a letter got through – and a time for celebration when a bundle of several very occasionally turned up all at the same time. There were many Jewish organisations that were active in Lisbon, including the JDC – the major American Jewish aid organisation that had moved its headquarters from Paris to Lisbon after the German invasion. And the tiny Portuguese Jewish community in Lisbon also worked closely with American Jewish communities.

Post from America seemed to be more successful – and this continued until America entered the war at the end of 1941. Lore and Inge had taken to sending letters for their parents via there (with some success), but this caused a certain amount of misunderstanding and family friction and so was discontinued.

In October 1940, Arthur Bodenheimer wrote to Henny and Hermann giving them the news that Lore and Inge were in Wales. This caused some confusion in Montory since there were financial arrangements that had once been made about schooling, accommodation and responsibilities between themselves and the Harrises (who no longer seemed to be involved), as well as with various Jewish organisations in England. Henny and Hermann were gradually losing all agency over their daughters' lives, which were being directed by other people in another country. Arthur also had further news concerning emigration plans:

> *Uncle Max has issued the papers and you will find them enclosed. For the time being, we will not send out the papers for the children. We consider it is too dangerous to allow the children to travel in English ships now because two or three ships with children have already been sunk, and we do not want to take that responsibility.*
>
> *Also, the cost of the travel tickets plays a decisive role. Uncle Max is not able to pay even a small amount as a grant. He will take you to his house when you are here, but that is all he can do. You know what my circumstances are. You know that my parents will come soon, and that we will have to stretch very much to the ceiling.*

Your cousin in Chicago [Meinhard] has answered in the same way. They have their mother and sister here for a short time and are not yet completely furnished. He might want to participate a little in the ticket. I enquired here with HIAS ['Hebrew Immigrant Aid Society' – an American Jewish organisation] and a request must be directed by you through the committee in Marseille, which will make a connection with the main committee in Lisbon.

Stay brave and know that many good wishes come from us all.

In October 1940, Henny and Hermann wrote again to Lore and Inge, sad that they seemed to be writing into a void as they had not heard from their daughters for the past four months. Henny said that Hermann was becoming increasingly depressed with their situation, especially when there was no news from them.

Some of the refugees who had been in Montory returned to their homes in Paris during the autumn months of 1940, and Henny reckoned that there were now only four refugee families in the village – and very few Jews. The previous day they had celebrated Yom Kippur and had gone to a neighbouring village to pray with others. She enclosed a list of questions (that she had been asking in every letter) which she hoped would be answered and thereby put her back in touch with her daughters' lives.

That same month, October 1940, the Vichy regime published the Law on the Status of the Jews, which essentially reversed the emancipation that had been granted to the Jews of France at the end of the eighteenth century and defined Jewish status in accordance with a racial criterion. There was a police order in France requiring all Jews to register with the nearest prefect, and those who refused added illegality to their statelessness.

By the time they wrote their November letter, Henny and Hermann had finally received a short letter from Lore and Inge – sent on from Else Wolffs in America and taking two months to arrive – which both thrilled and disappointed them. Both girls wrote primarily of disagreements between the two of them, asking their parents to give advice and offer diplomatic solutions to a problem that was no doubt by then long past. As Hermann said, 'You could have written something more beautiful.'

Expectations were high on all sides, and Hermann was upset that news of Lore's first job in an office had come via the Wolffs in Chicago, and not from Lore. But he was pleased with their end of year school reports that had been included:

I did not need to give you good advice. You have both grown up now and must unfortunately be responsible for yourselves and take care of yourselves. Stay well, my beloved children, work both of you so that you are busy, and when God wills, we will be able to work once more together. Your Vati.

Henny wrote of her happiness to know that they were both well and told them that she and Hermann had received 'a few lines' from Opa and from Louis Bodenheimer in Frankfurt and had heard good news about the elderly people in Emden, via Switzerland.

At 7 a.m. on 22 October 1940, 6,538 German Jews were expelled from their homes in Baden-Württemberg, on the French/German/Swiss border, piled into crowded trains and sent to the south-west of France. Two days later their train arrived at Oloron-Sainte-Marie, and in a freezing rainstorm they were taken by trucks to Gurs internment camp. Fortunately, by then the Quakers had a well-established soup kitchen in Gurs and were able to provide some initial comfort and nourishment. In the same month, Germany annexed the French departments of Alsace-Lorraine and Moselle, driving yet more refugees south-west. The arrival in the area of so many new refugees inevitably put increasing pressure on the services that could be provided for those already there.

It was soon evident that officials had severely underestimated the numbers of refugees involved, and the plans they had made were clearly not adequate. In November 1940, fifty of these refugees arrived in Montory. Their arrival required the local council to busy itself with 'credit for the purchase of food, repairs to premises, and bedding.'

November and December were birthday months for Lore and Inge and they each sent grateful and cheerful letters to their parents in response to letters that they had received with birthday wishes. It is difficult to know how many of these letters (that we now hold) ever got through to the recipients at the time. In her letter, Lore chatted away about being in Wales for the past four months, and her happiness at being there. She gave details of Inge's new address, with a family in Bottesford, near Nottingham, and stressed how 'awfully nice' the hosts were. Lore was keeping herself busy with writing letters, knitting, and reading – as well as taking part in the communal life of the hostel where she was still living in Wales. She wrote optimistically about the future:

> *You should not be discouraged because I know exactly that we will soon be together again. Sometimes it seems very dark, but it cannot always be like that.*

Inge wrote to her parents about her happy birthday celebrations with the family where she was living. Mrs Grimbley and her family had showered gifts on to her and she was delighted with them, as well as with the birthday tea that Mrs Grimbley had provided for Inge and two of her friends. She was, indeed, extremely fortunate in her new home, and the Grimbley family became very dear friends for the rest of her life. As Inge explained to her parents in those early days:

The people with whom I am staying are not Jewish, but I always do as you both taught me when I was small. I never eat bacon and so on. Mrs G always understands and is awfully nice about it. Now I know lots of nice people. I often get new dresses, underwear, and shoes, so there is nothing for you to worry about.

Lore wrote to her parents again in mid-November, acknowledging a letter that they had sent to her in August, but which had eventually arrived after receipt of one that they had written in October. It is a very long letter, describing her pleasure in the surrounding Welsh landscape, and giving a thorough account of her day-to-day existence – just the 'fully detailed' letter that her parents were always requesting.

She asks for details of their own life:

Now I want to know lots of things about you. What do you do in this old farmhouse all day? When do you think that you will go to the American Consulate in Marseille? Are you in good health? Do you think of us on Friday night at nine o'clock? We always think of you at that time.

She was pleased that Hermann had written his letter in English and realised that in some respects she no longer recognised her parents.

You must have learned a lot since we last saw each other, and I think you must have changed a lot since I last saw you. I have not grown much, and I think I am about as tall as Mummy. The other day I did my hair like you, and I think I looked something like you.

Reading her parents' letters, Lore had picked up some feelings of sadness and tried to encourage them.

Please don't worry about us. We are very well and happy. We often worry about you. You are not well; I know it from your letters. They are not happy, as they used to be. Please, please don't give up hope. I know we shall be together again soon – yes, soon. It is only a matter of months, so you must not lose hope. At night, when the moon shines into my bedroom, I always think that somewhere you are also looking at the moon. It is a nice feeling to think that don't you think?

Fond love to you both, and God be with you. Your ever-loving Lore.

That winter, the council in Montory appointed a merchant from the neighbouring village of Arette to supply potatoes and coal to their village. Seventy families were in need of oil, and the current allocation was insufficient. Ration cards were – at last – being produced, and 169 francs were allocated to this task. France was late in organising the rationing of food and other essentials for the population. The 'phoney war' between September 1939 and the summer of 1940 had lulled French politicians into inactivity. There had been a half-hearted ban on meat, alcohol and sugar on certain days but no serious attempt to organise food distribution when it was scarce. The Ministry of Agriculture and Food that was created on 17 July 1940 by the Vichy administration immediately declared that the number of calories needed to maintain life for an adult was between 1,000 and 1,200 per day (depending on age, work, etc.) This was, in fact, considerably less than the amount that was really needed.

Eventually, on 1 October 1940, it was the German occupying force that put in place a rationing system based on age, occupation and state of health – a system that provided barely enough to live on. At first, rationing affected mainly foodstuffs, but restrictions were quickly extended to all essential products – petrol and coal, metals, textiles, firewood, soap, tobacco, etc. The regulations were organised from the town hall of each commune.

Everyone had a ration book that was issued by the local town hall and local advertisements appeared extolling the merits of substitutes, such as chicory for coffee. There was also a complicated system whereby residents returned periodically to the town hall to collect coloured ration cards for specific foodstuffs. The colours changed from time to time in an attempt to prevent forgeries – but even so the black market began to thrive. Hermann and Henny were included in the distribution of ration cards at Montory and were allocated their share of food and other essentials on the basis of need – and not of race. After years of being treated as second-class citizens in Germany, they received the same (meagre) share as anyone else.

They continued to receive sporadic news from their friends who had once – like them – lived in Jever, but who were now dispersed. They learnt that by the end of December 1940, there were no longer any Jewish shops or companies in Jever. About thirty-five Jews from the town had been forcibly resettled in Hamburg or Bremen. Others had managed to emigrate – some to the Netherlands where, after the German invasion of that country, they had been deported to concentration camps.

But they both felt safe in Montory. Over the past six months they had adjusted to some of the conditions and had found friendly help, which they were pleased to reciprocate when they could. For the moment, until they could make arrangements to leave for the USA, they felt relatively settled.

And then everything changed again.

CHAPTER 11

Arette: Spring 1941

On 7 January 1941, Henny and Hermann Hartog were registered as refugees living in the village of Arette. A week later they wrote to their daughters:

> *For certain reasons, we unfortunately left Montory during the past few weeks and we are now 10km further away in a somewhat larger village, where the scenery is even more beautiful than in Montory. It was unfortunate that we left there because the local people were good to us, but here also the people are good, and friendly towards us. We are lucky that there are still good people who help us in our misfortune.*
>
> *We have now been here one week and have already been well received. Already, on our second day, the teacher invited us to tea.*

They were writing from their new lodgings in rue du Virgou in the village of Arette. Despite the many failures of their hopes and dreams over the next few months, Arette was to become their home – their safe haven amongst friends – for the rest of their lives. The welcoming teacher was possibly Madame Yvette Barrouillet, who was about 30 years old and lived not far from where Henny and Hermann were lodging, or the older Madame Cassou, who lived just around the corner. At the time, there were also two other teachers at the school, but Madame Barrouillet and Madame Cassou lived near to Henny and Hermann and were well known for being very kind people.

The reason for Henny and Hermann's move from Montory centred around the new refugee situation in their area of France. A few months earlier, in October and November 1940, over 6,000 Jewish refugees were sent by the German Nazis to the south-west of France from the Baden region of Germany, and from the neighbouring French regions of Alsace and Lorraine. They were mainly women, children and the elderly as young and middle-aged men had either emigrated or disappeared into Nazi concentration camps. They had been collected from over 150 local roundups, taken by road to major railway centres and then on the three- or four-day journey by train to Pau and Oloron. Nine trains (possibly freight trucks) were needed to transport the refugees, and when they arrived unexpectedly at the entry point to the non-occupied zone – at Chalon-sur-Saône – the station master was told that they were German military transports and must be allowed through.

The trains continued, and from the railway station the travellers were transported the last few kilometres to internment at Camp de Gurs by road. In one week in early November, the number of internees at Gurs quadrupled from 3,309 to 14,254. From Gurs, some of them were later given accommodation in nearby villages. The town hall of Arette recorded the arrival of refugees from Lorraine into the village on 24 November 1940. These refugees spoke both French and German fluently, and one elderly man, Jacky Tillous, in 2023 remembered a young girl, Barbe Grenner, who was in his class at school in 1941 and who spoke French, but with a slightly different accent from the local children.

At the same time as the arrival into the area of many refugees from Alsace and Lorraine, many of the refugees in Arette who had arrived during the summer of 1940 had decided to leave and return to their homes in the north of France. There were many refugees in the village at this time, and only a few of them were Jewish. By September 1940, thirty-seven refugees in Arette had left to return to their homes in Seine, Seine-et-Oise, and Seine-et-Marne. This, together with the influx of refugees from the east of France, meant that the local town halls had to manage a huge re-allocation of people and resources within the area. It was as a result of this massive change in the reception of refugees into the Basque-Pyrénées area of France that Henny and Hermann were moved from Montory to Arette.

Like Montory, Arette lies in the foothills of the Pyrénées, a mountainous range of high and wild peaks that stretches 450km between the Atlantic Ocean and the Mediterranean Sea. It forms a natural boundary between France and Spain and contains lakes, waterfalls, hanging valleys and dense forests. There are deep valleys and the isolated hamlets were few and far between. It was a place where local shepherds and farmers travelled easily and frequently along well-known trails. Later in the war, many such people who knew the trails well guided others wishing to evade the Nazis along these long, steep, treacherous and arduous mountain paths from France into Spain.

A week after their arrival in Arette at the beginning of January 1941, Henny and Hermann received a letter from Lore and Inge – the first for a long while. Hermann wrote back to them: 'It was a great joy and surprise for us when finally a letter from you arrived, and we are even happier that you received the six letters from us!'

Henny added to the letter: 'Vati and I were given some clothes for the winter here, but we are still very cold. Despite everything, we are healthy.'

Henny and Hermann arrived in the south of France, with more or less only the clothes on their backs, during the summer of 1940. The winters of 1940, 1941 and 1942 were exceptionally cold in France – amongst the coldest on record – and fuel was scarce, which added to everyone's misery. For everyone, it was a matter of survival. Most of the people in the villages of the Pyrénées were focused on surviving from day to day as best they could. Their main concerns were about food and about getting through each day. The future didn't look very promising. Henny and Hermann shared those experiences and those fears.

Several weeks earlier, Hermann and Henny had written to Arthur Bodenheimer in New York, asking for specific help. Their letter took a long time arriving, but Arthur and Sitta acted swiftly once they received it. They immediately packed a parcel to send to France.

> *We are very sorry that you do not have enough clothes and must be cold. At the beginning of this week, we sent you a box which contains pretty much what you wanted. We were not able to find exactly the shoes that you wanted as we were in a hurry but there are several pairs for you both. There are underclothes, as well as stockings, a pullover, trousers, a skirt, a jacket, two blouses, a scarf, a hat etc. The things are already worn but in good condition. We had thought during the whole time that you had not written about a lack of clothing, that you had your things.*

There were several aid agencies that gave help to the Jewish refugees – particularly HICEM, the Quakers, and the 'Joint'. HICEM was formed in 1927 to help European Jews to emigrate, was a merger of three Jewish migration organisations, and formed its name from all three: Hebrew Immigration Aid Society, which was based in New York; Jewish Colonisation Association, based in Paris but registered as a British charitable society; and Emigdirect, based in Berlin. The American Jewish Joint Distribution Committee (JDC, or 'Joint') distributed grants to local philanthropic institutions and in June 1940 had established its offices in Marseille. By then, HICEM's activities were partly supported by the Joint and in Marseille they worked together to provide refugees with tickets, information about visas, and transportation.

The aid agencies did not have an easy time. At the beginning of the year, on 30 January 1941, Theodor Dannecker – the German leader of the anti-Jewish SS Security Service in Paris – established the Coordinating Committee of Relief Organisations in France. It brought together most of the Jewish relief bodies, both those that operated on behalf of French Jews and those that were operating on behalf of foreigners. This body was later superseded by the Union Générale des Israélites de France (UGIF), in November 1941. In March 1941, Dannecker also established the General Office for Jewish Affairs in France, which became the main body for co-ordinating anti-Jewish actions and legislation. Most of the members of staff in this office were anti-Semitic and it was their job to prepare the legislative infrastructure for the future isolation of the Jews.

Back in the villages where refugees had been allocated, those playing host to them were sometimes torn as to whether they wanted them to stay or leave. For the most part, when refugees first arrived, officials were anxious to show hospitality and were sympathetic. In those areas where the authorities were able to adapt and cope with the demands made upon them, this remained the almost universal sentiment. However, as worries about food supplies increased, there was growing resentment that the refugees were taking more than their fair share, even possibly depleting stocks that had been put away for the winter.

During the previous winter, many refugees (such as Henny and Hermann) had found themselves in a desperate situation as far as clothing was concerned as so many of their possessions still remained in their earlier homes – which were now in areas occupied by the Germans. Indeed, one of the aid agencies – the AFSC – decided that one of the most useful services they could render would be to try to help some of them recover their baggage. This plan was seen to be particularly practical as everyone was finding it increasingly difficult to find clothes of any kind – used or new – to buy. If refugees could get their own luggage back, they would very likely have more and better clothing at less expense than if the aid agency tried to find things for them.

On 13 February 1941, about six weeks after their arrival in Arette, Henny was delighted to be able to tell Lore and Inge about a new neighbour in the village:

> *Here in Arette there is now a younger woman lawyer [Anneliese Elsberg]. We knew her and her husband [Karl] in Brussels. Her husband, who is a nephew of Frau Polak, is in a nearby camp, and Frau Elsberg is with us and has rented a lovely room in the village. She is very glad to be here, and we now realise how good it is that we left Brussels at the time that we did.*
>
> *Frau Elsberg has even sent us some of our suitcases with clothes and linen which have not yet arrived from Brussels. She wanted to pay for them out of her own purse in gratitude to us for looking after her husband. She also brought some important papers for us. You can imagine how pleased we will be to receive linen and clothes.*

When Karl Elsberg, whom both Henny and Hermann had known so well in Brussels, was sent to the south-west of France, he had first been interned at the camp at St Cyprien, and then sent to Camp de Gurs – and conditions were harsh in both camps. While he was in transit and in the camps, Anneliese managed to remain in Brussels. When she knew he was at Gurs, she travelled to find him.

By February 1941, Anneliese found refuge in Arette where she was able to rent the room Henny refers to. Over the next few weeks, she made serious efforts to release Karl from Gurs, and eventually her friendship with an Episcopal vicar allowed him to intervene and vouch for Karl's release into supervised residence. By July 1941, Karl and Anneliese were settled in the small town of Meillon, 6km from Pau and about 60km from Arette.

At the same time as Henny and Hermann were settling into Arette, they were also doing everything they could to hasten their emigration – and to make it as successful as possible. This was their absolute focus. Writing to his daughters in the middle of January 1941, Hermann says:

> *This week we have had a visit from a woman who is a language teacher and who will perhaps move here. Then we would learn more steadily for when we can at last be together with you again. Mutti already speaks French very well and I can understand it.*

In fact, both of them always struggled to understand the local Béarnese language that most of the villagers spoke with each other. The children in Arette spoke Béarnese at home and didn't start to learn French until they began going to school at the age of 5 or 6, and older residents usually preferred to speak their traditional regional language.

Hermann continues with details of their daily life:

> *We spend a lot of time here collecting wood, splitting it, chopping it up, learning a little French and English.*
>
> *Last summer, [in Montory], Mutti and I helped with the hay, and I have collected so many chestnuts and other nuts that we still have them, so that we can eat chestnuts twice a week. I wish that you two could eat again with us soon.*
>
> *Every day here we drink coffee that I make myself from acorns which I collected in the autumn. In Montory, many of the farmers were accustomed to drinking it.*

They tried to answer the questions and comments made by their daughters in the occasional letters that got through to them, and they did their best to explain what life was like for them now – a life so different from what they had all known just a few years before. In one of her letters in the middle of February 1941, Henny wrote:

> *Dear Lore, you say that our letters are not as happy as earlier. Now, dear children, we are well, but being a refugee is not a great pleasure. For such things, you have to be young.*

> *Sadly, Vati is busy sawing and chopping wood because we can only use wood for the open fire. The fire is on the ground on the stone kitchen floor, and Vati blows it to make the evening bread. The food always tastes wonderful to us because we are hungry.*
>
> *A dog called Stop constantly comes to our house, and a white cat, and we are sorry that we don't have any food for the animals – otherwise we would keep them completely.*
>
> *My dear children, we have not changed a lot. We have become a little older, Vati has become somewhat thinner, and I am a little more grey (because I no longer colour my hair). Let it go! We are still here with our love, and with our thoughts of you, and we longingly await the time when we will be together again. Your loving Mutti.*

In the same letter, Hermann writes:

> *The worst thing for us in France is that we have no work permit. I am busy the whole day – but with what? With gathering wood, chopping wood, buying foodstuffs. That is no working day for me. I don't even have a book to read here. But there will come a time when things will change and we all hope that it will be soon.*
>
> *Our care and love is always with you, despite the difficulty of the times. I kiss you both, my good beloved children. Your Vati.*

Such upheavals and reversals in family roles were not unusual among Jewish families during the war. Many Jewish men felt shattered and humiliated when they were no longer able to provide for and protect their families in the traditional way that they expected. And life in Arette was very different from anything that the intellectual and bookish Hermann and his cosmopolitan wife had previously experienced.

In the 1940s, when Henny and Hermann were in Arette, the houses there were mostly quite basic in their facilities, and Henny and Hermann shared this lifestyle. Very few households had running water or indoor sanitation, so women carried buckets of water from a neighbour's pipe or well, sometimes several times a day. This chore was also taken as an opportunity to converse with neighbours and catch up with local news.

The houses in the village usually had an outside smooth plaster rendering, often painted grey or pale pink (and sometimes with a few flaking areas) and were usually home to three or four generations of the same family. The name of the house was the name of the family, and this was the address that they were known by. The hearth and home of a family were the centre of gravity for village society and newcomers tended to remark upon both its centrality and its vitality. Everyone knew each other, helped each other, and shared common activities.

Above left: Henny and Herman, Nauheim July, 1936.

Above right: Henny Hartog (née Scheuer), 1937.

Below left: Hermann on the steps of their home in Wilhelmshaven, 1936 (Inge peeping around the pillar).

Below right: Adolf Scheuer, Henny's father, 1938.

Above left: Berta Hartog, Hermann's eldest sister, 1939.

Above right: Oskar Hartog, Hermann's brother, about 1900.

Hermann (far right) and his siblings – (left to right): Oskar, Berta, Sara, Henny, outside Wallstraße 46, Aurich, 1932.

Above left: Inge, Henny, Lore (and Hermann's shadow), summer 1938.

Above right: Karl/Charles and Anneliese Elsberg, Meillon, July 1941.

Below left: Gaston Derrez.

Below right: Josephine Migazzi (née Borau) in Rue Paillassère, Arette 1935.

Above left: François Casabonne making cheese outside his farmhouse, 1970s.

Above right: Daisy Grimbley in her garden in England, 1941.

Above left: Jever synagogue, schoolroom entrance, 10 November 1938, after the pogrom.

Above right: Inge *Kindertransport* pass, 18 November 1938.

Above left: Gaussstraße 16, Frankfurt where Henny lived before her marriage.

Above right: Schlosserstraße 23, Jever, Henny and Hermann's first home together.

Right: Montory main street.

Arette, outside the Derrez house (now Casabonne's).

Kitchen of the Derrez house, where Henny and other refugee women met.

The Castagné house by the River Virgou, Arette.

François Casabonne's farmhouse, Arette.

Above left: Deportees from Camp de Gurs (with permission of Amicale de Gurs).

Above right: Oloron Ste Marie railway station.

Right: Cattle truck at Drancy former internment camp.

Stolpersteine for Berta, Sara and Oskar in Aurich.

Frankfurt wall of remembrance.

Site of Hermann's schoolroom, GröschlerHaus, Jever.

Lore and Inge in England, 1940.

Henny and Hermann were known to be living at *chez Castagné* since the owner of their house was a Monsieur Charles Castagné, who was their landlord. People usually kept their doors permanently open to welcome their neighbours. As one elderly lady in Arette, Madeleine Larragueta, remembers of the day in late 1942 when the Germans eventually occupied their village, everyone significantly shut their gates and closed their doors as the soldiers came down the street.

Most of the streets were not much more than dirt tracks and there were hardly any cars in the village. There was a very unreliable and infrequent bus service between Arette and the town of Oloron about 20km away, but the bus rarely had sufficient space for everyone and their luggage and often needed to make long detours to outlying villages. As petrol became unavailable during the war, the service became defunct. People went to places on foot, or by bicycle, or used farm carts, and children played outside in the street. When the weather made the paths to outlying hamlets wet and muddy, people coming to the village from farms in those places would often stop off at a house on entering the village and change from their boots to less cumbersome footwear – to attend school, or Mass, or catechism classes. They did the reverse on the way back home afterwards. The streets in the village were also frequently used for herding sheep or cattle to and from different pastures.

Most houses had gardens where flowers and vegetables were grown, and a courtyard where hens, rabbits and perhaps a pig were raised for food. There were numerous small shops in many of the streets. Rue d'Escamet (always known during the 1940s as Rue Paillasère) runs south-west from the church in the centre of the village towards the bridge at its edge and one resident could easily remember at least a dozen shops there at that time. Also, in the centre of the village, next to the church, is what local people still call the 'chateau'. It is an old sixteenth-century secular abbey with a large parkland of plane trees, all surrounded by high walls, with just a small door on to the main street of the village.

There were few men in the village when Henny and Hermann were there. The departure of the men and the young people had created a real void in the village – an absence that was shockingly and keenly felt in every house, farm and workshop. Some of the men had been mobilised to fight after the declaration of war and left their homes in 1939 or 1940. And after June 1940, many of them were taken prisoner by the Germans. Many of the men who were left worked as shepherds or lumberjacks and were absent for long periods, either with their sheep in the mountain pastures, or working for the timber companies in the forests. Here – as in Montory – during the summer the shepherds took their flocks to the higher mountain slopes where the grass was lusher and so the *brebis* (the adult female sheep) produced a better milk for the making of the cheese. During those months the shepherds lived frugally and mostly in solitude in their huts on the mountain, cared for their sheep, made the cheese there, and brought it back down to the villages in saddle-packs on mules.

They also chased the chamois and other mountain animals and possibly engaged in a bit of smuggling along the mountain paths and across the mountains in all directions. The beginning of the transhumance was celebrated with a fete in the village, and then the shepherds departed – at least by 20 June – and they returned by 20 September. Meanwhile, much of the rest of the agriculture had to be carried on by women and the elderly in the village, who were also – together – raising the children and looking after their homes, gardens and animals.

Everywhere in France, in February 1941 – especially in the cities – people reported a scarcity of food. Even with ration cards, many people no longer had enough to eat. Every woman became an accountant as well as a household manager as she coped with feeding her family when there was often scarcely any fresh meat, no butter, seldom any eggs – and often not even any potatoes.

Henny and Hermann's names appear on the list in Arette for the distribution of ration cards, as do – later in the year – the names of their fellow German refugees, Liesbett and Gerhard Preiss and Liesbett's mother Gertrud Schück. Also the name of a Jewish gentleman whose origins were in Poland, Abram Köppelmann.

The postal service did not function well between England and the south-west of France and letters from Lore and Inge were few and far between. Henny and Hermann rejoiced when they arrived.

> *My dear Lore and my dear Inge,*
> *You have given us great pleasure with your detailed letter. Hopefully that means that you will soon answer Mutti's further questions in detail, so that we really learn about you, your lives, where you live, and everything else. Then we can think about you, because although we are so far away from you and can write to you, we are even more concerned about you.*

The details of everyday life were important to them in trying to connect to the reality of their daughters' lives. Inge managed a rare response to her parents, writing in English from an address in Nottingham:

> *Dear Mummy and Daddy,*
> *I am sure you will be surprised to hear from me. I am staying here with Mr and Mrs Grimbley in the country. I am sure I could not be more happy anywhere else. I mean of course with you I could, but I mean away from you. I am going to school. Lore is not staying with me. We write to each other once a week.* ***Please*** *do not worry about me. We have got a piano here and I am trying to learn how to play it. In the family in which I am they say that they are pleased to have me and try to keep me as long as they can.*

Lore wrote long and detailed letters about the difficulties of finding a job that suited her, but her parents were not completely sure that she viewed the situation as seriously as they did. Henny told her:

> *I regret that you cannot find any work, and if it is impossible for you to be in business you must – for better or worse – work in a household, and what you learn in a household you will be able to use later. Consider it as a temporary thing. It is important that you earn something because you will see that unfortunately your poor parents can no longer give you anything. Hopefully, you will soon find some work. It hurts us badly that we are not able to help you both.*
>
> *You see for yourself that life has taken us away from you, but we must not despair, and we want to hope for a time when we will all be together again. The thought of you and Inge gives us strength, and may the dear God grant that you become good girls.*
>
> *You rarely receive post from us, and you must not be sad about that. You are sensible and know how expensive a letter to you is. We will write to you in detail once a month.*

A few weeks later, on 10 March 1941, Henny wrote a reflective and nostalgic note in her letter to Lore and Inge:

> *Today it is exactly 20 years since Vati and I had our civil marriage ceremony, and on 13 March was the synagogue marriage ceremony. At that time, we would never have believed that such difficult times could come for us.*

There were further concerns from them both. Henny wrote:

> *Unfortunately, our suitcases have still not arrived from Brussels, and we must reckon on the loss of our clothes – 4 of Vati's suits, 8 dresses of mine, shoes, linen, coats etc. Arthur has sent us a parcel with some clothing but so far that has not yet arrived.*

And Hermann added:

> *With our emigration, so far nothing has succeeded. A letter came from Aunt Sara last week and they are well. We have had good news from Frankfurt and Emden, via Switzerland. Uncle Oskar was very ill with pneumonia but has been well again for a long time. They always ask after you, and we copy the contents of your letters to*

> *them. Almost all the people from Wilhelmshaven and Jever are in Hamburg. The old people from Aurich are in an old people's home in Emden.*

For those Jews still living in Germany, the list of foods they were no longer allowed to buy grew ever longer. In 1941, in addition to the already prohibited foods, it included canned foods, fish, poultry, smoking goods, coffee and milk. Jews could no longer buy apples or tomatoes and were limited to particular vegetables.

The Nazi government had already (in 1940) prevented Jews in Germany from buying shoes, lingerie and clothing. And they were also not allowed to buy material with which to make or darn their clothing or repair their shoes.

On 14 February, Hermann wrote in his letter to Lore and Inge:

> *We have had news from the Committee (HICEM) in Lisbon that you are registered by the American Consulate in London. At that time (October 1939) registration between Hamburg and London was still allowed. It would be better and easier for you to connect with them through Bloomsbury House or another committee, or with another woman. Therefore, you must stay in contact with Mrs Harris, or with Lord and Lady Hartog, so that they can act for you. You will not be able to do it on your own without help and protection.*
>
> *Dear Lore, it would be good if you could soon get your passport extended. And also enquire from where Inge can get a passport. We are also now trying to get ours extended – they expired in July 1940.*

Hermann sounds hopeful and positive in this letter, and his and Henny's main concern at this time remained to get away from France and get to the USA, using the visa arrangements they had been organising for the previous two years or more. It continued to be a frustrating and complicated process. They told Lore and Inge:

> *After we received the affidavit a few months ago, we are still missing further papers, and even when these are here, we are still missing the important money for the journey. We are now waiting for Uncle Max to send the recently required affidavit for impeccable morals and politics, and then we will have our papers together. After that, it is not out of the question that we will go to Marseille. The worst thing is the expensive travel.*

It is clear from their letters that while they fully intended to try to emigrate from France to the USA, they also recognised that money for the fares was going to be a huge obstacle. Money could be sent from America to France through the AFSC –

if there were any funds in America that were available. As the AFSC noted at the time:

> *Although it was possible for friends or relatives to send as much as 50 dollars a month to people in France, there was often a tragic delay in making such transfers due to the many formalities required. Numerous requests were received by our office in Philadelphia and by our office in Marseille to help transfer money from America to France for needy individuals.*

And the money required for the transatlantic fares was going to be considerably more than fifty dollars.

Meanwhile, daily life was getting more and more difficult for many people in France. Reports from Paris in March 1941 highlight that provisions were hard to find, often unreliable, and only available at odd times in the day. There was almost no meat, no potatoes, no fish, no pastry, and bread rations were being tightened. Attacks on fundamental liberties increased as political parties were dissolved or forbidden, the headquarters of trade unions closed, a curfew imposed, and requiring a pass for many public places became routine. Leisure activities such as sport – football and rugby – became restricted, skiing and mountain hiking forbidden, and a censorship extended to cinema and theatre programmes. People became less trustful of their neighbours and more wary about voicing an opinion. Everyone gradually became more silent.

But, with one third of France not occupied by the Germans until November 1942, little active resistance against the Nazi and Vichy regimes took place in the unoccupied zone during 1940 and 1941, a period in which many anti-German French people were not entirely sure whether Vichy was a friend or an enemy. When Pétain visited Marseille on 3 and 4 December 1940, he was greeted by ecstatic crowds chanting *'Vive Pétain!'* and *'Vive la France!'* At that time, he was hailed as the only man who could save France. There were some patriotic individuals who reacted instinctively to resist the occupation of their country, but most French people then were content not to be involved with any military or political activity. Such groups of resisters that existed at this time were formed mainly through family, friends or professional contacts.

In fact, the Vichy administration was clearly anti-Semitic. In August 1940, the regime repealed a decree that banned the publication of anti-Semitic propaganda and in October 1940 it issued the *Statut des Juifs*, which was followed up in June 1941 with a second *Statut* that described a broad definition of who should be considered Jewish. This set the trap for later prosecution of the Jews as they were hunted down.

The existing Jewish community was not large in the Basses-Pyrénées, with about 400 people, most of whom lived in the Saint-Esprit area of Bayonne.

The Jews were known as being well integrated into the local society, and their synagogue was renowned for its beauty.

Vichy replaced the republican slogan *Liberty, Equality, Fraternity* with *Work, Family, Country*. Completely in line with Nazi ideology, the Vichy administration planned to 'purify' the nation and 'strengthen its moral tone' – while at the same time suppressing any 'harmful' individualism. 'Purifying the French state' required dealing with the Jews and the political focus was on that community. The special statutes were designed to exclude Jews from all professions, including teaching, and to confiscate their property. Foreign Jews were interned in special camps like Camp de Gurs and all French Jews were required to register – a registration that subsequently made it much easier for the French police, acting together with the Germans, to arrest and deport them.

Vichy was hierarchical and authoritarian, and it endorsed conservative traditions and the Catholic faith. In its efforts to rid France of 'Undesirables', the regime ruthlessly persecuted minority groups, especially the Jews – exactly like the Nazi occupiers of their country. Those who supported the Vichy regime in France did the work of the Nazis for them in their own country.

The least that Henny and Hermann could hope to do during this time was to support each other within the safety of their home in Arette – a place where each could depend upon the other, and where they could depend on good neighbours. But, at the same time, they desperately wanted to leave.

'When we receive the moral and political affidavit from Uncle Max – and that could be any day now – we will also make contact with the Consulate in Marseille. Hopefully, we will then succeed in leaving for America, for which we have already been waiting for more than two years. With God's help, a happy time will soon come for us all, when we will be able to work together, as we have done all our lives,' Hermann wrote in his February letter to Lore and Inge.

And at last, just as they had hoped, the necessary papers arrived from America and they were given permission to travel to Marseille. They left immediately, in the first few days of April 1941, with no time to tell their daughters what had happened and what they were doing.

At last – at last! – it seemed as though their dream of emigration might really come true.

CHAPTER 12

Marseille

16 rue de la Couronne
Aix en Provence
Monday 14 April 1941

My dear children,
As you can see from the above address, we have moved to another place. We are now near Marseille, where the American Consulate is, and we hope that we can better and more quickly operate our emigration to America from here.

Whether we stay here or not depends on many things. It is much more expensive for us to live here and we do not know if we can get by here. If it is not at all possible, we will go back to Arette. In any case, we have many worries and our greatest joy is when we receive good and frequent letters from you.

We have struggled with the simplest things around us, like how to deal with wood ash, smoke and the like. You have to understand that your parents have become very poor because of these unfortunate times, and you must take any job if you do not have the opportunity to get work in these intellectual things.

Did you realise that it is now Pesach?

Your ever-loving Vati

Henny reinforced Hermann's comments, and their shared concerns, in her part of this letter:

You are the only thing that remains for us in these unfortunate times. In the morning, I must go to the American Consulate but unfortunately, we are missing many important papers, so that our onward migration is out of the question, and what will then happen the dear God knows.

Dear Lore, you have to be your age now, and as a child of very poor parents, you urgently need to begin work, no matter what it is. Nowadays, nobody asks any longer whether the work will make them happy. The most important thing is to earn money. If you could see how we live, you would resolve everything. Don't be posh and hold back. Today we only achieve something in our situation if we are resolute and brave.

It is lovely that you spent your birthdays so nicely and that you, dear Inge, are with such lovely people. Be good and grateful. What would we do if there were no good people in the world?

For our onward migration, it depends on what happens politically, and on whether those in New York and Chicago want to make sacrifices for us for the tickets for the ship.

I am very tired and must get up early in the morning. Stay well.

Thousands of kisses, Mutti.

Rue de la Couronne, where they were now living, was a very narrow cobbled street near the Jewish quarter of town with tall, narrow buildings of yellow sandstone rising to four floors on either side. The wide stone doorway at number 16 had little embellishment but contained a solid door that led directly onto a steep flight of internal stairs. In this building, Henny and Hermann rented a room during their stay in Aix.

The day after writing her letter, Henny left their lodgings in rue de la Couronne and went to Marseille on her own. The journey – whether she took the train or the bus from Aix – took about an hour, plus the walk to the consulate offices in Place de la Prefecture once she was there. (The public square has since been renamed Place Varian Fry.) When she had left for Marseille, Hermann returned to the previous day's letter to say something very important to his daughters on this very critical day. He took a fresh sheet of paper and wrote:

My two dearly beloved children,
This morning Mutti has gone to Marseille to see what will work for us at the American Consulate. So, I want to write a few more words.

Everything is very difficult for us here, even more difficult than in the village. But your mother is so courageous and has supported me so well and strongly in every emergency. I have to write this to you without her knowing it, so that you can keep in mind for your whole life what kind of mother you have. She never despairs and bears all difficulties and every emergency with me. You must never forget that, no matter what fate brings, and what else happens with us and with you. You are not so small anymore and must already understand that. May God protect all four of us and bring us together again! In your whole life, always hold tightly, tightly together.

Opa, Uncle Louis and Aunt Hedwig, and Uncle Oskar and the Aunts ask after you in every letter.

I kiss you with much love. You are our happiness and our hope. Your Vati

Then he added this sheet of paper to the rest of the letter in the envelope, sealed it, and posted it to his daughters in England.

While Henny went almost daily to Marseille, Hermann occupied himself at the synagogue in Aix. There had been a very large Jewish community in the city until the early 1930s, but by May 1941, when the Hartogs were there, this was reduced to thirty-three families – according to the census carried out that month by the Vichy government – and Gabriel Milhaud was the chief officer of the community. The synagogue, which had been built in 1836, was in rue Mazarin – about a six-minute walk from Hermann's lodging at rue de la Couronne. He went to the synagogue services every day, and on Saturday afternoons he gave a lecture. He was delighted to find a harmonium there to play, but regretted the fact that the synagogue did not have a piano. We do not know whether Hermann took part in the services at Aix as a cantor, but there was a strong musical tradition within the community as Gabriel Milhaud was the father of the composer Darius Milhaud, and such musical connections would have given Hermann a great deal of pleasure.

As Henny was to find out, there were hundreds of people in Marseille who had come to the port in order to leave France and there was massive tension amongst the crowds. Everyone facing the challenge of obtaining a visa to America from the offices in Marseille encountered tremendous problems. Some visas were eventually issued, and some people with visas eventually managed to find a ship to make the journey, but many more did not. Applicants could wait for hours in a queue for the American Consulate – six to eight hours was not uncommon – just to obtain information. People arrived hours before the offices opened and queued around the block, and even then they were sometimes not able to be interviewed by anyone before the offices closed in the evening. This was repeated for every committee or official that needed to be involved with the decision. Sometimes answers to officials' questions had to be verified with friends and relatives in America, or decisions had to be agreed between family members, and so cables and letters flew backwards and forwards across the Atlantic in an urgent effort to finalise a successful visa application. This procedure could sometimes be accelerated with bribes, but Henny and Hermann had nothing to use as a bribe, even if they had wanted to.

It was all exhausting, frustrating, and extremely stressful, and Henny needed to return to Marseille day after day to procure the necessary documents and papers. She was only allowed to go if she had an appointment at a consulate office, and she was required to return to her residence afterwards. Different offices and committees issued different necessary papers, most of which were only valid for a certain period of time, so some documents could become invalid before all of those required were amassed.

Meanwhile, Henny and Hermann were not registered for food rations in their new surroundings, and food had become very scarce in Aix, and particularly in overcrowded Marseille. Only local products, such as olives and wine, were freely available, and even fish became unavailable as fishing expeditions from Marseille were reduced to minimise espionage and illegal emigration. There were shortages of not only food but also medical supplies, petrol, and clothing. But the black market flourished. People were desperate for both food and emigration visas.

Aid agencies operated in the town to try to help these desperate people. The AFSC, HICEM, and other American and Jewish organisations, for example, had reception offices and tried to help with relief of all types, employment questions, and also the complicated issues around emigration. These issues seemed to become increasingly difficult every week as emigration regulations tightened and more and more documentation was required.

Some documents had to be acquired before others could be requested, they all had to be obtained before one of them became invalid (otherwise the whole process had to start from the beginning again), the dates had to coincide with the expected date of passage, and they all had to be paid for. Affidavits were required, as well as income tax return statements, transit visas for countries between France and America (such as Spain and Portugal), a French exit visa, police certificates, a financial affidavit, safe conduct visas, stamps from internment camp documents, and proof of moral and political blamelessness, as well as a successful personal interview with the consul. Under the armistice agreement, Vichy officials shared applications for exit visas with the Nazi Gestapo, so this had to be cleared too. If all of this went well, the applicant would be given a letter stating that a provisional visa would be granted when they had given proof of a definite reservation on a ship to America, and proof also of the ability to pay for the travel.

Even when this proof was possible, there was no guarantee of a visa because this could not be granted until a definite quota number could be obtained from America. And even if a quota number became available, there was, again, no guarantee of a passage if no ships were available. It was not easy even for the aid agencies to get information about the availability of ships, their routes and sailing dates. By the spring of 1941, liners from Lisbon were booked three to nine months ahead. The shipping route from Marseille to America via Martinique closed in late May 1941.

It was all absolutely overwhelming, and Henny and Hermann were caught up in this endless, difficult and constantly disappointing scenario – all the time worried not only about their emigration but also about merely surviving from day to day. They knew that the biggest obstacle in their efforts to emigrate was their lack of funds for the passage by ship. They simply had no money left, and shipping lines were only accepting payment in dollars. They contacted everyone whom they hoped would help and put most of their hopes in their relatives in America. A few days after they had started the emigration proceedings, they heard from Henny's cousin, Arthur Bodenheimer, in New York.

> *I have sent you ten dollars through the Postal Telegraph and Cable Company, which cost almost two dollars in expenses, and with that I have done the utmost that I can for you. I have sent a telegram to Uncle Max and asked him to do something if he is in a position to do so. Further, I asked him to get in touch with his daughters [Mildred and Barbara, in Bronx, New York, in the hope that they and their husbands could help]. Please direct all future correspondence to them directly because the letters that I have so far forwarded have not been successful.*
>
> *Six weeks ago, I paid for the tickets for the ship for my dear parents and I still have to pay for their journey from Germany to Lisbon. My parents have now sold the house in Scheffelstraße [in Frankfurt] and so expect to be able to come soon. You will not hold it against me when I explain to you that I have the duty and obligation to care first for my parents and parents-in-law. I have to reckon that sooner or later dear Sitta and I will have the care of four old people, for whom it is almost hopeless that they will be able to earn anything, and what that means you can count on your five fingers. My parents don't have any money here, our savings are almost all gone on the tickets for the ship, so it is quite absurd to write at length about your request concerning 800 dollars for the tickets for the ship. It is impossible for me, and Uncle Max has rejected the request outright.*
>
> *It is not that we don't understand the difficult situation that you find yourselves in, but that for us – who have not yet been here for three years ourselves and still don't have the income that we actually need – it is impossible for us to do more for you than we have already done, and with that I would like to close this chapter.*

This was a bitter blow, and both Henny and Hermann were left reeling from it. However, they hoped to find some way forward and they determined to stay in the Marseille area for as long as they felt they might have some success. If they were to leave the only place from where they might be able to get on a ship, they were not at all sure they would have another opportunity to return. Time was of the essence. There was not enough time. Everyone was terrified of being left behind as the trap seemed to be closing.

But, in order to be sure of somewhere to live in case they were unsuccessful, on 21 April 1941 Henny wrote on behalf of them both to the mayor of Arette:

> *Monsieur Mayor,*
> *For two weeks we have been in Aix, where we have been granted a provisional residence certificate for four weeks, but it is not certain that we can stay here. Therefore, please continue to keep our refuge.*
> *We thank you again for your kindness,*
> *Yours sincerely, Hermann Hartog,*
> *Henny Hartog*

The day before Henny wrote this note, Pétain had visited Pau, the main city in Béarn and just 50km from Arette. All the main civic leaders were there to welcome him with an enthusiastic reception. Traders had been requested to hang Nazi flags along the streets and to decorate their windows and facades. Portrait posters of Pétain were distributed free of charge, and special trains laid on to bring residents from the surrounding villages and valleys to celebrate this glorious occasion. There was an official reception, a ceremony at the *Monument aux Morts* (the city's war memorial to those killed in the First World War), a special Mass, and a tour of the castle – as well as the presentation of numerous gifts.

Although Arthur had not mentioned all the American relatives in his letter to Henny and Hermann, he had in fact received an earlier letter from Hermann's 30-year old cousin, Meinhard Wolffs, who was living in Chicago:

> *We are not in a position to be able to help Hermann and his wife. My brother and I have been drafted and could be called on any day to join the army. I cannot let them know by letter. How difficult it is to write such letters over there saying that we cannot help! My intention to support Hermann is really strong, and I did so before I had the responsibility of my mother and sister, but unfortunately it doesn't work today.*

Henny and Hermann eventually left Aix and Marseille to return to Arette on 29 May 1941, nearly seven weeks after they had left the village with such high hopes and expectations. They had been successful in obtaining provisional emigration visas, but they could see no prospect of raising the money for the fares to America. Henny started writing a letter to Lore and Inge while she was on the train, but was defeated by the conditions of travel and her own emotions:

We are leaving Marseille to go back to Arette, where we can live better than in Aix, where we have been for seven weeks. From the train we can see the beautiful Mediterranean Sea, and if we were happy, that would make me happy.

After a five-day journey from Aix to Arette, they arrived back rather changed people. They had struggled with so many things during their time away, not least the difficulty in finding sufficient food whilst away from their designated village. As Henny wrote to her daughters:

Unfortunately, since March we have not had any state support and life has become much more difficult for us. There is not much to say about us. Vati has lost 15 kilos and I have become slim again, and quite grey-haired. Your parents have not become younger in this difficult year.

I wanted to tell you more, dear children, but my head is very heavy.

Both Henny and Hermann were very glad and relieved to read in a letter that was waiting for them from Lore that she had eventually found a job and were pleased she had received it through some links within the Jewish community. Lore had found clerical work in an import/export company, and the mother of her boss had been born in Jever. Henny remarked in her reply:

I congratulate you! Make an effort so that your boss is satisfied, and you keep your position and improve it. How happy Vati and I would be if we could earn money!

Hermann noted, 'Jever was always a lucky place for us. You can confidently tell your boss that Mutti and I spent our happiest years there.'

The same letter that had brought news of Lore's new job also brought unwelcome news about Inge: she wanted to leave school when she came of an age to be able to do so. Henny and Hermann had come straight back from tussles with emigration officialdom in Marseille to questions about the education system in England, and they felt at a great disadvantage in the conversation as they tried to participate from a distance, during wartime, and with limited knowledge or understanding of Inge's educational possibilities and her teachers' recommendations. As ever, they also knew they were several weeks late to the discussion because of delays in the postal service. As soon as he could, Hermann relayed their joint decision to Lore and Inge:

Mutti and I have thought for a long time, dear Inge, about the question that you want to leave school and become a hairdresser.

> *We have found it difficult to assess the situation and have concluded that Lore should go to Inge's class teacher and ask her about Inge's school performance and education. If the teacher says that she is below the average of the class, then she must finish the school year.*

He sounded optimistic about their emigration prospects in his letter:

> *When we have the money for the fare, and a place on a ship, we will receive the visa and can travel. Of course, we did everything straight away to speed it up, and wrote to Arthur so that he can take matters in hand from over there. It might take a long time, but there is a prospect now, and then with God's help the time will not be far away when we can at last meet again, and better times will begin for us.*

In fact, it was extremely unlikely that the Hartogs' name would ever rise to the top of the quota list with which America restricted the number of immigrants to the USA. On 1 July 1941, one month after Henny and Hermann returned from Marseille to Arette with their provisional visa for America but no prospect of money for the fare, the United States tightened regulations again. From that date, the State Department of the USA centralised all visa control in Washington DC, so all applicants now needed to be approved by a committee in Washington and also to submit additional paperwork, including a second financial affidavit. All visa applications in process were voided, including those with provisional approval from consular offices elsewhere. At the same time, Nazi Germany ordered the United States to shut down its consular offices in all German-occupied territories. So, the consulate in Marseille became nothing more than a post-box. After July 1941, many of those refugees fleeing Nazism were turned back, and emigration from Nazi-occupied territories became almost impossible. The hopes of thousands of refugees were utterly crushed.

And then, in December 1941, the United States entered the war.

When Henny and Hermann fled Germany, they never expected to be in Belgium or France permanently. They were just in transit – temporarily – and on their way to the United States of America. They were grateful for the generous welcome that had been extended to them by France, but they saw their future as being across the Atlantic. Now that emigration had become almost impossible, they were forced to consider that they might be obliged to stay longer – and in very different circumstances from those that they might have envisaged. It was, in some respects, a demoralising situation.

They had seen emigration as a process that would eventually succeed when their names came to the top of the list, once all the necessary documents had been obtained. But the entire system had changed dramatically. Those with plenty of money for fares (and bribes) might jump the queue, and people with international reputations were often helped to emigrate by prestigious organisations with influence, especially if their immigration would enrich the host country in some way. But Henny and Hermann were 'ordinary people' without wealth, international reputations, or influence to be courted.

Fortunately for them, there were people in Arette who cared about them and who showed their concern and empathy in very practical ways. Henny and Hermann might never have expected to find friendship, some happiness, and a sense of community within an isolated and pastoral setting in the south-west of France, but their neighbours would make that possible.

CHAPTER 13

Arette: Autumn 1941

Henny and Hermann were received kindly when they returned to Arette at the beginning of June, and to their previous lodging *chez Castagné* in rue du Virgou. They were relieved to be back in a place where they could rely on the friendship and support of neighbours – and where they were entitled to ration cards. As Hermann wrote to Lore and Inge a few weeks later:

> *You will know that we are again living in our village. As we have no money, we cannot stay in a town. It is very difficult for us here because we have no opportunity to earn money.*

He had even written to his older sister, Sara, who was then still living in the old people's home in Emden, to ask if she could help with money for the fare to America and she eventually replied during August: 'I cannot fulfil your request for the time being, and I think about it day and night. I am very sorry. It really hurts, but it can't be changed.'

On 22 June 1941, Hitler declared war on Russia, so the course of the war took yet another turn, and inevitably events escalated world-wide.

By the time that Hermann wrote to Sara, on 8 July 1941, he was aware of the new regulations in America concerning immigration and during the rest of that summer both he and Henny had to come to terms with the likelihood that their emigration would not happen. Both of them were intensely sad at this turn of events and Hermann wrote about his bitter disappointment that their relatives in America could not manage to raise the (very substantial) sum of money they needed for the fare. To have come so far in the emigration process, and to be denied success because of a lack of resources and an extreme tightening of the regulations over which they had no control, was a very cruel blow. They had to face the reality, and they had to let Lore and Inge know how this affected them. In that same letter of 8 July, Hermann wrote:

> *We hear that more specific regulations are again coming from America, so all of our work is probably over, and we start again from the beginning. We have little hope that we can go to America, and whether or not we survive the war lies in God's hand because no one knows how long this war will last nor what will become of us. I must write clearly to you, my two beloved children, about what I want for the next little while, and maybe beyond.*
>
> *If we cannot go to the USA, then you should also not emigrate there, but rather stay in England if possible. You have been to school there, grown up there, and you are used to England's conditions. You will be happier there than with strangers in America.*

It was summertime, and the weather was getting hotter, but Henny found it possible to work in the cooler rooms of the house where they did the cooking. Their small house was in rue du Virgou and their landlord, Charles Castagné, lived in the same street, a little further along on the other side of the road in a larger house, with the River Virgou running past the small garden and outhouses at the back of his house and towards the mill next door. Madeleine Larragueta remembers playing in this garden with the Castagné's little girl, Ginette. She knew there were refugees living in the house opposite but does not remember seeing them.

Henny was enjoying the company of a little cat that had attached itself to her and that liked to sit on her lap: 'She should catch mice for us. We don't know if she will, but she distracts us a little.'

During the summer of 1941, the citizens of France – in both the occupied and non-occupied zones – increasingly recognised the presence of police terror, informers and collaborators in their communities. People shared less with each other in their conversations, and letters became comparatively bland. Jewish correspondents in Germany who had been moved to ghetto-like accommodation wrote only about how healthy they were, and how well the officials treated them. In France, friends kept their serious conversations for a time and place where they could be secret and away from those who might inform on them. From this time onwards, Henny and Hermann rarely gave much personal information in their letters abroad but focused solely on their correspondents.

Hermann continued to hold out some desperate hope that it might be possible for them to get to America, partly because he was fearful of the alternative of remaining in France when the Germans occupied so much of the country. He was also upset that they rarely received news from England. By the time that he and Henny wrote to

Lore and Inge at the beginning of September, it had been three months since they had last had a letter from them (and it would take another four months before Lore would receive their letter, on 8 January 1942). Hermann told them of their latest thoughts:

> *We have very little hope of reaching America and are resigned to having to wait here until the end of the war. How long that will take, no one knows, and we just hope that we reach the end of the war in good health and finally see you again after all these years.*

Henny added: 'We feel quite abandoned.'

In fact, after July 1941, it became virtually impossible for anyone to emigrate to America from a Nazi-controlled country.

Their little cat, whom they now called Mimi, was being useful catching mice (but Henny was upset when the mice were eaten by the cat). In most respects, their daily life carried on much as it had before they left for Marseille.

> *Hardly a day passes without any rain, but when the sun shines it is very hot. On the other hand, the nights are really cold. Vati is often busy collecting wood, and then he has to chop it. We collect blackberries and the farmers often give us windfall apples with which we make a spread for bread. Otherwise, we have the bare essentials for eating.*

Mrs Grimbley, who was caring for Inge in England, wrote to them in August and her letter arrived quite quickly via airmail. She let them know that she was now also caring for Lore, who had become lonely at the hostel in Wales when most of the other children had left after the summer. She gave them an update on Inge's education, which was not altogether welcome:

> *Inge has been at school all the time we have had her, and I wish she could have stayed longer, but now she is shortly going to a training centre, where she will be with other Jewish girls and boys. The boys learn farming and other heavy work on the land, and the girls do gardening, poultry and beekeeping, cookery, laundry, and other domestic work.*

Hermann wrote to Lore and Inge on receipt of this news:

> *I don't like that Inge has gone to a farm school, and I would have preferred her to have been talked out of being a hairdresser. If it can still be changed, see if you, dear Lore, can bring this to an end.*

> *I would prefer any job with an education rather than housekeeping or agriculture.*

Henny was equally unimpressed with the news:

> *Such a school is very good preparation for Palestine and is seen as Zionist. But we don't want Inge to go to a kibbutz in Palestine. Only if there is something right for Inge should she leave school, otherwise she must stay. Who had decided that Inge should go there?*

But it was too late to make any difference, and their letter took weeks to arrive. It was very difficult indeed to be the parents they hoped to be in such a situation as they found themselves. Meanwhile, they were truly grateful for Mrs Grimbley and the care that she offered to their daughters:

> *Do not forget to greet the Grimbley family sincerely from us. They must certainly be very good people, and you can thank the dear God that there are people who assist you dear children.*

In August and September of that year, persecution of the Jews took a new turn and thousands were rounded up in the occupied zone of France and sent to the internment camp at Drancy, in the north-east of Paris. The searches, arrests and deportations were carried out by the German *Feldgendarmes* (German units with police powers) working with French police officers.

In Arette, local people and neighbours befriended and assisted Henny and Hermann. All refugees in the village were in fairly frequent contact with the town hall, which stood in the middle of the village, as they had to register there, receive their ration cards, deal with any refugee status administration, etc. The mayor was the elderly Pierre Casabonne, who had been mayor since 1919 and was aged 78 in 1941. His secretary was Gaston Derrez, who was married to Amélie Haristouy, whose mother had been a Casabonne and a relative of Pierre Casabonne.

Gaston was 57 years old and Amélie was 51 – similar ages to Hermann at 54 and Henny at 44 – and they were both sympathetic to the plight of refugees and not in sympathy with the German occupation of their country. During 1940 and early 1941, and especially in the non-occupied area of France, there had been no particular resistance to the Germans, although an individual might help to hide someone or offer unqualified assistance, perhaps from the basis of their religious faith or from a feeling of fellow-humanity – or because they felt strongly the Basque tradition of serving their 'first neighbour'.

From the summer of 1941, French public opinion began to shift, and there was increasing dissatisfaction with the Vichy regime and its collaboration with Nazi

Germany. Resistance took many forms, many of them not particularly overt. Many women took part in resistance as something that had to be done to show their refusal to accept the conditions of the armistice, to keep their moral principles of patriotism and honour, or to uphold their religious or political ideals. Such resistance as existed in the non-occupied zone extended only to small groups of family members or friends, who did what they could to stand fast to a position of principle just where they were. This thread of resistance was reinforced as people became more aware of the escalating persecution of Jewish people. But not all French citizens approved of even subtle support for resistance, and some saw any activity that did not support the Vichy regime as being illegal and criminal.

There are people living in Arette today who remember Gaston Derrez and who saw him working at the town hall when they went to school as children, as the school for boys was in the same building. They remember the stories their parents told about Gaston being prepared to help refugees and others wishing to flee the Nazis and get over the mountains into Spain. He was well placed to prepare the necessary official paperwork, provide false identities, etc. Some of them remember that Henny and Hermann were on good terms with Gaston Derrez and his wife.

Lore and Inge had earlier been given the name of Amélie Derrez in Arette as a point of contact for their parents, but Henny and Hermann no longer mentioned her or Gaston in any of their letters. They did not mention the names of any of the people who helped them. People were beginning to wall themselves into a silence that would not bring recrimination, denunciation or suffering to anyone else. When we talked with villagers in 2023, one elderly lady told us:

> *We are talking with you now. We are telling the stories, and maybe laughing about some of them, but at the time and for a long, long time afterwards nobody said anything. We have only recently started to talk about those times. You did not talk then. You did not even talk to your wife or husband about things. You might suspect that your husband was taking people over the mountains, but he never told you, and you didn't ask. You never said anything when children were around. If they didn't know anything, they couldn't pass it on. Everybody was absolutely silent, and they were silent for many more years after the war had ended, because they were frightened.*

Nowadays, nobody in Arette – apart from one or two distant relatives – remembers Amélie Derrez. She and Gaston lived on the main road in Arette, in rue Marcel Loubens, about a five-minute walk from where the Hartogs lived. Amélie befriended Anneliese Elsberg several months earlier when Anneliese lived in the village, and helped her with her efforts to get Karl released from Gurs. She remained in contact with them both. When Henny and Hermann returned from

Marseille, she befriended them and the newly arrived German Jewish refugee family of Liesbett and Gerhard Preiss, and Liesbett's mother, Gertrud Schück. The Preiss family had lodgings in a house called Maison Pellisson, which was owned by the Rapin family. It stood in the centre of the village, across the square from the church, in Route de Lanne.

Amélie and Gaston had no children and seem to have devoted themselves to the support and welfare of the refugees in their village. Amélie was particularly helpful to the Jewish women and invited them to her house every afternoon. There they had the opportunity not only to be with one another while they sat in her kitchen – no doubt around the table in the centre of the room, covered with the traditional brightly-coloured oil-cloth – but also to listen to *Radio Londres*, which countered the propaganda broadcast by the German and Vichy radio programmes and gave important and reliable information about the course of the war and developments in France. *Radio Londres* was broadcast by the BBC from London to Nazi-occupied countries in Europe. For France, it was broadcast in French and operated by the Free French who had escaped from occupied France. Listening to *Radio Londres* in France was, in fact, a banned activity in the unoccupied zone from July 1941 and so was done in secret. Those listening to it risked a heavy fine and confiscation of the radio, or even prison. And in every village, there were those who were ready to denounce their neighbours to the authorities. Those listening to the radio at the long table in the welcoming kitchen of Amélie Derrez's house were doing so in the very heart of the village.

In France, in 1941, newspapers were the main source of information, but supplies were rationed and few people in Arette possessed a radio. The Germans and the Vichy government broadcast a great deal of false information from their own radio stations, and it became an act of resistance to be able to offer the means to hear reliable messages.

Henny and Hermann were both involved alongside other local people when extra help was needed with farm work – such as during harvests. One of the autumn tasks when more hands were helpful was the stripping of the ears of corn after their harvest. It was often also a social event, taking place in the evening after the meal. Helpers would gather together in a barn with the heap of corn in front of the benches on which the people sat. The job was to strip away the leaves that still enveloped the kernel, but it became an opportunity to sing, laugh and talk with one another until the work stopped at about midnight. A young Belgian refugee living in the Béarn at this time has left a memory of such an occasion:

> *Stripping the corn brightens up many autumn nights. Sometimes there is a pair of laughing young girls, sometimes a farmer with a beret pulled down over one eye, or a Jewish refugee who looks so vulnerable and foreign to this pastoral life that it breaks your heart.*

During those autumn months, Henny was also offered welcome help from another woman in the village. While neither Henny nor Hermann was allowed to be in paid employment, Henny was offered the opportunity to help a family with some domestic work. Louise Borau (always known by the local people as 'Louise de Rose') lived with her daughter Josephine Migazzi and Josephine's two children, Elia and Gilbert, in rue d'Escamet (or rue Paillassère, as the locals called it) and owned and ran a small grocery store that was attached to her house. It was a substantial and roomy house with grey plaster, red shutters, and an ornately decorated wooden balustrade along the large balcony that overlooked the garden at the side of the house. The shop was to the right of the building and customers entered through a glass-covered entrance where opening the door caused a chime to sound. Louise wanted to help Henny and Hermann, whom she recognised as being 'very good people', and offered Henny domestic work in her house so that she herself had more time to attend to the shop so that she could provide employment for Henny, and in exchange help her with foodstuffs and perhaps some money and material gifts.

Louise had a piano that had been in her family for many years and when she realised that Henny liked playing, she invited her to do so while she was in their house. Louise came from a very musical family and encouraged Henny, especially when she recognised that Henny played very well. Louise's granddaughter, Elia, doesn't remember Madame Hartog, as she was only 4 years old at the time but, later, both her grandmother and mother often talked to her about Henny and how much she used to enjoy playing their piano – which Elia herself often played in later years as she was growing up. Her younger brother, Gilbert, who was born after the Hartogs had left Arette, also remembers his grandmother talking about them. For Elia, when we met in her house over eighty years later, it was a very real shock for her to hear the name again. 'Madame Hartog was like a member of our family.'

Opposite Louise's house and grocery shop lived Joseph and Jeanne Carassou with their daughter Anna and her two children. Anna's husband, Jean-Baptiste Pourrillou, had been killed the previous year, on 13 June 1940, in the fighting around Arras. Before leaving Arette, he had been employed by the Post Office and after he had been called up, Anna took over the delivery of telegrams. When a telegram arrived at the Post Office, a bell attached above the door in her house would ring stridently and Anna would rush off to deliver it in or around the village.

These houses, like most others in the village, had gardens where people grew vegetables. Some women had a spinning wheel and could spin yarn for knitting warm clothes, and most women sewed, darned, and made clothes from whatever was available. There was sometimes barter among the villagers – spun yarn in exchange for some cheese, for example.

A little further along the road from where Louise de Rose had her house and shop was a small factory where *espadrilles,* a type of light shoe or sandal, were made. It had been in existence since 1925 when the owner, Emile Pée-Laborde, opened for business and gradually increased the number of buildings where people from the village worked at making the sandals. By the 1940s, it employed nearly 100 people and most families in the village had at least one person working there. It was an important place of employment for Arette, as was the small sawmill next door, also owned by Pée-Laborde, where several men in the village worked to produce beams, planks and sleepers for boats, which lorries then transported to Biarritz.

Nothing was easy, but in the countryside it was possible to get food, even if you had to eat frugally, and not many people in the villages were seriously hungry. However, most people lived poorly and had to be content with very little and very little choice. Generally, on the farms, a vegetable garden and keeping some animals allowed some nourishment, although with the large families of this period, it was never easy to stretch the amount of food to be sufficient.

Wheat flour became expensive and then largely unobtainable, and local people used flour that they made from corn or from chestnuts and adapted their methods of cooking bread (or bread-like products) to accommodate the different grains.

At Arette, it was not usually difficult to acquire milk, and even young children on the farms had to milk the cows and were expected to help with the general daily farm work. The sheep provided milk for the local cheese that people made at home. Some farmers kept a pig, although there were official restrictions about their killing and the distribution of meat and pig products (which usually involved many neighbours).

On 6 October 1941, Hermann was glad to receive a grant of 817 francs from Monsieur Kerschner at the AFSC in Marseille to help them to stay alive, and a few days later he was delighted to receive a bundle of long letters from their Jewish friends who had once lived in Jever but were now living in Hamburg. The letters were full of news of family members, previous members of the Jewish community that Hermann had known so well for so many years, and memories from those times. Marie Feilmann wrote:

> *Do you remember, dear Pastor, when you came to us with Lore by the hand? I remember so well how the child felt the first time that she was able to look over the table in the room behind the shop. Where has the time gone? The children have all grown up and friends and relatives are scattered to the four winds.*

Julius Schwabe reminisced:

> *Yes, dear friends, how nice it was before in Jever when you took the religious services so beautifully. I see you as a young cantor. I see you as a house guest in the Schlachtstraße [with the parents of Julius Schwabe, Clara and August Schwabe, who was a watchmaker].*

> *I see your dear wife and your two children. I see you in my thoughts playing skat. Philipp [Sternberg], Manfred Isaak, Rudi [Gutentag], or also Herman Gröschler, Wolff de Taube, Josua [Weinstein], and many who are still on earth, and also those who are already above. Like Josef Haas and his wife, Rudi and his wife.*

There were also letters from Hedwig and Julius Gröschler and from the Aunts Cohn. All the letters mention and lament the recent death of Rudi Gutentag, which had clearly shaken their community. He had been much loved and had continued to 'work for our community on an honorary basis, as he did in Jever', as Netty Cohn wrote.

Marie Feilmann commented: 'I thought of you at his bier. You would hardly have been able to give the eulogy for your emotion.'

Henny and Hermann might well not have known exactly what was happening in the different Jewish communities in Germany at this time, but these would be the last letters that they would ever receive from their former friends and neighbours. That month, October 1941, Germany began the systematic deportation of Jews and within a few weeks the killing was in high gear with some extermination camps working at full capacity. Word about what was happening spread quickly amongst the Jewish communities and nervous breakdowns, depression and suicides amongst Jews became more and more common.

Deportations of Jews from Hamburg began on 18 October 1941, and Julius Schwabe committed suicide on 28 October 1941.

That same month, Henny and Hermann moved a few doors further along the road to be directly opposite the Castagnés' house, in the second of their properties. It was still in the same road with its houses and shops on both sides of the road, and still a short distance from the town hall, and the Derrez and Preiss homes, as well as close to the river and the mill. While the new house was still small, it had definite improvements on their previous lodging. Henny described their new accommodation in a letter to her daughters on 19 October:

> *There is an entrance from the rear, a cement floor to the kitchen, a small staircase leading up to a small bedroom for us (furnished with the usual refugee furniture) and next to that a beautiful white wash-room with a proper WC. We are not used to such luxury any longer.*

A day later, their luggage at last arrived from Brussels – after nine months.

> *There were many things missing from both the box and the chest, especially shoes for both of us, Vati's new suit, a travel bag and its contents, pullovers, gloves, my best summer dress, blouses, scarves,*

> *umbrellas and many other things – but the main thing is that we have something to wear.*

On the same day the luggage arrived, unknown to Henny and Hermann, Henny's uncle and aunt (and Arthur Bodenheimer's parents), Hedwig and Louis Bodenheimer, were deported in the first deportation from Frankfurt to Łódz. According to a note in the Reich currency files, Louis' considerable fortune was used 'for the benefit of the Reich'. He was 65 years old, and Hedwig was 69. Five months earlier, on 30 May, Arthur had written from New York to Henny and Hermann: 'My parents have been given a place on an American Export Line ship for 30 January 1942. God alone knows what will happen before then.'

But Henny and Hermann only knew about those who were still alive and so able to write to them. They had news from Opa, and from Hermann's brother and sisters, who all reported that they were healthy and well.

October was a month of Jewish holidays, which Henny and Hermann spent quietly with the Preiss family and Abram Köppelmann – their whole Jewish community in Arette. They were also busy squirrelling away items for the colder months to come.

> *We are now very busy looking for chestnuts. We eat them in every form and like them very much and are creating a lovely winter supply for ourselves. And I have never eaten as many walnuts as here. They taste best peeled and sprinkled with sugar – like the finest chocolate from earlier days. Vati is always working hard: wood, chestnuts, fetching groceries, everything is difficult. The chestnuts, which we eat every day, replace many things for us.*

Henny remembered Lore and Inge's birthdays in November and December:

> *On your birthday, dear Lore, the Preiss were with us. We celebrated you. I even put out a white cloth with coffee, nuts, medlars, even some cake, some of which we had prepared home-made from chestnuts. Making the chestnut flour is very time-consuming and tedious, but getting wood is even worse and Vati's powers hardly suffice – let alone mine!*

As Hermann noted: 'We help each other here, and we have enough to eat.'

They then became aware that Hermann's sisters were no longer in the old people's home in Emden, and they became very worried. In fact, the old people's home was more or less emptied of its inhabitants in October 1941 and they were deported to the concentration camp at Łódź, as was Hermann's sister, Henny, who was deported from the Polaks' house in Cologne, where she lived and worked. Somewhat ominously, Sara had written in her latest letter to Henny and Hermann that they should not expect a letter from them for a long time. Some of the residents in Emden were instead deported to the concentration camp at Theresienstadt, in German-occupied Czechoslovakia. Theresienstadt was a ghetto that was established in November 1941 by the SS as a transit point before the extermination camps. Its conditions were deliberately engineered to hasten the death of its prisoners and about 33,000 people eventually died there – mostly from malnutrition and disease.

Henny and Hermann were still concerned about Inge's educational and work prospects, but it wasn't easy to advise from such a distance and with such a time-lag in correspondence. Henny wrote to Inge for her birthday and included some pithy advice. As well as suggesting that she instead consider nursing, or working with children, she told Inge:

> *Remember something for life: work on the land is the hardest work and earns the least. You have to think about the future, my dear, and if you are smart you will refrain from working on the land.*

Since sending their girls to England for safety, it had been increasingly difficult for Henny and Hermann to remain engaged with their education and career prospects and to have any idea how to advise them for the future. They did not know the people with whom they lived, nor the language they now spoke, nor any other aspect of their circumstances. This was just one more part of their lives in which they felt powerless, and they bitterly regretted that they could offer only marginal guidance to their daughters. They wanted to understand the context of their children's lives, but they were ignorant of so much that mattered to them all, and managing the situation by postal correspondence had become almost impossible.

By the end of November, Hermann felt that 'we are doing a little better', but he was worried about his siblings. However, as he wrote to his daughters on 24 November:

> *One must not lose courage, and when we have letters from you, that sets us up. One day this will come to an end, and then it will be like a bad dream in the memory. But for the time being, we must all hold out.*

At the beginning of December, Inge wrote to her parents to tell them she was at an agricultural school in East Lothian, Scotland, with other Jewish refugee children. As Henny and Hermann had guessed, the farm and home was a Zionist school set up to teach agricultural techniques to the children in the expectation that they would settle in Palestine after the war. As it happened, the school closed not long after Inge was sent there, and she was moved elsewhere.

In France, the role of refugees in providing manpower for work in agriculture and some industries took on greater significance as the promised return of French prisoners-of-war from Germany failed to materialise. During the second half of 1941, the Vichy government decreed that all destitute male Jews between the ages of 18 and 55 who had entered the country after 1 January 1936 were to be put into forced labour groups, *Groupes des Travailleurs Etrangers* (GTEs). These groups quickly became a substantial workforce in southern France, mainly in agriculture, industry and forestry. Individual GTE units contained anything between just over 100 to several thousand workers. Some units were entirely composed of Jews, and others contained workers from different national backgrounds. But the vast majority were Spanish Republicans. The GTEs aimed at keeping 'Undesirable' refugees on the margins of society and the labour market while using them to plug gaps in the economy.

On 23 December 1941, Hermann was drafted into the system and issued with an identity card as a member of the *Groupe des Travailleurs Etrangers* (GTE) 526 at Izeste. His registration card was number 2179 and he would receive 300 francs per month working with other members of the group in timber work in the forests around Izeste, which was just over 30km east of Arette. Hermann was nearly 55 years old and the work would be very arduous. GTE 526 was a large group with hundreds of men – mainly Spanish Republicans, but also some Jewish refugees – working in the forests, and they lived for months together in the camp nearby.

However, at the end of 1941, in an attempt to be seen to be improving workers' conditions, the Vichy government allowed workers to apply to leave the GTE and return to their families if appropriate work could be found near their homes. This seems to be what happened to Hermann. After he had been told that he would be drafted into GTE 526, Henny talked with Amélie Derrez, and the two women came up with a plan that would make it unnecessary for Hermann to go to Izeste in the new year. Both Henny and Hermann owed a great deal to their neighbours who were willing to give them shelter, food and work during their time in Arette. Some of their neighbours possibly did so as a demonstration of their deep Catholic faith.

It had been a hard year of frugality, shabby clothing, disappointment and hardship of many kinds for everyone. On the last day of 1941, Henny wrote a short note to Lore and Inge. In it, she wished for all of them a better time in the coming year, and she told them that she had received a postcard from Opa in Frankfurt. In the previous weeks, all his relatives and friends there had been required 'to leave for Poland' and deported from their homes. He had written on the postcard: 'Lore's Opa is left completely alone.'

CHAPTER 14

Arette: 1942

> *There are many good people here, and again and again people ask us about you and about news from you. Stay well, and in everything that you do, think about your parents, who have the greatest happiness and also the greatest concerns among friendly people.*

So Hermann wrote to his daughters in his letter on 25 January 1942. He and Henny were certainly amongst good people, and during the following few months in Arette they were probably happier than they had been for a long time – but also they had 'the greatest concerns'.

It has been difficult to establish for how long – if at all – Hermann worked in the forests near Izeste with GTE 526. We know he was issued with an identity card/registration document for working with this group, and we also know that at the end of 1941, those workers who wanted to leave a GTE were allowed to return to their families if alternative employment was available locally. Once Henny had talked with Amélie Derrez about the placement, Hermann was able to leave the group because he was offered alternative local employment with a farmer called François Casabonne. As François explained thirty years later to Lore and Inge:

> *I knew Monsieur and Madame Hartog very well indeed. Monsieur Hartog was sent to a foreign workers' company at Izeste. Through my cousin, Madame Derrez, who was a member of the French resistance, I had him taken away from this company to work for me. He came to my house every morning at daybreak, went back at midday to eat with Madame, returned as soon as he had eaten and went home just as night was falling.*

'*Casa bonne*' means 'good house', and this good family's farm and farmhouse is in the area of Arette called Bugala, about a fifteen- or twenty-minute walk from where

Hermann was living, up the side of the steep hill to the north of the village. To get there, he could either take the road through the village or cross the river near the mill just opposite his front door, follow the footpath alongside and over the River Virgou, until he crossed the river again and started climbing up the hill. On his way, he would pass the neighbouring farm belonging to the Tillous family.

François Casabonne had not grown up expecting to be a farmer. The family farm would have passed to the first-born of the family, François' elder brother, Jean Noël Casabonne. He was the eldest by five years. However, when Jean Noël was killed early in the First World War – at Zonnebeke on 27 March 1915, aged 21 – François became the son who would inherit and manage the family farm. By the time Hermann worked for him, François, a couple of years younger than Henny, was married to Marie and they lived and worked on their farm with their five children. One of Marie's friends, Joséphine Lagrave, would often walk with her family up the hill from the village to the Casabonne farm on summer Sunday afternoons to visit for a few hours. Joséphine's daughter Madeleine remembers those afternoons, and the warm friendship between their families. Of François she says simply: '*Il était un homme formidable.*' ('He was a wonderful man.')

So Hermann, a month short of his fifty-fifth birthday, was employed by François as an agricultural labourer, and thereby averted being part of the Nazi/Vichy forced labour on the land. Jacky Tillous, who was then a 9-year old boy living on the adjacent farm with his family, remembers seeing a tall refugee 'from the north' working in the Casabonne fields next door. Jacky was 92 years old when we talked with him at the end of 2023, and his memory was razor sharp. He remembers that the worker helped with all the farm jobs and shared the work in the fields, such as the harvest. He also remembers that François Casabonne often talked with his agricultural labourer for some time at the end of the working day, and that the refugee worker would sometimes stay for a while in the evenings at the Casabonne house. 'It was a bit unusual.'

Jacky knew of this man by the name of 'Sénicourt', but there was never a refugee with that name in Arette, and François' grandson said that François never employed a second refugee worker – 'He was too frightened.' Maybe Jacky was told this name to make sure no harm came to Hermann from village gossip or the chatter of children. Jacky remembers that the man eventually 'disappeared very suddenly'.

In his letter to Lore and Inge at the end of January 1942, Hermann wrote – from Arette:

> *We will have to see what happens next, because the time will certainly come when I can use my strength again. Up until now, we have been able to be at peace here, recuperating from the hard times.*

It seems that his logging and forestry work at Izeste was behind him, and he was looking forward to a better future – probably made possible by François Casabonne's offer of employment.

Hermann's mood was also lifted by some money arriving for them – although both he and Henny were disconcerted that some of it seemed to originate from Lore and Inge.

> *We thank you very much for it, but don't do it again. We always write very clearly what you should do, but it is a very pleasant thought for us that you would not let us be without funds. It is your money, dearest children, and we thank you a thousand times, but with a very sad heart because we definitely don't want your nest egg and we are doing better now. Please never do anything like this again, because it is not ours to have!*

The money – 2,000 francs – had been forwarded from London to Hermann by Howard Kershner from the AFSC in Marseille.

We know about Hermann's registration with the GTE and, therefore, the amount of money that Hermann had in savings, because this information was recorded as part of a registration process that had been ordered in a census for all foreign Jews at the beginning of January 1942. Hermann completed the census information in Oloron in February 1942. This information later made it very easy for the French police to draw up lists of the names and addresses of Jews living outside the internment camps – and to arrest them. But Henny was fairly cheerful about their situation during the wintry early part of 1942:

> *We have had quite cold days here. It was really freezing, and has been raining for a few days, but when the sun shines in winter, you can breathe easily and sit outside. Except for frostbite on my hands, my health is good, and Vati has even become a little fatter. We have, thank God, enough to eat.*

She was, however, concerned about comments in Lore's letters about her friends and social life – which were so very different from anything that Henny had ever known in Germany when she was growing up as a young girl within her close family circle and local Jewish community. Lore was then 17 years old and living in a very different world from one that her parents could recognise. Henny tried to counsel:

> *I would like to say that you must be extremely careful with your friends. Keep your good reputation, and do not give your heart to a young man – no matter how nice and good he may be. So don't let*

the friendship become too serious, and we also worry because you have no experience in these things. In your passion and enthusiasm, you often see only the beautiful and not the bad. Be both smart and sensible.

But her motherly advice to Lore invoked rather more the life she had lived in Frankfurt at a similar age than anything that Lore was experiencing in wartime England or that she herself was in Arette:

And take care of your good things! That means dusting off coats, clothes and hats with brushes, hanging clothes etc on hangers, always stretch shoes over lasts in the evening. That's a few more minutes work a day but you will then look like a lady and still be pretty, and to be pretty like you is a special grace that you must protect and also defend. So pay attention to your posture and your body and face. Don't spoil your complexion with too much powder and make-up. In the evening you must always cleanse your face with fat cream before you go to sleep.

Remember, dear Lore, that we have to save stockings. Buy celluloid fibres that are held between the shoe and the stocking at the back of the heel, then the shoe does not rub the stocking to pieces. Always check your stockings in the evening when you have time.

Henny would dearly have loved to have been with her daughters as they grew up and found it very difficult to be so far away. 'How I would like to help you with everything, my dear Lore! At night when I don't sleep, I think especially about you two. I often fear for you then.'

For his part, Hermann enjoyed engaging with the questions that Lore had posed in her letters as she read different books and developed her ideas about life and religion:

I read your views on religion with interest, and I thought about my own youth. I wasn't at home when I was 17 either, and only came to Aurich for one week in the year, in July. You will probably orientate yourself differently about religion, will think a lot, and come into contact with people in both religious and non-religious circles. You will become more or less loyal to it, and perhaps finally, after many years, you will have a firm attitude towards questions about religion, and many other questions. There are good and bad people in both places, in the religious and non-religious. When we were still in Wilhelmshaven, I sent you some good letters to read about these questions, and I had already thought about talking to my thoughtful child about many questions and clarifying some things. Hopefully later.

He was also keen to advise on practical aspects.

I am so worried that you don't have any funds. You will not have forgotten what I said to you, that you must always have some money, because you never know when an emergency might come. We have had to experience a lot of this in the last few years. Imagine if you suddenly had no more work. How would you live? And in my opinion a large inflation of sterling in England is not to be expected. So save, and also influence Inge in this way. We are very pleased that you celebrated your birthday beautifully and that good friends treated you well, but at the same time it hurts us because we can't contribute towards it.

Both Henny and Hermann missed their girls very much indeed and longed for their letters. Inge was never a great correspondent, and this saddened them: 'We get the feeling that Inge has already a little forgotten about us,' Henny wrote on 15 February 1942.

Inge was upset when she eventually read this, but it was perhaps inevitable that someone with her very limited education and lack of confidence in expressing herself on paper would not find it easy to correspond in what was now to her a foreign language to people she hadn't seen for over three years.

Parents like Henny and Hermann had to try to accept the disappointments of the situation in the hope that sending their children away to England had been the right decision. They still believed that they had done the right thing. As Hermann wrote to Inge in their February letter:

We still have no news from the dear Aunts and Uncle Oskar, and we assume that everyone is in Łódź together. We thank God that we are here at this time, and we are even more grateful to the good God that we were able to get you to England in time.

Henny added: 'Mrs Grimbley misses you very much. Just write to her. She must be a magnificent woman to whom we owe a great debt of gratitude.'

Lore had asked whether they would like to go to live in England later, and Henny's reply was:

We would very much like to live there, where you are! But we will have to earn some money, and you can't do that if you can't speak

> *the language. When you get older, it is very difficult or impossible to learn a foreign language. So it is not very possible to take a stand on these questions today. Have you thought that after the war, you might have to help your parents to return? Maybe Vati and I can start something together with your and Inge's help?*

Hermann finished his part of their February letter to Lore by saying:

> *We only wish that you both stay healthy and be happy and at peace. One day these times will be over. Everything in life is a transition, and many things can be taken too seriously as an individual fate.*

A few weeks later, Henny and Hermann were delighted to hear that a son, Peter, had been born to Anneliese and Karl Elsberg at the village of Meillon where they had refugee lodging together. The Hartogs and Elsbergs were in fairly frequent communication by letter, as were the Elsbergs with Amélie Derrez.

Although Hermann was still working for François Casabonne, and Henny was helping Louise de Rose with housework and visiting Amélie Derrez in the afternoons together with Liesbett Preiss, there were still their own household jobs to complete. As Henny wrote to Inge in February:

> *Tomorrow Vati is going to the mountains to cut down trees so that we have wood, because there is no coal here. This is hard work for him because he is no longer young. We are both well but have become older and my hair has become quite grey.*
>
> *The sun shines brightly but it is freezing at night. It is not warm in our large kitchen with the stone floor, despite the fire in the stove, and my hands are stiff and red from the cold.*

Henny and Hermann received occasional postcards from Henny's father, who sent them to Arette via Max Ruda in Zurich. He was feeling very lonely in Frankfurt, with so many of his family and friends already deported. After March 1942, Jewish people in Germany had to display a Star of David both on their homes and also stitched on to their outer clothes. Their vibrant and lively communities had disappeared and those Jews still in the town had to walk (sometimes quite considerable distances) to be with each other once they were no longer allowed to use the public transport. In that same March, Lore and Inge both wrote short letters to their grandfather, in reply to one that had arrived from him after a very long time in the post. It made Lore aware that writing in German again was something that she was finding increasingly difficult, and she expected that she had made many mistakes. Inge reminded him of activities they had enjoyed together in the past, in

Wilhelmshaven: 'I often go swimming here and I like it. Do you still remember how we used to walk home?'

Lore told him about working in her office and also about her living arrangements:

> *I now live alone in a large room and cook for myself. You should see me. All my friends are talking about it because everyone thinks I am not much of a housewife, but I will show them. My room is very close to a beautiful park, and I often go there to read. There is usually a concert there too and if I don't feel like going out then I open the window and I can hear the music.*

During March 1942, François Casabonne let Henny and Hermann have a small plot of land adjacent to one of his fields so that they could cultivate a little garden and grow some vegetables. It was a corner of a field that was unsuitable either for growing cereals or pasturing animals and the Hartogs were delighted to have the opportunity to grow some of their own food – like most other people in the village. Jacky Tillous remembers that his family grew swedes and Jerusalem artichokes, both for themselves and for the pig to eat. Henny was happy and feeling ambitious about their gardening plans, and at the end of the month, she wrote in their letter to Inge:

> *By chance, we got a piece of earth from a good farmer, where Vati works, which he dug up for us, and it will be a beautiful vegetable garden, because vegetables are rare here. I have a lot of work to do before it is alright, but I enjoy it and I work in it like a peasant woman. I have already planted peas, garlic, lettuce; now come onions, carrot, spinach, cabbage, radishes, beans, potatoes, beetroot, and I am already looking forward to the harvest. Do you also enjoy gardening, dear Inge?*

In fact, while Henny enjoyed working in the garden very much, it exhausted her. She often worked there in the evenings, after the work for the rest of the day had been done, and she quickly discovered that she had very little experience in growing vegetables. Although François had initially dug over the land, maintaining the garden was a constant battle against weeds and vermin. One of Hermann's jobs on the farm was to trap moles, but as François Casabonne later explained to Lore and Inge: 'He trapped the moles in my fields, but he did not destroy them in his own garden because he thought that they were good for aerating the soil.'

Henny and Hermann were happy during these early months of the year as they lived amongst friends, benefited from their kindness and generosity, and shared village life with their neighbours. In February, Hermann wrote to Lore and Inge:

We have made good friends here. Also, in educated circles you can find good and decent people everywhere in the world. It is always important that you remain an excellent person even under the most difficult circumstances, and that you don't lose your self-respect. Then you will also retain confidence in your own strength, and with God's help get back on track in life. That is what I have told you so many times, and it is what I would like to bequeath to you for your whole life.

They missed their daughters dreadfully, but they knew they were safe in England and in good hands there.

'Not a day goes by when we don't often talk about you, and every hour is full of longing for you. I am often up at night and then stare to see your picture in front of me. We want to ask you so much and tell you so much,' wrote Hermann on 21 March. Henny added: 'We are glad every day that you two beloved children have found a refuge in England.'

Hermann was looking forward to the spring work on the farm, and wondering whether he might accompany the shepherds up the mountain when they took the sheep to the higher pastures later in the year. François Casabonne had a herd of cattle, which were usually sold for meat, and a flock of sheep (the local *brebis*) that were kept for their milk and the cheese the shepherds made from it.

Maybe I will go up into the mountains with a flock of sheep for a few weeks or months in the summer. They make cheese there. Yes, life is rough, and you have to be satisfied with anything.

In the same letter, Henny and Hermann talked about their preparations for the forthcoming festival of Pesach, which would begin on Wednesday 1 April. Henny had a lot of cleaning work to do as part of the traditional preparations and she wanted to keep their celebrations as festive as possible.

'You will remember, just like us, the times when we spent those beautiful days together,' she wrote to Inge. 'I have started the work for Pesach and even if it is not possible to keep everything as before, we try to keep everything that is possible.'

Hermann was focused on the actual celebration around their table with their other Jewish friends: 'We will celebrate the seder evening here with friends, and with every song we will think of you, my beloved Lore and Inge. When will things change?'

At the beginning of 1942, Henny applied for an identity card from the French authorities. Both her and Hermann's passports had expired, Hermann had an identity card of sorts from the time when he was drafted into the GTE, and she was keen to have an official form of identity. Correspondence and form-filling took some time, but an identity card was eventually issued to her on 15 April, and is currently in the archives at Pau.

As Hermann wrote in his March letter to Lore and Inge, he was 'really nervous, mainly because I am waiting for news from Poland.'

In February, he had written much the same thing:

> *We have been waiting for news from your aunts and Uncle Oskar for two months now. We don't know anything about them – where they are, how they are doing, whether they are healthy, and if they can endure the road accidents. This is our whole life now – "waiting". We can be content with our situation here, when we think of the fate of our acquaintances.*

We do not know what Henny and Hermann managed to glean from the radio or from their friends' letters about the situation of Jews who had been sent 'to Poland', or 'to the east'. It is remarkable that Hermann writes of 'road accidents' as some of the first victims of the Nazi killing machine in Poland were murdered in coaches that were filled with poisonous gas. But this was deemed to be too slow a method for killing thousands of people, and so more efficient evil systems were soon invented and introduced.

At the beginning of 1942, Hermann's sister Sara was living in the ghetto at Łódź, at 26 Gnesener Strasse, in what was called an old people's home but was in reality a place for collecting together elderly people before murdering them. On New Year's Day, she wrote a letter to a relative in reply to greetings that she had received from them. In it, she also gives news of her brother Oskar's recent heart attack and death.

> *Dear Wolff family,*
> *We received your card yesterday, as well as the 32 Marks that Herr Wolff sent us. We were very happy with it and send our best wishes for it. I hope you are all fine. We are healthy so far. Only Oskar had a heart attack last week but thank God he quickly passed away. I'm always with Rosa, also here in the retirement home. She is healthy too. We are very sorry that Adelheid C and Frau Haas are so ill. I heartily wish them both a speedy recovery. Frau Maiberg went to her husband today. Herr Weinberg is here with us. His sister is gone too. Now, dear Frau Wolffs, you are heartily greeted by your siblings Hartog. Please greet Adolf Wolff and mother.*
>
> *Your sibling Hartog.*

This letter was never sent because the post from the inmates of the ghetto was just set aside and never posted. It was, however, recorded in the system and was discovered in 2016 by college students from Emden who were visiting the archives at Łódź.

Less than six weeks after writing this letter, on 12 February 1942, Sara was taken 30km north-west of Łódź to Chelmno, where she was murdered. In May, her two sisters were also taken to Chelmno and murdered there – Henny on 3 May and Berta on 12 May.

Chelmno (or Kulmhof, in German) was the first stationary facility where poison gas was used for the mass murder of Jews. However, a yet more murderous killing process had recently been agreed at a conference at Wannsee, near Berlin, on 20 January 1942. It was planned to establish a network of extermination camps to carry out the genocide – the 'Final Solution of the Jewish Question'. The process of deportation and murder was initially expected to start slowly, but in fact it escalated quickly. The Heads of the Jewish Affairs departments in France, Belgium and Holland met with Adolf Eichmann, who had been appointed to be responsible for the carrying out of the Final Solution, in Berlin on 4 March.

Theo Dannecker, the chief Nazi responsible for the removal of Jews in German-occupied France, proposed that 5,000 Jews be deported from the occupied zone, and on 27 March, Convoy number 1, carrying 1,112 male Jews, left Compiègne in France for Auschwitz. Most of the men had been arrested in the Paris region during the previous year. In this first convoy, the Jewish deportees travelled in third-class train carriages with German soldiers (commanded personally by Dannecker) escorting them. A few of the Jews died while they were on the train. Most of the rest of the men on this first convoy had died by August from conditions in the camp.

It is not easy to know how much Henny and Hermann were aware of events in the rest of France or elsewhere, but we know they were listening to the radio broadcasts of *Radio Londres* and also that they were in some sort of contact with the Jewish grapevine, including Max Ruda in Zurich. People in Arette who knew the Hartogs recognised that Hermann had seemed aware of what was likely to happen from a very early date. François Casabonne told Lore and Inge that it was said in the village that Hermann already feared what would happen to him if he was arrested. This would not be surprising. Hermann had spent some weeks in Sachsenhausen concentration camp in 1938 and knew something of what the Nazis were capable of.

Henny also was not unaware. As the months passed in 1942, and she and Hermann became ever more afraid of what might happen to them, Henny asked Louise de Rose to take care of the jewellery she had left, as well as other valuables. Both of Louise's grandchildren, Elia and Gilbert, remember that their grandmother Louise refused, because she neither wanted the responsibility of taking them, nor the consequences if the authorities discovered that she held jewellery that did not belong to her. She tried to convince Henny that there was no need – the Germans would not find her in Arette. As Elia remembers her grandmother's story:

> *Madame Hartog would always say to my grandmother, "The Germans are coming", and my grandmother would say, "No, you will be alright here. You will be safe here." And Madame Hartog would say, "No. You will see, Madame Louise. You are wrong. The Germans are coming." And they did come. It is quite normal that Monsieur Hartog did not want to give himself up to the Germans.*

Elia mentions Hermann's reluctance to be taken by the Germans because she remembers a story that circulated in the village during and after 1942 in which Hermann is said to have wanted to kill himself rather than be 'taken by the Germans'. Since he was working on a farm, maybe poisonous material was more readily available, and he is said to have tried to poison himself, 'but someone saved him'. 'My grandmother told me this.'

Madeleine Larragueta remembers 1942 as the year her playmates disappeared. She and her younger brother were friendly with two Jewish children from a refugee family that lived in a house further along her road, rue de Baigt. The children were about the same age as them, 6 years old. Sometimes they would run round and round the house together, sometimes they would play in the garden, or in the attic of the barn. One day, they were playing as usual when:

> *A man suddenly appeared, saying "Quick! Quick! We have to go. Get out, get out!" There was a car outside and the children got in. They all went – the adults and the two children. We never saw them again.*

Madeleine and her brother fled for home.

In March 1942, as Henny and Hermann started work on their garden plot in the freedom of Arette, further restrictions were placed on Jews living in the occupied zone of France. They were forbidden to visit public spaces such as cinemas and swimming pools, had to obey an overnight curfew, were restricted to shopping between three and four in the afternoon, and banned from owning radios, telephones and bicycles. These were measures that had been imposed by the occupying Germans and were enforced by the French police.

Friends in America were still trying their best to find a way for Henny and Hermann to leave France, but it had become impossible, and everyone now began to recognise that. On 21 March 1942, Henny wrote in her letter to Lore and Inge:

> *Recently the HICEM has been trying to get us to continue our onward emigration, but we no longer believe in it. Frau Alice Weil*

and her husband, who used to live in Vienna, want to give us another affidavit, but that doesn't solve the question of travel expenses.

The next month, on 16 April 1942, Pierre Laval, who had earlier been removed from office by Pétain (in December 1940) for negotiating privately with the Germans, was returned as prime minister. This was a position of enhanced power in the Vichy government and with Laval's promotion, Pétain became increasingly merely a figurehead for the regime. Laval had gained the trust of Hitler and was willing to collaborate fully with the Nazi programme of oppression and genocide.

Meanwhile, life continued as usual in Arette. Henny and Hermann remained sad and disappointed that letters arrived so infrequently with news from Lore and Inge, and when there was any post from England it often brought news that worried them about Inge's education and work prospects, as well as what seemed to them to be continuing difficulties about Lore's social life. Both girls tried to reassure their parents and explain their lives as well as they could, but it was not easy.

On 19 May, Inge wrote cheerfully to them:

You ***never*** *have to worry about me. Thank God, I am not as naïve as you imagine. You don't have to think that I always put up with everything. No, it is just the opposite. I have been learning here differently for a long time. I am the quietest in this home (except for singing). I often play the piano and often with music (with two hands). I can play the mouth organ and would like to have one some time.*

Lore, who was 17, was frustrated that her parents disapproved of her going dancing once a week, having many non-Jewish friends – even amongst the young men – and of her not cultivating a social network of 'good families'. She despaired of ever explaining adequately to them what life was like for her generation in an English town. During the summer, she wrote them a letter from where she was living in Nottingham, in the midlands of England, in which she included:

Dear Mother and Father, please try to understand. I can assure you that people out of the very best families go to dances here...To give up a boyfriend just because we happened to be born in different religions is worse than ridiculous...It is quite impossible to get to know good families without having someone to introduce you and we just don't know anyone like that, except for Lady Hartog, and she is in London.

There were so many aspects to all of their lives that separated Henny and Hermann from their growing daughters, but to some extent by 1942 everyone was grateful for the letters because they showed that the people who mattered to them were still alive – regardless of what the letters said. Fortunately, Mrs Grimbley also wrote to Henny and Hermann and reassured them by being a support both to them and to Lore and Inge. So, Henny and Hermann kept themselves busy with all that they needed to do in Arette. In their June letter, Hermann wrote:

> *We also have too much to do. Mutti and I work every day in our garden in which beans, peas, potatoes, and tomatoes and much more are sown. I also help in all the agricultural work – haymaking and the like. We have not heard anything from the Aunts and Uncle Oskar for eight months. Yes, it's not so nice any more.*

Henny wrote only briefly:

> *Have you already half-forgotten us? We have had hot dry summer weather for a long time and rain was necessary. Since our garden used to be a meadow, there is a lot of work to cultivate it. I am sorry for writing so badly. I am very tired from lack of sleep.*

During this hot summer, many French people became increasingly restive at their government's failure to address the shortages of food, clothing and fuel. Diseases such as tuberculosis were becoming more common and there was increasing high mortality amongst disabled and elderly people. Hunger was affecting more and more people, and many were losing weight. Children often arrived barefoot at school and fainted during lessons. It was clear that the collaborationist stance of Laval was not popular with many ordinary people in France, and non-Jewish people often changed their former negative opinions about their Jewish neighbours. People did not like what was being done in their name, and they started to make that clear. On 14 July 1942, there was a large demonstration in Marseille. One hundred thousand people turned up on the streets of the city to demonstrate against Laval and Hitler, to cheer for Charles de Gaulle and his Free French Forces, and to sing the *Marseillaise*.

By then, French people had been able to see for themselves what deportation by the Nazis involved because it was not possible for the authorities to conceal the extent and scale of the expulsions. News of persecutions and round-ups circulated, despite the attempts of the authorities to detain and arrest people during the night and keep other people away from convoys and train stations. As a young non-Jewish refugee from the countryside in the non-occupied zone remembers about one night that summer:

> *That night, Pierre was completely shaken to the core. In the deep silence, suddenly horrible screams were heard coming from the*

neighbouring village. The following morning, we learnt that during the night all the Jewish refugees had been rounded up.

Many more non-Jews started to offer help to those Jews threatened with deportation.

At the beginning of June 1942, Heinrich Himmler, Chief of the German SS, declared that Europe should be 'rid of Jews' within a year. Further persecution of the Jews in the occupied zone of France began on 6 June, when all Jews over the age of 6 years were required to wear a yellow Star of David in public. It had to be clearly visible and sewn firmly onto the upper left side of their outer clothing. The star had the word *Juif* (Jew) printed in bold black letters in its centre. Yellow stars could be obtained from local police stations but had to be paid for from the monthly clothing ration.

On 11 June, representatives for Jewish Affairs in France, Belgium and Holland met again with Eichmann and agreed an escalation of the deportation programme for all Jews. Dannecker suggested an allocation of 100,000 Jews from France but this was subsequently reduced to 40,000 – half of whom would be French Jews and the other half would be foreign Jews. Vichy offered to protect its own French Jews by taking a higher number (of foreign Jews) from the internment camps in the non-occupied zone. Inmates from these camps could be sorted and selected very quickly and so internment camps, such as Gurs, in the non-occupied zone became a holding area and a waiting room for deportations to Auschwitz.

It was decided that French police would be responsible for detaining and deporting the Jews, and those detained would be foreign Jews who were considered fit enough to work – both men and women. Children would also be taken, 'so as not to separate families'. Those already in internment camps would be selected first, so from the summer of 1942, the internment camps could no longer be seen even nominally as places of safety or protection for foreign Jews.

Deportation trains for Auschwitz left France on 5, 22, 25 and 28 June 1942, each carrying about 1,000 people. The train that left on 22 June was the first to carry women as deportees. The Jews were arrested and rounded up by local French police, and no one knew where the deportees were going. The Germans did not give the Vichy government a destination, and the Vichy government did not ask. On 4 July 1942, Vichy gave Germany permission to deport foreign Jews from the non-occupied zone.

The biggest round-up (*rafle*) of Jews in France took place in Paris on 16 and 17 July 1942 in an area of the city where many Jews (French and foreign) lived, near the *Vel d'Hiv* where Henny had first been interned when she arrived in the summer of 1940. About 4,500 French policemen were involved in rounding up and detaining 13,152 people, of whom over 4,000 were children. This was a huge operation that was meticulously organised by the French police force who used carefully prepared index cards to identify and arrest the people on their lists. Very detailed instructions were given to each Jew who was detained that itemised the documents they needed to bring with them as well as the food, clothing, utensils and toiletries they were allowed. As the police collected the detainees from their addresses, they checked that the gas and electricity were turned off and that keys and pets had been left with a neighbour.

This event shocked many people, not only in Paris but throughout France. A few days afterwards, the cardinals and bishops of France eventually broke their silence of the past two years and signed a document denouncing what had happened.

On 5 August 1942, the secretary general of the French police, René Bousquet, sent a communication to the prefects of the departments in the non-occupied zone with instructions for the delivery of 10,000 foreign Jews to the Nazis by 15 September 1942. It seems that although this was not publicly announced, people knew or guessed that this was going to happen, and rumours flew around. Everyone at Camp de Gurs waited for the worst.

Foreign Jews were deported first from the internment camps, but not from the region's villages. The first convoy to be sent from the non-occupied zone to the occupied zone went from Gurs to Drancy, in the north of Paris, on 6 August 1942. In the barracks of the camp at Gurs, a list of those whose last names began with the letters A to M was read out and those inmates packed up their bags to leave. There were 800 men and women. They were taken by lorry from the camp to the railway station at Oloron, and from there in sealed and crowded cattle cars, each with straw on the floor, a jug of drinking water, and one bucket to serve everyone in the wagon as a toilet.

Another convoy of 850 men and women left Gurs for Drancy on 8 August 1942, this time containing those Jews whose last names began with the letters N to Z. After 25 August, when another train carrying 1,184 Jews from internment camps in the non-occupied zone, sixty of whom were from Gurs, had departed, the camps were left more or less empty. About 4,620 Jews had been deported but at least 10,000 had been promised to the Nazis. The shortfall in numbers had to be made up from elsewhere – from the surrounding towns and villages where Jews lived amongst the local population.

Everyone at Camp de Gurs had become increasingly apprehensive towards the end of July, especially when leaders of the *îlots* were told to provide the authorities with lists of names with nationality, religion, marital status, etc., included. There had not been any announcement about an imminent transfer to a different camp, and then came news of the raids carried out in Paris. So inmates began to fear a similar situation at Gurs. It seems very likely that Henny and Hermann were aware of some of what was happening and knew the rumours that were circulating. They looked for help wherever they could. Unfortunately for everyone in Arette, the mayor, Pierre Casabonne (who was a cousin of François), was seriously ill during the summer of 1942, and died aged 79 on 12 August 1942. He had been a strong support to Henny and Hermann and had loyally kept their refuge when they were away the previous year. He also oversaw a town hall that allowed Gaston Derrez to give help to refugees. There was unlikely to be much official help available now from the town hall.

Searching for any other source of help, Hermann decided to send a letter to a Frenchman whom he had met twenty-four years earlier – during the First World War, in Aurich. On 23 August, he wrote to a 'Monsieur René Gardez, Castillones, Lot et Garonne,' Henny wrote the letter for him, in French:

> *Dear Sir,*
> *You will be very surprised to receive this letter. Unfortunate events have brought me to your region, and I take this opportunity to remind you of the cordial relations we had in 1916 at the hospital in Aurich, where you were then a sick prisoner. I myself was hospitalised sick, and we were sometimes together. It would be the greatest pleasure to have news of you.*
>
> *Having arrived in France in May 1940 from Brussels, I live with my wife as a foreign refugee in Arette for an indefinite time, and I allow myself to recall your memories. I would be happy to hear your news and to renew our relations. In this expectation, I shake you warmly by the hand.*

It didn't make any difference. The letter was 'returned to sender'.

On 25 August, the social assistance office of the UGIF in Oloron sent a letter addressed to Henny, 'Madame Hartog, Arette'.

> *Madame,*
> *We kindly ask you to pass by our office as soon as possible.*

We do not know the purpose behind the letter. Maybe it was to notify Henny of her arrest. Perhaps it was to offer assistance of some sort. Perhaps it had a different administrative function. The UGIF was not asked to carry out any of the tasks involved in the deportation process – this was the role only of the French police.

Henny never saw the letter. She was no longer in Arette when it arrived. The letter still exists, with its envelope, which has been opened. In Amélie Derrez's handwriting on the envelope is written, in French, 'opened 27.8.42. To inform the committee if necessary', and she has initialled this.

On 26 August 1942, a huge round-up began throughout the villages of the non-occupied zone. French police carried with them their prepared lists of names and addresses and went in their black cars from house to house, arresting people. Behind them came lorries to pick up those they arrested.

When the police arrived in Arette that day, it was broad daylight and the friends, neighbours and well-wishers of Henny and Hermann, Liesbett and Gerhard Preiss, Gertrud Schück and Abram Köppelmann gathered around. A lorry had come to collect them all, once the police had arrested them, and Louise's granddaughter Elia remembers her grandmother recounting that it had seemed just like a film – it could not be possible that this was happening. Louise did not allow Elia to be there because it would have been too painful an occasion to witness.

François Casabonne was there, and many years later told Lore and Inge what had happened.

> *There were at that time many people like them under house arrest in Arette. The Preiss family, Monsieur Köppelmann, I recall their names.*
>
> *One morning in 1942, the police came banging at the doors of all the people. I went to the town hall to try to save Monsieur and Madame Hartog, but nothing could be done, and they were taken back to the camp at Gurs, and since then I have heard nothing of them.*
>
> *I shall always remember the moment when they left for the camp at Gurs, and Madame Hartog, still smiling, giving heart to her husband and their companions in misfortune, after having given instructions to Madame Derrez about what to do with what was left of their store of food.*

François Casabonne was not the only witness to comment on the calm, dry-eyed self-control of some Jewish women in the middle of extreme unrest and confusion at this time. While their demeanour might have looked like (and been) extraordinary strength and courage, rather than female frailty, it also shows one aspect of the typical upbringing of a woman in a bourgeois Jewish family before the Second World War: her dignity was an essential part of her Jewishness, even in the face of horror and dishonour. It would seem that Henny maintained this right to the end of her life.

Elia remembers that after the events of that day it was always said that someone – she did not know who – had called out as they were being bundled into the lorry, 'Give the jewels to Louise!' (her grandmother). Gilbert, Elia's brother, confirms this story and they both say that their grandmother wanted to have nothing to do with receiving any valuables as the refugees were forced to leave.

When they arrived at Camp de Gurs, Henny was allocated to *îlot* J with Liesbett Preiss, and Hermann was sent to *îlot* H.

The internment camp at Gurs was an appalling place, especially in wet weather when the deep mud everywhere made it almost impossible to get around. Over the following few days, the Post Office bell in Anna Pourrillou's house must have rung wildly several times as telegram after telegram was sent from Gurs to Arette, as Henny and Liesbett requested help from Amélie Derrez:

> *28 August 1942. Henny Hartog to Amélie Derrez:*
> *Please send someone urgently with trunk, backpack, add clogs, shoes, apron, bath robe, old coat, shoe polish, sewing equipment, towels to go to Pau.*
>
> *28 August 1942, Liesbett Preiss to Amélie Derrez:*
> *Please send clogs, rain coat behind the door, things to eat, preserves, pans, leather shoes, galoshes, two summer dresses for my mother, with warm thanks.*

The following day, 29 August 1942, Henny sent a letter from herself and Hermann to Amélie and Gaston Derrez:

> *Dear Friends,*
> *Because of recent events I have not yet been able to write to you.*
>
> *There are no words to tell you how difficult it was to leave you and there is no comfort for any of that.*
>
> *Yesterday I sent you a telegram and please excuse us for charging you for it all. I have a little work here – I have been made Head of our barracks, and with these small duties I am able to forget a little. Do not send this news to my daughters; they will certainly get to know.*
>
> *In case we don't see you again, take all the food that is left at Madame Castagné's (oil, gherkins, about 50 kilos of potatoes) and sort everything else out with Madame Castagné.*
>
> *There is almost no luck for us now – short of any evidence.*
>
> *We thank you again for all your goodness and kind-heartedness. We will never forget what you have done for us. Perhaps the good Lord will allow us to thank you one day in some other way.*
>
> *With our very best wishes, we wish you farewell, and we hope to see you again one day.*
>
> *Hermann Hartog. Henny Hartog.*
>
> *From both of us please say hello and many thanks to Monsieur and Madame Casabonne, Madame Marianne, and everyone who has been kind to us.*

The following day, 30 August 1942, Liesbett Preiss also wrote to Amélie and Gaston.

Letter from Liesbett Preiss to Amélie Derrez 30.8.42
Camp de Gurs, îlot J, Baraque 7

Dear Madame and Monsieur,
I am now settled in Camp de Gurs and have become a little calmer. I would not want to miss thanking you heartily for your great goodness which has touched me profoundly. You cannot imagine how much you have helped me with your goodness and kindness. I will always be very grateful to you and your husband, and I will never forget the help that you have given to me.

I send my very best wishes, and I ask you to please send my respectful greetings to Madame Caristny,

Liesbett Preiss

I am sorry to ask for one more kindness from you. I have left some wool that I have already paid for with the lady who lives opposite my landlord. Would you please look for it and put it in the case. Thank you.

There was one last telegram for Henny to send to Amélie, probably on 29 August (the date stamp is not easily decipherable):

Do not send any more luggage neither for us nor Preiss, Schuck, important letter from Mardet send immediately to Madame Berthe Sonin, îlot J barrack 7 Hartog

As Henny said in her letter, she had been appointed 'Head of our barracks'. This was a new role for their cohort of deportees and was aimed at trying to avoid the disorder that had occurred in the previous deportation a few days earlier when there had been a hostile rebellion amongst those being sent away that had caused extra confusion and delay. So, some changes in the administration of the next deportation were made. Instead of all the deportees packing their bags in their barracks and then trudging the length of the central road to the main gate where they were collected together in huge aeroplane hangars – one for the men and the other for the women – this time, the inmates packed their bags and went to another barrack that contained fewer people than a hangar and was designated only for those leaving the following day. *Ilot* E at the camp, which had become empty after previous deportations had left, was re-opened and the barracks there were used exclusively for the following day's deportees. Henny was responsible for the list of names of those in her barrack, and for managing all the different formalities for them.

Before they left, the deportees received back any permits or valuable items that had previously been left in the registry office of the camp. The AFSC kept a presence at Camp de Gurs and tried to help those who were leaving. They took care of any of the valuables or jewellery, including money and documents, that people wanted to have looked after by someone trustworthy. Henny and Liesbett Preiss had already left small amounts of money with Amélie Derrez, who had made out a receipt for them. Eventually, she passed Henny's money to the AFSC so that it could be passed on to Lore.

While she was at Gurs, Henny wrote to various people to let them know what had happened. She wrote to Anneliese and Karl Elsberg, and she sent a telegram to Lore, which has never come to light. She also asked her neighbour in the barracks to write to Lore after she had been deported.

Early on 31 August, the guards who were especially appointed to the convoy arrived at Gurs and so everyone knew that departure was imminent. The camp was sealed and no one was allowed to leave. A roll-call was taken on each *îlot* and those being deported packed their bags. There was extreme nervousness, distress, and heightened tension and anxiety amongst the whole camp population. Anyone who attempted to hide or evade deportation was discovered by the police with their dogs.

That evening, the deportees were gathered together in the barracks on *îlot* E. They were given an evening meal and all the lists were checked again. The lorries to collect them started arriving at midnight – one lorry was allocated to the people of each barrack. They stopped on the roadway at the entrance to *îlot* E and each lorry 'loaded the contents of one barrack', as was described in the official instructions. Every aspect of the 'operation' was deliberately designed to humiliate and dehumanise those leaving on this journey.

When the convoy left Gurs, the lorries carried about 500 men and women to the train station at Oloron. The cattle cars they then climbed into, and which were then closed and sealed, were equipped with just straw on the floor and the usual toilet bucket and jug of drinking water. On 1 September 1942, Henny and Hermann, Liesbett and Gerhard Preiss, and Gertrud Schück were deported on this convoy to Drancy, an internment camp in the north-east of Paris. The train made its way to Paris via other internment camps in the southern part of France, picking up new deportees on the way. When the train stopped at the camp at Rivesaltes, Henny managed to send another quick message to the Elsbergs.

A few days later, on 7 September 1942, Elisabet Bernhard did as Henny had requested and wrote to Lore.

> *Dear Miss Hartog,*
> *I suppose you got the cable which your mother sent to you before the departure. I made the acquaintance of your parents here in the camp, and though we stayed only a few days together – your parents had to*

leave while I stayed until now – I felt a real deep sympathy for them. I suppose when you are neighbours under those dreadful circumstances you feel that comradeship of fate which is more than friendship.

Your mother has been my neighbour on our barrack, and she asked me to write to you before she left. She looked well, she was very quiet (so was your father – and both were very courageous) and not afraid of the long journey. Your parents asked me to tell you that you must not be afraid, and not be worried if you hear nothing for a long time. Sooner or later all our sufferings will be finished and then your mother will write again to you. She thought about you and your sister a great deal and I hope that you can be together with your parents sooner or later. These are hard times for all of us!

Sincerely yours, Elisabet Bernhard

Back in Arette, Henny and Hermann's landlord searched for more information about what had happened to them, and on 6 September he sent a letter to the commandant at Gurs:

Monsieur the camp Commandant,
I have the honour to ask you to kindly inform me ***as soon as possible*** *if* ***Mr and Mrs Hermann Hartog****, *my former tenants in Arette, who left the locality to rejoin Camp de Gurs at the end of August this year,* ***are still resident at your camp.***

**Jews from Germany*

Yours sincerely,
Castagné (signed)
Castagné, Charles retired L.F.C. (Légion Française des Combattants) (French Legion of Veterans)

He received a reply on 9 September, sent via the mayor of Arette.

Following your letter of the 6th instant concerning those named Hartog, Hermann, and his wife, I have the honour to inform you that those of interest have left Camp de Gurs.

Commandant of Camp de Gurs

Finally, on 12 September, the last telegram arrived from Gurs to send Anna Pourrillou rushing down the road again. It came from Siegbert Plastereck who was himself detained at Gurs and worked with the aid agency HICEM, who had a presence in the camp. His job there was primarily to try to get the internees out of the camp, legally, through another aid agency. His telegram merely said: 'Hartog

Hermann and Henny and Preiss Gerhard and Liesbett are not present at the camp. Plastereck.'

Today, when you stand on the platform of the quiet railway station at Oloron-Sainte-Marie, it is not easy to envisage the scenes of confusion and despair that must have been part of these departures. The deportees had no idea where they were going. All they knew was that it was *'une destination inconnue'* – 'an unknown destination'. The railway lines from Oloron stretch a long way into the distance. For Henny and Hermann, in September 1942, they initially stretched as far as a run-down residential suburb of Paris – Drancy.

CHAPTER 15

Drancy and Auschwitz

Mercifully, Henny and Hermann were only in the internment camp at Drancy for two days, because it was a terrible place to be, especially by the beginning of September 1942, when thousands of other Jewish deportees had already passed through the camp during the previous summer months.

Internees were housed in the buildings of a huge, unfinished construction project that had started as a low-cost modernist housing scheme for Parisian workers in a north-eastern suburb on the edge of the city, about 13km from the centre of Paris. Building started in 1931 and the designers had planned to create a housing scheme that would improve the lives of local people in their 'Silent City' (*'La Cité de la Muette'*). It was still unfinished in May 1940 when it was confiscated by Nazi authorities after the German invasion of France. After being briefly used as a police barracks, the buildings were converted into the main detention centre in the Paris area for holding Jews and other 'Undesirables'.

When the policy of extermination of the Jews was agreed, the internment camp at Drancy became an antechamber for Auschwitz. The first convoy taking Jews from Drancy to Auschwitz left on 22 June 1942, and another sixty-one transports would follow over the next two years until 17 August 1944. Thousands of Jews passed through the camp, which was designed to hold 700 people but at its peak held more than 7,000. The camp was under the authority of Dannecker until July 1942, and then of Heinz Röthke, who ran a strict regime but was a cold and distant personality who took little part in the everyday running of the camp, which was given to the French police (at least until July 1943).

One particular section of the building complex was used as an internment camp. It consisted of a U-shaped set of buildings, all five storeys high and each with their own stairwells. In front of the three wings that created the U-shape was a courtyard, and a road, Avenue Jean Jaurès, ran across the far side of the courtyard. The whole camp was surrounded by a double barbed wire fence 3m high, watchtowers and guard posts. The main entrance was guarded.

Living conditions were atrocious at Drancy, and the food supply was so disastrous that inmates were often hungry. Between August and October 1942, during which time Henny and Hermann were briefly there, forty detainees died of hunger in the camp.

Every aspect of life at Drancy was humiliating for the Jewish refugees. On arrival, they were assembled in the courtyard where they had to hand over their ration cards and any remaining valuables. The courtyard was covered with clinker over the clay ground, so when it rained there were large muddy puddles everywhere.

Accommodation was in the unfinished rooms, which were of an irregular shape, roughly 20m long and 7m wide, narrowing to 3m in the centre of the room. The minimal furniture included some wooden bunks for sleeping but the palliasses laid on them were very dirty. The untreated concrete floors were dirty and would have been difficult to clean even if cleaning materials had been available. Any windows overlooking the outside of the camp were boarded up and didn't fit well (neither did any doors), so the rooms were very draughty. With between fifty and eighty-five people in each room, the camp was often overcrowded, filthy dirty, and infested with vermin.

Until June 1943, the Drancy camp was guarded entirely by French gendarmes, who were housed, with their families, on the eastern edge of the camp. Supplies came from the prefecture of the Seine, and the administration was also French.

By the time Henny and Hermann arrived at Drancy on Wednesday 2 September 1942, in a deportation of over 1,000 other Jews from the non-occupied zone in the south, Drancy was a transit camp for Jews being transported to the extermination centres in Poland. Between 7 August and 22 October 1942, more than 10,500 Jews would travel the same way. Drancy was only a temporary staging post for them.

Henny and Hermann were destined for the convoy from Drancy to Auschwitz on Friday 4 September, on Convoy number 28.

Before deportation, all deportees had their hair shaved off, and the men were shaved of their moustaches and beards. This took place in a hut in the barbed wire enclosure in the courtyard. They then had their baggage searched and were allowed to take one parcel, a satchel, and a blanket with them.

Once these further humiliations had been endured, those waiting for the convoy were not allowed to return to any of the rooms but had to wait in a stairwell that had been allocated to them. No one was allowed to go anywhere else. Buckets were placed in the stairwell to serve as toilets and the whole area became squalid and foul-smelling.

While they waited, the freight cars were being prepared at the station. They were cleaned, fresh straw was laid down, and a toilet bucket and a bucket of water were placed on the floor of each wagon.

Early on the morning of Friday 4 September, buses were waiting outside the camp to take the deportees on the ten-minute journey to the train station. Opposite the camp, in Avenue Jean Jaurès, was a hotel that had a view over the camp and its courtyard from the windows in its upper storeys. Relatives of those interned would sometimes pay high prices to be able to see their loved ones from this vantage point.

The camp was close to the centre of the town of Drancy and near to two railway stations that had good networks to the east of the country and beyond, to Germany and Poland. Until June 1943, the station 'Le Bourget' was used to transport the convoys of Jews eastwards.

Each deportation consisted of one locomotive, three passenger cars for the security guards accompanying the convoy, and twenty freight or cattle cars for the deportees. At the station, fifty to seventy people were pushed into each wagon – men and women, children, unwell people, pregnant women and the elderly – before the wagon was sealed. The commandant of the camp, Heinz Röthke, might have been at the station since he was often present as convoys departed.

Convoy 28 carried a total of 1,013 men, women and children on 4 September, and it arrived in Auschwitz three days later. About 100km west of Auschwitz, the train stopped briefly at Kosel and those men and boys between the ages of 15 and 50 who were considered fit to work were taken from the train to be part of the forced labour teams in the area.

At Auschwitz, sixteen men and thirty-eight women from this convoy were selected to work in the camp. Everyone else, including all the children, were murdered in the gas chambers immediately. Henny and Hermann Hartog were amongst them.

Nobody who loved and cared about them knew exactly what happened to them. It would be many, many years before people could discover some of the events of this time, piece together some parts of the story, and acknowledge what Jewish people had lived through over these years.

But Auschwitz was not the end – in some ways it was the beginning of another journey of discovery.

CHAPTER 16

Afterwards

Shortly before the Second World War had even begun, Hitler had shouted to his service chiefs, assembled on 22 August 1939 at the Obersalzberg, his mountain residence near the Austrian border: 'Close your hearts to pity. Act brutally. The strongest man is right. The greatest harshness.'

And so it had happened. This rhetoric was largely ignored by other societies in other countries, and their inability to recognise the imminent dangers of Nazism had become the epitaph of a generation. Although people in many countries were terrified of the Nazis, few people outside Hitler's close circle could have had any idea at that time that events would unfold as they did.

On 8 November 1942, about nine weeks after Henny and Hermann had been murdered in Auschwitz, American and British forces landed on the beaches and in the ports of French North Africa in order to open a new military front against the German Army and its allies. Partly as a response to this aggressive action, four days later, on 11 November, the Germans occupied southern France in disregard of the 1940 armistice, thus making the entire country a zone of occupation. From that day until the end of the war, the Vichy government continued to exercise authority throughout the country, but only on the condition that it continued to do as it was told. The Germans left the French civil servants in their positions in the previously non-occupied zone, but they now came under their supervision.

The people of Arette were surprised that the Germans arrived in their village so soon after the occupation of the southern zone of France. It was terrifying suddenly hearing the sound of soldiers' boots on the road. They closed their gates and shut their front doors against the newcomers. They were not welcome to traditional Basque hospitality.

Over eighty years later, as my husband and I strolled cheerfully around Arette on a warm Friday afternoon in October 2023 with our guide and friend Janette Ananos, we turned away from the riverside onto a very narrow, unmarked path leading back to the centre of the village. We appreciated just how narrow it was as we struggled slightly, single-file, through the foliage, and Janette explained that this was a path that had once only been recognisable to those people who lived in that part of the village, who knew the locality very well and were familiar with its hidden passages. Partway along the track, and rather concealed by the surrounding vegetation, was a house, creating a sharp corner in the path, which then ran very close to the windows of the house, that we had to navigate, along with the brambles and nettles.

When the Germans had arrived rather more quickly than expected so many years ago, the people living in that house had been horrified to hear the sound of soldiers' boots coming along the path, down from the village towards the river, and straight past where they were living. For them, and for many people in Arette, that was almost a secret path. If the Germans knew about it, what other Intelligence did they have? And the people who were living in the house at the time had a son who had recently disappeared over the mountains into Spain to evade being taken as slave labour to Germany. What did the Germans know? Who had denounced them? What was going to happen now?

In Arette, in late 1942, the newly arrived Germans took over the mayor's large villa – almost next to the imposing town hall – for their lodging, and also installed themselves in the hotel in the centre of town. They set up barbed wire in front of the villa, blocking any access to the road running past their lodgings from the main road to the town hall, thus obliging the local children to make a detour around a few more streets in order to get to their school classes, since the town hall building also served partly as a school. Jacky Tillous, who already had a fairly long walk to school from his home on the farm at Bugala, remembers the children's mild resentment at the extra distance.

Blankets were requisitioned from the local people who were also required to give up some of their meagre supplies for their occupiers. Two years later, when the Germans departed as quickly as they had come, leaving the place in disarray, one resident of Arette was wryly amused to see her blankets fluttering from the balcony of what had previously been the mayor's villa as she went to Mass at the church opposite.

Arette became a changed place once the Germans occupied the area. It was clear there were some villagers who were hostile to the newcomers and did their best to help anyone adversely affected by their presence. At the same time, there were others who wished to find favour with the occupiers and collaborated with them, and who subsequently denounced other residents. Everyone became much more distrustful of their neighbours and retreated into a greater silence, except with very close family members and maybe a few dependable friends.

Madeleine Larragueta remembers that when she was a small child there was a rabbi living in the house on the corner of her street who wanted to leave for the mountains when the Germans arrived. One man in the village:

> *...who was very religious – Catholic – and very far-right and wanted to do what was right for France, when the Germans came and asked where the rabbi was, he told them that he had left for the mountains. Afterwards, whenever my father saw him again, he would always ask him why he had told them. He would tell the man, "It wasn't necessary to do that".*

After their occupation in November 1942, the Germans sealed all the French borders and carefully checked, and sometimes confiscated, all packages in and out of the country. This border control was generally done by French people acting on German orders.

On 9 November 1942, the day after the Allied landings in North Africa, the Vichy government broke off diplomatic relations with the United States. With American interest no longer officially welcome in France, and since the whole of the country was now occupied by the Germans, the AFSC was required to bring to an abrupt end the relief activities the organisation had undertaken in France for at least the previous two years. This was a real blow to the many American Quakers who were involved with the organisation, but much of their work was still carried on by the non-American workers who remained in France during the rest of the war, despite the increasing danger.

In the summer and autumn of 1942, Germany had looked almost certain to win the war. It was at the same time that Vichy's collaboration with the Nazi police on their dealings with the Jews had mainly taken place. Forty-two thousand Jews were deported in just six months during that year. What had eventually slowed down the co-operation between the French and German authorities on this subject was the pressure that the Church and the French people eventually put on the Vichy administration, particularly following the deportation of Jews from the unoccupied zone during the summer and early autumn of 1942.

Wednesday 26 August 1942, the day that Henny and Hermann were taken from Arette, was one of three days during which the French police arrested over 6,500 Jews in the unoccupied zone and quickly transferred them to Drancy. The French people's reaction was very negative. On Sunday 30 August 1942, in response to the strong emotion expressed by many people, the Archbishop of Toulouse and Narbonne, Monseigneur Jules Saliège, wrote a strongly worded letter against the deportations, which was to be read in every church of the diocese that day. He wrote:

> *That children, women, men, fathers, mothers should be treated as a wretched herd, that members of the same family should be separated from one another and embarked for unknown destinations, was a sad spectacle reserved for our times to see. These Jews are men. These*

Jewesses are women. All is not permitted against them. They belong to mankind. They are our brothers like so many others.

The letter was banned by the prefect but still read out in most churches. It was also taken up and transmitted by the BBC. Similarly, Monseigneur Vansteenberghe, Bishop of Bayonne, published an article with the title of *Fraternity* in the diocesan bulletin of 20 September. He was the only bishop in the occupied zone to protest in this way. The Germans demanded and obtained a ban on its publication until the Liberation.

The people in the villages slightly higher up the mountains that circle Arette remember this second half of the war, after the Germans occupied their part of the country, as a very dark period. Many of those who had signed up for the French Army at the very beginning of the war had already been taken prisoner when the armistice was signed two years previously, and now the entire commune was occupied by the German Army.

People found it increasingly difficult to travel to the villages and towns in the lowlands to conduct their business, and there was a curfew of eight o'clock in the evening – punishable by death. This curfew was strictly enforced as a means of controlling the movement of people across the nearby border into Spain. German sentries took over some of the huts traditionally used by the shepherds on the higher reaches of the mountains during the transhumance, and German soldiers vigorously patrolled the footpaths on the mountains.

For the people of Montory, where Henny and Hermann had lived for a few months in 1940, the war really came home to them in 1942 when the Germans arrived in the area, set up guard posts on the mountains, and patrolled the routes into Spain. Listening to the men talk now, this was the focus of their war: outwitting German patrols on the mountain paths that they knew so well and helping refugees and others escape into Spain.

In February 1943, the Vichy government brought in even stricter measures to enforce the *Service de Travail Obligatoire* (STO), which was a forced labour workforce to be sent to Germany from the occupied regions of France – that is, all of France. Young local men resisted this in their hundreds and evaded conscription in whatever way was possible for them. For some, this meant going into hiding, for others it meant joining the local Resistance group, and for others it provided the final motivation to climb over the Pyrénées into Spain and join Charles de Gaulle's Free French Forces in Algeria or Madagascar to fight against Hitler.

There were guides (often local shepherds) who became part of the Resistance movement to oppose the Nazi invaders by helping those who were desperate enough to attempt the journey. They knew the routes, knew the dangers, and had been keeping a careful watch on the German mountain patrols to understand their movements and learn how to outwit them. But it was a very secretive way of working. There were denouncers in every village, happy to collaborate with the Germans, and secrecy was essential for getting into Spain. Although large numbers of young men preferred to take the route over the mountains, or go into hiding, rather than be sent to work in Germany, the logistics involved in helping them were almost overwhelming for the newly created Resistance movement. Those who did this work usually did so in spite of the danger to themselves and their families, or they cut themselves off completely from their family in order to spare them any connection.

At the time, and for a long time afterwards, no one talked about the *passeurs* – the people who guided others over the mountains and 'passed' them on to others to take them further along the journey. Often family members had no idea what one of their own was doing, and certainly the neighbours were not included in any talk. Sometimes, it was only much later – when some of those individuals who had been helped returned to the area to offer their thanks – that a picture began to emerge about what had gone on during that time.

The war came to an end for the people of Arette, Montory, and other nearby villages in late 1944 as the Free French Forces moved eastwards and liberated the towns and villages of France from the control of the Germans as the German soldiers disappeared from the Basque country on their retreat back to Germany.

Local people in Arette recall the hunger that people experienced at this time, alleviated only by what they could grow themselves and share with each other. The queue for bread often stretched right round the square in front of the church – and then the bread was black, where you could see a mixture of assorted grains inside. And poverty was actually at its worst after 1945 because the Germans took everything with them.

'Everything was stolen by the Germans. They took everything,' said Jacky Tillous.

Elia Migazzi told me:

> *It brings back bad memories to remember these stories. It hurts to remember, to know that Monsieur and Madame Hartog were exterminated in this way, and that Monsieur their grandson is just over there. It does something to you. It is a sad memory, a very sad memory.*

Adolf Hitler committed suicide in his bunker in Berlin on Monday 30 April 1945 and two weeks later, on Tuesday 8 May 1945, Nazi Germany surrendered to the Allies. Four countries representing the Allies – the United States, Britain, the Soviet Union, and France – took joint authority over Germany and stripped it of its sovereignty and former state. The war was over in Europe, although it continued for another four months in Japan. The Allies divided Germany into four occupation zones, which they each administered. Frankfurt was the headquarters for the American zone, and Aurich, Jever and Wilhelmshaven were all in the British zone, where the headquarters were in Bad Oeynhausen, about 200km south of Wilhelmshaven.

As soon as the war in Europe ended in May 1945, Jews all over the world who had survived tried to find information about their friends and relatives, and it was at this point that the full horror of their extermination began to be more fully realised. When evidence of the extermination camps was shown, people throughout the world were shocked and repelled. Jewish organisations and aid agencies tried their best to give help to survivors and the International Red Cross took a lead in tracing people.

What had happened to everyone? Had they survived? If so, where were they?

In Arette, Amélie Derrez wrote to everyone she could think of to try to find news of Henny and Hermann, including trying to get in touch with Lore and Inge to see if they had news. She had a typewritten page of contact details for both the Hartog and the Preiss families and she made her way systematically down the list.

First, she wrote to Karl Elsberg, after she had received the joyous news from him that he, his wife, and second son were alive and well in Italy, and in his reply on 13 February 1945 he said to her: 'Unfortunately, there is no longer any hope that our friends Hermann and Henny Hartog are still alive. With us, everything is unchanged.'

On 27 February 1946, nine months after the war in Europe had ended, Karl Elsberg sent a letter to Lore from where he was living in Italy:

> *Madame Derrez from Arette sent me your letter and asked me to reply, because she knows us as Hermann and Henny's best friends. I have tried to find again those friends who are so close to us, or to find out something about their fate. I write to all the arrival points and committees on the mainland, here in Italy, in France, Belgium, Switzerland. Unfortunately, without any success, as well as my requests to Ruda. We had the last direct message from your parents in autumn 1942, from Camp de Gurs, and then from the deportation camp at Rivesaltes. Of the whole circle of friends who had gone through so much, we are the only ones left.*
>
> *No news has yet been received from those who were deported from Gurs, or about these poor people. Can we still hope? I don't think so. Because even the deportees who fell under Russian rule should have had the opportunity to inform their relatives a long time ago. There is not even a clue that they were transported to any of the camps, especially since they were constantly being transported onwards.*

We had to leave the last greetings cards from your parents behind in France. Due to the challenges and deprivations from 1939 to 1942, your parents were already in ill-health. I think I have to accept, therefore, which might be a small consolation to you, that our dear Hermann and Henny died a natural death.

The Elsbergs had eventually escaped from France to Italy. Their first son, Peter, had been taken away from them to be looked after in an institute in Limoges, France, but had died there in April 1943, aged just over a year old. Their second son, Nicolas, was born in France in February 1943. When the Germans occupied the non-occupied zone, the Elsbergs were moved to Eaux-Bonnes (further south from Meillon, the village where they had been living, and close to the Spanish border), but were taken north again to the internment camp at Dun-le-Paleteau, where Jews from all over France were collected for deportation to Drancy. While Anneliese and Nicolas were protected by a local doctor, Karl was arrested twice. When he was arrested the first time, he was released because he answered at an interrogation that his son was French. The second time that he was arrested, Karl managed to leave the lorry that was transporting him for deportation. The three of them eventually made their way to the Nice area and at the end of the year escaped from Nice to Aosta, in Italy. There they were protected by an Italian partisan and his family and managed to survive the war in Italy before emigrating to the USA in 1946.

From their new home in Springfield, Massachusetts, Karl wrote to Amélie Derrez on 22 February 1947, with news and some advice about packages that Hermann had left with her five years earlier. While Henny had left some jewels and a little money with Amélie before she was deported, Hermann had apparently given into her keeping his prayer shawl and his *tefillin*, or *phylacteries* – the set of small boxes with leather straps that contain tiny scrolls of parchment inscribed with verses of the Torah, or Jewish law, and are worn by Jewish men during prayers. In his reply, Karl advised:

Regarding the package that our Hartog friends left with you, you can give it to a synagogue. These are religious clothes, and the band with the writing is a band that is used in the synagogue to wrap the religious laws. You can send everything to the synagogue. My compliments on the reproduction of the drawing on the band, but I cannot read Hebrew.

Anneliese died in the USA in 1968 and Karl in 2001.

Amélie Derrez also tried to get information about Henny and Hermann from an organisation in Paris, the SER (*Service d'Evacuation et Regroupement*), which had been set up by Jewish resistance fighters who had been freed from Drancy or who had escaped from the last deportation train. They were dedicated to trying to find any survivors and they set up an office in the centre of Paris, at 23, Boulevard Haussmann. The reply Amélie received on 20 March 1945 could only say: 'I regret to inform you that the two persons were deported from Camp de Gurs on 5 or 6 October 1942' – so their information at that time was not very reliable. Ultimately, the SER was obliged to close down since there was 'a lack of returnees'.

Amélie Derrez wrote to Mrs Grimbley on 29 January 1946, after she had exhausted all other possible channels. She wrote in French:

> *Madam,*
> *Excuse my writing to you, but Madame Hartog had spoken to me about you in such kind terms that I have decided to write you a word. Could you please give me news of Lore and Inge? I know how much you love the latter, which makes me believe that you know where they are.*
>
> *I did some research to find their unfortunate parents, but without success. Perhaps their daughters would have more luck than me. I would hope so, but I believe that like many others they were the victims of the Germans. I ask you, if possible, to reply to me in French because I have no one who can translate.*
>
> *I look forward to your news, and I say to you, 'Thank you very much'.*

When Mrs Grimbley received the letter, she immediately passed it on to Lore, who replied herself to Amélie Derrez. Madame Derrez was delighted, and sent a letter to Lore:

> *My dear young girl, unfortunately, I do not have any news of your parents. I was, in fact, a great friend of them, and their departure caused me great sadness. I tried to search in Paris, without success. Nevertheless, I do not despair. God will help us.*
>
> *If I have correctly understood your letter, you ask if I know any friends of your parents. Amongst my papers, I have the address of Mr Max Ruda in Zurich. I correspond with Mr Charles Elsberg who escaped to Italy with his wife and little boy. I have asked him to write to Mr Ruda because they speak the same language, so it is easier for him than for me.*
>
> *I speak English very badly. I am too old to learn what I have forgotten. But you, write in French. It is the only way to learn our beautiful language.*

Give me news of Inge and some details about yourself. Since when have you been married? Do you have children? I will let you know of anything that I learn. In the meantime, I kiss you like your mother used to, strongly.

The small amount of money that Henny had entrusted to Amélie Derrez eventually found its way to the AFSC, which had its main office in Pennsylvania, America. On 3 March 1948, the AFSC Committee wrote a letter to Max Bodenheimer ('Uncle Max') to say:

Our agency has been trying to contact Miss Lore Hartog but has not received a reply. We are holding a small sum of money which was left in her name by Hermann and Henny (née Scheuer) Hartog with our representative in southern France, before they were deported in 1942.

Through the location service of the Unite Service for New Americans, we understand that a Lore and Inge Hartog were brought to the United States by you and by Arthur Bodenheimer. If you know the present whereabouts of Lore Hartog, could you tell us how we can reach her?

Max Bodenheimer's widow, Hettie, sent the letter to Arthur Bodenheimer who wrote back to the AFSC to explain that his uncle had died two years ago, that Lore and Inge had never arrived in the USA, that Lore had since married and changed her name, and that she had also changed her address from the one that they had been given. In due course, arrangements were made to send the money to Lore, who shared it with Inge.

The Allies who were occupying Germany immediately after the end of the war formed an International Military Tribunal (IMT) together, and from 1945 to 1946 the former leaders of Nazi Germany stood trial for crimes against peace, war crimes, and crimes against humanity. The first trial in Nuremberg, which opened on 21 November 1945, revealed a great deal about the character of Hitler's Nazi system. Although the regime had glorified the men who appeared on trial, and hero-worshipped them, these men in the dock now no longer looked like the supermen they had been portrayed as. Although they had been given unrestrained power by Hitler, they now seemed quite 'ordinary people' who had relished both the increasing power and the opportunity to use it without self-control. They had manipulated, perverted, and corrupted the law – and brutalised themselves and others in the process.

In his opening speech for the trial, the American Prosecutor, Robert Jackson, spoke of crimes that had shown themselves to be: 'so calculated, so malignant, so devastating, that civilisation could not tolerate their being ignored, because it could not survive their repetition.'

Henny and Hermann Hartog, like millions of others, were the victims of an evil government that had pursued policies to eliminate humanity. The first group that the Nazis wanted to eliminate were the Jewish people – and Henny and Hermann were Jews. Other groups followed: communists, homosexuals, travellers, black people, Slavic people – anyone who threatened the ideal of the Nazi 'pure Aryan race' – until humans were no longer viewed as 'real people'. This elimination of minority groups succeeded through terror and through the destruction of natural human links – such as an attachment to family members. And it was achieved through a bureaucratic system that included a secret police unit and by completely ignoring the rule of law.

It took many, many years to discover some of the particulars of what had actually happened to those family members and friends of Henny and Hermann Hartog who had been unable to emigrate from Europe before or during the Second World War. Here are a few details of some of the people who have already been mentioned in this story, apart from Hermann's siblings, whose fate has already been told. Most of these people had very little knowledge of the fate of each other.

Lore and Inge's grandfather – Opa: On 15 September 1942, Henny's father, Adolf Scheuer, then aged 78 years, was deported from Frankfurt on the ninth convoy from the city – and the largest, with 1,367 people on board. He was required to leave his home on the appointed date and report to the cellar of the *Großmarkthalle* (the wholesale market hall), which was about a 2km walk from his home. Along with others on his convoy, he was detained for some hours in the huge underground cellar of the market hall and generally mistreated. Meanwhile, the ordinary work of the wholesale market carried on in the halls above. From the market railway station next to the hall, he was taken to Theresienstadt, where he died three months later, on 10 December 1942.

On 16 June 1942, Benjamin Polak – who had employed Hermann's sister (Henny) as his housekeeper – was deported on the first deportation from Cologne to Theresienstadt, along with his wife Emmy and son Helmuth. A few weeks later, on 10 July, he died there of pneumonia. Emmy and Helmuth also died in Theresienstadt – Emmy on 10 March 1944 and Helmut on 16 October 1942.

From the earlier Jewish community in Aurich, the teacher Moritz Lachmann died on 12 August 1942 in Łódź. His wife, Friederike, had died in January 1942, and he had been able to let their children in the USA know about this.

Inge's friend Marta Cohen did not survive the war years. Marta, who had lived almost opposite the Hartogs in Wallstraße in Aurich and was just a few months younger than Inge, had been forced by the Nazis to leave Aurich (with all other Jews) in February 1940 and go to a children's home in Cologne with her younger brother Manfred. Meanwhile, her parents were moved to Vegesack to do forced labour. Marta and Manfred returned to their parents in October 1941 when Marta left school, and the following month the whole family had to go by train to Hamburg and then on to Minsk, where they had to live in the ghetto. On 28 July 1942, the whole family was murdered with others in a van that had been converted into a mobile gassing unit. Marta was 15 years old.

Almost all of Henny and Hermann's Jewish friends from Jever who had not emigrated were murdered by the Nazis. They were all forced out of the town in March 1940 and sent mainly to Hamburg or Bremen, although a few went to Dortmund or Berlin. There they were required to live in 'Jew Houses', usually in crowded conditions – certainly compared with their former bourgeois lifestyle – and were subject to the increasing restrictions placed upon them as Jews and 'Undesirables'. From these 'Jew Houses', they were eventually deported to Theresienstadt, or Auschwitz, Riga, Treblinka or to some other extermination centre.

The Aunts Cohn – Emma, Frieda, and Netty – were deported from Hamburg to Theresienstadt in July 1942 and did not survive living there.

Julius Gröschler, one of the former leaders of the Jever synagogue community, and his wife Hedwig were deported from Hamburg to Theresienstadt in June 1943 and then murdered in Auschwitz in October 1944.

Erich Levy and his wife Ruth (who had converted to Judaism on her marriage) lived in a 'Jew House' in Berlin until 1945, when the Allies allowed them to return to Jever.

From Neustadtgödens, Samuel de Taube and his wife Rosa (who lived in Wilhelmshaven in 1938) went to England on 25 August 1939 and returned to Horsten (3km from his former house at Horster Grashaus) in 1947. Rosa died in 1948 and Samuel in 1949.

Robert de Taube (Samuel's son) was interned at Sachsenhausen after the pogrom in 1938 and when he was released on 9 December 1938, he went to Wilhelmshaven. He was forced to leave Wilhelmshaven and settle in Berlin in 1940. While there, he took on the false identity of 'Auguste Schneider, landscape gardener' and so managed to evade deportation to Auschwitz. Meanwhile, the Nazis leased out his family estate near Neustadtgödens to various farmers. After the war, Robert returned there and eventually managed to get back the family estate during a protracted struggle between 1946 and 1954.

In Aurich, in a trial in December 1948 of those responsible for the 1938 synagogue fire, four men were charged with arson, breach of the peace, serious deprivation of liberty, and crimes against humanity. They were the Nazi district leader Heinrich Bohnens, the painter Hermann Theesfeld, the businessman Karl Rector, and the government secretary Harm Flügge. Bohnens and Flügge were interned until 19 June 1949.

Four years after the end of the war, in 1949, those responsible for the pogrom in November 1938 in Jever were brought to justice. In a first verdict, the main defendants (who invoked 'emergency orders') were acquitted. However, the Chief Public Prosecutor's Office appealed against the acquittal and in a new trial, a verdict of several years in prison was given – but then successfully appealed. The penalties were mitigated.

Ten officers and gendarmes from Drancy camp were tried on 19 – 22 March 1947 before the Court of the Seine. The trial was not much discussed in the national press. Only two were convicted and they were pardoned later.

In France, Amélie Derrez died on 14 June 1950 at Arette, aged 60. Her husband, Gaston Derrez, died on 8 December 1958, aged 74, and François Casabonne died on 10 September 1980, aged 81.

Lore and Inge remained in England, which is also what Henny and Hermann had wanted. Letters from their parents had been arriving increasingly infrequently and always delayed, and now they just never came at all. Like so many of their Jewish friends around them who had parents in a different country, no news arrived from anywhere, but they did not give up hope that their relatives were still alive.

Even though Lore and Inge were living in relative safety in England, it wasn't an easy existence for them. As a *Kindertransportee*, Inge was always under the guardianship of the Children's Movement, which later became the Jewish Welfare Committee. Lore had had a guardian relationship with the Harrises, but when she was evacuated to Wales, with Inge, they both came under the jurisdiction of the Welfare Committee. Their move into the Grimbley family was welcomed not only by the two girls but also by the committee. As they became older and more independent, both Lore and Inge rather resented the frequent visits by the committee members to 'keep an eye on them', but Inge, in particular, was glad of their support with expensive items such as a winter coat, or with arranging (and paying for) necessary eye and dental treatment. Lore was in paid employment soon after leaving school, but it was several years before Inge earned enough to look after herself. They both always remembered the occasional hunger of that period, and the need to sell a piece of jewellery from time to time in order to be able to keep going.

Lore married the young man who had been the subject of her last letter to her parents – David Ronald Hepburn (always called Ron). He was a tall, fair-haired Englishman who came from a protestant Christian background and who gave Lore all the love, kindness, dependability and support that she needed. In an earlier letter, Henny and Hermann had expressed their strong disapproval of Lore becoming romantically attached to a non-Jew and in a reply to them on 18 August 1942 (which they would probably never have received) she made her feelings clear:

> *There is **nothing** that I would not do for you, but darlings, to give up Ron, I can't, I just can't do it. When Ron was here I showed him*

> *your letter and perhaps it is strange but he seemed to understand you better than I do. He has asked me to write and tell you all about us and as he said,*
>
> *"I am sure your parents will understand us if you write and tell them what we think of each other, and also that we try and please them as much as we can."*
>
> *Whether our love will last all our lives or will only be passing does not make any difference to our religion, that will go on for ever.*

Lore and Ron were married at a civil ceremony in London, near Ron's family home, on 19 May 1944, when Lore was 19 years old and Ron 22. On their marriage certificate, the occupation of Lore's father is registered as 'teacher' and Ron's as 'deceased'. At that time, they did not know that Hermann had been murdered twenty months previously.

When they married, Ron was serving with the British Army, but when he was demobilised, they went to live in south-east London, near Ron's mother and sisters. Their son, Peter, was born in 1950.

Inge remained working in Nottingham until Lore moved to London, when she also went to live in the capital and enjoyed working as a pharmacist's assistant for several years. She and Lore kept in close touch with each other and with the Grimbley family.

Once Lore and Inge realised that their parents, grandfather, aunts and uncle had all probably been murdered by the Nazis, they joined those other Jews who sought some sort of restitution from the new authorities in Germany. Germany's restitution measures ranged from compensating former owners and heirs for assets wrongly seized during the Holocaust to – still today – making substantial financial contributions to victims' funds and survivors' pensions.

In November 1947, the US military government in occupied Germany announced Military Law No. 59, which became the foundation of the first programme of restitution of Holocaust assets. Similar laws enacted in the French and British zones between 1947 and 1949 enabled the return of property that had been seized by the Nazi regime under duress.

Dispossession is a fundamental aspect of genocide. Seizing property had been vital to the dehumanising effect of persecution by the Nazis, and had been closely linked to later emigration and deportation. Restitution – of property, assets, health, and missed lifetime opportunities – was an essential component in rebuilding post-war society and creating a new politics in a different and more humane character.

On 4 May 1950, Lore and Inge made a statutory declaration under oath that they were the only heirs of not only Henny and Hermann Hartog, but also Hermann's siblings – Berta, Sara, Henny and Oskar.

In the following years they made claims for restitution for the confiscation of the Hartog house at Wallstraße 46, in Aurich, which had been registered in the relevant local land registry in Berta's name, as the eldest of the siblings. The house had been seized by the Nazis on 22 October 1941, when Berta (then aged 69) had already been 'evacuated' to the 'old people's home' in Emden. The house had become 'the responsibility of the Reich Minister of Finances' and 'the assets of the property of the Jewess Riwka Berta Sara Hartog' had been 'confiscated for the benefit of the German Reich'. Three days after receiving the official notification of the confiscation, Berta had been deported, with the other Jewish residents from Emden, to Łódź.

After being seized by the Nazis, the house at Wallstraβe 46 had been rented to a foreman in the navy whose name was Habbe Reuter. He had moved in during November 1941 and official letters from the tax offices in Aurich and Emden repeatedly state that he was renting from 'the former owner, Frau Hartog', paying a rent of 50 Reichsmarks per month. This is even on a document dated 1 June 1949 – although Berta Hartog had been murdered on 12 May 1942, more than seven years previously. Almost ten years after moving in, Habbe Reuter was still living in the house in 1951 (and at that time working as a carpenter), along with a pensioner, Hildegard Saathoff, and an agricultural worker, Willi Jahnke.

On 27 September 1951, Chancellor Adenauer delivered a historic speech in the Bundestag, during which he asked forgiveness for the crimes of Nazi Germany and stated that he was ready to commence negotiations with world Jewry on the issue of Holocaust reparations.

In 1956, the Federal Republic of Germany (FRG) – the new state in West Germany – passed the Federal Compensation Act (BEG), which covered many aspects of compensation for Nazi injustices not covered by the Allied restitution laws. It provided payments, when necessary, as compensation for physical injury and damage to health, restrictions on personal freedom, harm to economic and professional growth, and damage to personal property.

This enabled Lore and Inge to make claims for Inge's poor health as a result of living in Germany under a government that restricted her nutrition (resulting in rickets, which needed treatment and correction once she was in England, as well as untreated eye disorders). They could both also claim for being disadvantaged in their education. Lore had only been able to continue a secondary education because she had been sent overseas and away from home to acquire it, but Inge – two years younger – had had her educational opportunities severely stunted. In fact, she had barely been to school throughout her childhood. As Lore and Inge pointed out in their claim, their parents had expected and wanted them to continue into a university education, and this had been completely denied them.

In the 1950s, Lore and Ron moved out of London with their son Peter, first to Surrey and then to the Sussex countryside, where Ron had relatives living not far from their home. In 1955, Inge (then aged 29) won some money in a lottery and chose to use it to visit Arthur and Sitta Bodenheimer in New York, as well as Rosa Wolffs and her daughter and son, Else and Meinhard, in Chicago (and originally from

Aurich). She was away for six months and was very happy to meet so many people from the past who had managed to start their lives again in America. A few years later, Inge went to live in Sussex, not far from Lore and Ron, and she married Peter Sinden in 1961. She and Lore met very frequently, and the two families spent a lot of leisure time together.

In the summer of 1973, Lore and Inge, with their husbands, decided to 'go on holiday to France'. My husband and I knew nothing of the real reason behind their visit, which was to try to find the last address where they knew their parents had lived – Arette.

They were travelling with an old address, the name of Amélie Derrez, and a road map of France. There was no internet, no mobile phones, and only Inge's husband knew even a poor smattering of schoolboy French. Amazingly, they found the village and were introduced to François Casabonne, who was then 74 years old. François' grandson Pierre (the current mayor of Arette) remembers that the visit was not at all easy as neither group could understand the language of the other.

However, François wrote out an account – in French, of course – of what he remembered about the Hartogs, and his own part in their story. By that time, neither Amélie nor Gaston Derrez was alive, but someone managed to find the pile of letters to and from Henny and Hermann that had last arrived or been sent more than thirty years previously, and gave them to Lore and Inge. They had been extremely carefully kept and included the last telegrams from Camp de Gurs that Anna Pourrillou had delivered to Amélie Derrez from Henny and Hermann, Liesbett and Gerhard.

Lore and Inge did not understand a word that anyone said to them while they were in Arette, but they were immeasurably grateful for the extraordinary kindness that had clearly been shown to their parents, and then extended to themselves.

I remember very well Lore and Inge, with their husbands, visiting us soon after their return from France. They still told us nothing about their journey, nor why they had gone, but they had returned with a few old telegrams, which they asked me to translate. Everything was quite confusing as we had no idea what we were looking at, but when I translated the request from Henny (in muddy Camp de Gurs) for her '*sabots*' as 'clogs', Lore was incredulous and refused to believe me.

> *Clogs! That's impossible! My mother was a city woman. She came from Frankfurt and was very refined! She had really dainty feet and only wore very fashionable shoes. That can't possibly be the correct translation.*

How very difficult it was for us all to begin to understand the changes that had taken place in so many lives during the 1930s and 1940s, how much everyone had had to adapt to new ways of living and surviving, and how much the kindness of strangers had mattered.

Inge's husband had François Casabonne's account translated into English and wrote back to him (in a letter that he also managed to get translated). In it, he told François how grateful they all were to everyone for the kindness shown to the entire Hartog family, and told him that since their return, the memory of the beauty of the village and mountain surroundings, the peacefulness of the Basque countryside, and the empathy of the people of Arette had all meant that the nightmares Inge had constantly experienced since the 1930s in Germany had finally disappeared.

After Ron died in 1993 and Inge had divorced Peter some years earlier, the two sisters became increasingly close again. Inge died unexpectedly on 28 December 2015, and Lore just a few weeks later, on 7 February 2016. Soon afterwards, whilst clearing out their homes, my husband and I came across the letters.

Although Lore and Inge didn't exactly keep the letters secret, we only vaguely knew that they had once existed. They were never talked about and we had no idea that they were being kept carefully in a leather wallet in a cabinet next to Lore's bed. In all their house moves over the years, and periodic de-cluttering and cleaning, the letters had never been thrown away – but they also looked as though no one had opened them for a very long time.

The wallet contains letters between Lore and Inge and their parents from the end of 1938, and also random other documents such as a passport, official documents from German and French sources, postcards from friends, etc. There are no letters between Lore and her family when she was first at school in England, which must have seemed a very 'normal' time compared with what came later. Some of the letters are those received by Lore and Inge in England and kept, and others are those that had been preserved by Amélie Derrez and later passed on to Lore and Inge in the 1970s when they visited Arette.

This is not a complete collection of a correspondence. We do not know of other letters that might have been thrown away, those that never arrived, or those that somehow just got lost. Even in the surviving letters, there are gaps in chronology, and silences in the text. These letters had to go through a censor, so there were some things that could never be said for fear of the letter being delayed or destroyed, for fear of putting someone else in danger, for fear of causing trouble for oneself or one's loved ones.

The letters prove that letter-writing is by no means a perfect vehicle for maintaining a relationship from a distance, especially when a dialogue cannot be sustained. The increasingly long gaps of weeks and then months between their receipt merely underscored the grief associated with loss of personal contact as well as the possibilities for misunderstanding. Henny and Hermann bitterly regretted their inability to be effective parents to their daughters, however much counsel and guidance they tried to convey through their words. Their letters, as well as those of their daughters, came ultimately to tell merely the often trivial details of their daily lives, and remembrances of happy times that they had once spent together.

In the end, it mattered only that a letter confirmed that the correspondent was still alive, that it sent a message of reassurance that they still deeply loved the recipient, and the affirmation that they all continued to hope and pray for better times. The Nazis fractured so much that German-Jewish people had once known as a happy and stable family life – it was not only the paper that the letters were written on that had become fragile.

The silence that sometimes emanates from these letters is also like the shroud of silence that still surrounds the activities of those who had once helped people like Henny and Hermann. From the very little that Lore ever spoke about her parents, or about the years during the war, I had understood that there were two women in particular who stood out as saviours for their family – Daisy Grimbley and Amélie Derrez. The Grimbleys had continued to be close friends with Lore and Inge, who both remained good friends with the daughters of the family well into everyone's old age. But nobody knew anything about Amélie Derrez, and none of us knew (until the 1970s) anything about the help that François Casabonne had given to the Hartogs.

We now know that Amélie Derrez and, probably, her husband Gaston were members of the burgeoning Resistance movement in France. During late 1940, 1941, and 1942, when Henny and Hermann were in the Basque-Pyrénées, there was little local appetite for resistance against the Nazi occupation of the north of their country. But there were people who helped the refugees amongst them, and some who particularly wanted to help the Jewish refugees.

Gaston Derrez is still remembered by people in Arette as a secretary to the mayor who was well placed to be able to help with the paperwork, false identities, etc., required for those wishing to evade the Nazis. And he is known to have done this willingly. He remained in post after the occupation of the unoccupied zone by the Germans in November 1942, and seems to have continued to be helpful – especially as increasing numbers of young Frenchmen escaped the Nazis over the mountains into Spain from where they could join the Free French Forces in Algeria or Madagascar.

Although elderly villagers in Arette still remember Gaston Derrez, when I ask about his wife, they look puzzled. No, they don't remember his wife. I give her first name, and the one or two details I know about her, but they remain perplexed. She was related to the Casabonne family, a well-known and very respected family in Arette, but they are still puzzled. She and Gaston had no children, and it seems that the memory of Amélie Derrez has vanished from the area and only silence surrounds her and her activities.

Amélie and Gaston Derrez, and François Casabonne, possibly pursued their activities of quiet resistance against an occupier as a result of their Catholic faith. Although they actively helped the Jews who took refuge in their village, the silent tolerance of their neighbours was also necessary if everyone was not to get into trouble. Passive goodwill and benevolence of others was equally important as activity. Who else knew about the Jewish women listening to *Radio Londres* in Amélie's house? Who else knew that the agricultural worker on the Casabonne farm was really an erudite Jewish teacher? Did Hermann Hartog and François Casabonne only talk about farm work as they chatted late into the evening, or were politics, philosophy and religion also part of the conversation? How many people knew that Henny was welcomed into Louise de Rose's house and given work, some extra food, and the opportunity to play the piano? Who used to know about the care and concern showed to the Hartogs by their landlord, Charles Castagné? Henny and Hermann survived as long as they did partly because of the generosity of the people in Arette who kept them safe for as long as they could and allowed them some happiness.

There were no doubt other people who nowadays remain in the silence who were willing at that time to respect other human beings, tolerate different nationalities and faiths, and act independently to help people to survive. They were immensely courageous and there were not many of them.

The Nazi experiment did not entirely succeed. Millions of people were killed by it, but friendship, the Jewish faith, empathy between people of different nationalities, love between family members – that all survived.

When writing this story, which is a true history, I have had to admit to myself that there are probably more holes in the narrative than there is substantive text. But perhaps this is what a family story looks like – lots of holes. Of course there are things missing, knowledge that we don't have, evidence that has not yet materialised or been verified. Even as we peer carefully through those holes from a distance of more than eighty years, it is very difficult indeed to fully comprehend what really happened at the time, or to appreciate how people could ever move forward from the wartime horrors.

In the year 1945, when the war in Europe finally came to an end, Germany as a nation was facing *Stunde Null* (Zero Hour). So were most people – everywhere – as they individually tried to come to terms with what had happened, where they found themselves now, and how they might find a way into a better future. What could the future look like?

Maybe it was going to be impossible to move ahead without first trying to face the past, to make some atonement for the extreme suffering, to make sure that the events and the people were remembered – and vow never to allow humanity to forget what had happened.

CHAPTER 17

Memory and Memorials

Elie Wiesel, a survivor of the death camp at Buchenwald who remembers – as a young boy – being there the day that the Americans arrived to free them, has frequently reminded the world of the need to remember what happened during the years of National Socialism. In a speech in front of the then president of the United States, Bill Clinton, at the White House in Washington in 1999, he stressed the need to be active in our remembrance if we wish to be vigilant against evil. Not only was there 'so much violence', there was also 'so much indifference'. As he expressed it: 'In the place that I come from, society was composed of three simple categories: the killers, the victims, and the bystanders.'

After the war, people in the cities of Germany gradually cleared away the rubble from their streets. Throughout the country, as people picked up their brooms to sweep clean their neighbourhoods, they also hoped to sweep away the stories of the lives of some of the people who had once lived there. Meanwhile, they also swept away some of their own memories. Some people even claimed, afterwards, to remember nothing at all.

> *'Where did the Jews in Jever live?'*
> *'Jews? No, there were never any Jews living here in Jever.'*

Individuals and societies remember people and events in different ways. We sometimes talk about 'choosing to remember' – or, indeed, 'choosing to forget'. An 'active memory' can remind us of past injustices and then lead us on to address contemporary issues. The collective memory of a particular group can influence not only how those people see historical and current events, but also how they understand and interpret the world around them. While memory connects us to those who have lived before us, it can also lead us along a path of recognition, healing, reconciliation, and possibly forgiveness.

In much the same way as Virginia Woolf is alleged to have said that 'nothing has really happened until it has been written down', there are those who maintain that 'nobody is really forgotten if we say their names'. In both ideas, there is the notion that something of significance must be remembered and recorded if it is to have its proper meaning and value. Something that otherwise might seem transient or ephemeral can be given weight, substance, and meaning by being remembered and documented.

About six million Jews died in the Holocaust, as well as millions of other victims. *Holocaust* is a Greek word meaning 'sacrifice by fire'. If, after the flames, all that remains of the particular essence of a person is a memory – their laughter, their way of smiling or speaking, their unique quirkiness – it has to be recorded and passed on. A certain permanence can thus be given to those people who can otherwise only be remembered in fragments of letters, photographs, journals. Giving back their name to a victim of the Holocaust returns to them some of their identity – an identity that was incrementally, gratuitously, and aggressively removed from them by the Nazis as part of a deliberate process of humiliation and dehumanisation.

In the Jewish tradition, when a righteous person dies, it is customary to add 'May the memory of the righteous person be a blessing' after mentioning the deceased person's name. When referring to an indisputably evil person, such as Adolf Hitler, it is customary to say 'May their name be erased', or even, 'May their name and memory be erased' after mentioning the name.

Jewish tradition places great importance on a person being remembered after death. A person is remembered by their children and by later generations, and also by their actions, the impact that they have on others. Within Jewish tradition there are some sources that say there are three deaths. The first is when the body ceases to function; the second is when the body is consigned to the grave; the third is that moment, some time in the future, when their name is spoken for the last time.

Even until the end of the twentieth century, French politicians insisted that France was not to blame for its country's actions under Nazi occupation during the Second World War. The official political point of view in France after the war was that Vichy had been an illegitimate regime that did not represent the country's values. However, Vichy France had not only collaborated with the Nazis and carried out what was demanded of it by them, but had also enacted its own measures against the Jews.

After the war, the places where the Jews in France had been interned were destroyed, abandoned, or returned to their original function. At Camp de Gurs, trees and other vegetation grew over the swampy ground, and the barracks (never very robust) collapsed. On 29 April 1979, forty years after the building of the camp for the Republican refugees from Franco's Spain, a group of former internees met there to form the *Amicale du Camp de Gurs* (Friends of Camp de Gurs).

Since then, the *Amicale* has fought hard for the site and the few remains of the camp to be a central point of remembrance in France and initiated the construction of a national memorial there in 1995. It has become:

> *...a place of journey and silent reflection, in the middle of huge trees, set against the backdrop of the Pyrénées. The beauty of nature and the sadness of the deportations are inextricably mixed.*

Nowadays, from the informative display at the small car park, the visitor is guided round the site by memory information boards. The path through the camp is on a raised boardwalk across the often muddy terrain – a luxury not afforded to the earlier inmates – and passes through the reconstruction of a barrack (one of the original 382 that once stood in this enormous town of flimsy wood buildings). Like the original cabins, this reconstruction was made from thin slabs of wood covered with tarred cardboard.

The central road running straight through the camp remains, as does the cemetery – which since 1963 has been carefully tended each year by the citizens of Baden, from where so many Jews were expelled and sent to Gurs. The only other original remains of the camp include thirty-five concrete blocks that once supported the enormous cisterns for water, which was barely drinkable, and at the edge of the forest, a few concrete slabs are still visible in the soil. These slabs are the same dimensions as a barrack, 24m by 6m, and were once the bases for the kitchen barracks. At the original entrance into the camp, the metal uprights for the barrier across the road are also visible. Otherwise, the forest has covered everything, and the visitor is encouraged to imagine how people might once have experienced the camp.

> *A dark forest, vaguely hostile, marshy ground, the sound of the wind, the song of the birds. And yet, you must imagine a real town of misery here. A closed universe, away from everyone. A huge camp, without trees or grass, without shade in the summer, with nothing to protect against gusts of wind or rain in the winter. You must imagine the loneliness, the cold, the hunger and the vermin. You must imagine the permanent anguish; the anguish of never hearing news from your family, the anguish of suffering, the anguish of death, the anguish of deportation. Nature has covered everything again. Yet every square metre of this place has known pain.*
>
> *Can we forget?*

Before leaving Camp de Gurs, the visitor is reminded:

> *You are leaving a place symbolic of xenophobia, suffering and cruelty. This place could only exist through the abandonment of conscience and irresponsibility, in the name of principles that have little regard for human dignity.*

> *Over four and a half years, from April 1939 until October 1943, a merciless mechanism was able to work, beyond any humanitarian feeling. Sometimes justified by reasons of national security, sometimes for exceptional reasons, sometimes by the desire for repression, sometimes by institutional anti-Semitism, this mechanism contributed to crushing thousands of men, women, and children.*
>
> *Don't you have to think about this?*
>
> *Can we be certain that this will not happen again?*

Genocide – the deliberate and systematic extermination of a national, racial, political, or cultural group – is an act that is out of the ordinary and disturbs the natural order of things. It affects places as well as people, so that locations are no longer used for their original purpose but turned into sites that facilitate genocide. The Nazis and their collaborators misappropriated sports halls, old people's homes, housing estates, market halls, forests, and fields and turned them into sites of murder.

In 1993, the *Amicale* was successful in having one of three national memorials installed at Camp de Gurs (the others are at *Vel d'Hiv* in Paris, and at Izieu). It was designed by the Jewish artist Dani Karavan and has three elements: a large concrete slab supporting the framework of a truncated barrack; a large concrete slab surrounded by barbed wire; between the two, a railway line symbolising the deportation from the Camp de Gurs to the extermination camps such as Auschwitz. The entire path is 230m long and was inaugurated in October 1994.

The railway line is symbolic – there was never any railway at Camp de Gurs. The visitor is encouraged to enter the memorial and 'walk the length of the railway in silence, in tribute to the men, women, and children who here knew suffering, mourning, and misfortune'. In total, almost 65,000 people passed through Gurs.

The railway track that took Henny and Hermann and other deportees to Drancy after they left Camp de Gurs passed through the railway station at Oloron-Sainte-Marie, 15km away. Many years later, on 24 April 2009, a memorial plaque to remember the arrival of the Spanish Republicans in 1939 and the departure of the Jewish deportees in 1942 was installed on the exterior wall of the station, facing the town, with the heading: 'Let us remember'.

From Camp de Gurs, most of the deportees, like Henny and Hermann, were taken to the internment camp at Drancy in the north-eastern suburbs of Paris and from there to Auschwitz. On 4 September 1942, after leaving the camp at Drancy, Convoy 28 of freight wagons, packed full of Jewish deportees (including Henny and Hermann), left from the nearby railway station at Le Bourget to travel to the death camp at Auschwitz. On 3 July 2016, almost seventy-four years later, a commemorative plaque was installed on the station forecourt at Le Bourget:

> *In 1942, and until June 1943, almost 40,000 Jews, men women and children, coming from the camp at Drancy, were deported from this station to the extermination camp at Auschwitz. From July 1943 until the liberation of France, the deportation trains left from the station at Bobigny. Almost all the deportees were assassinated. Fewer than 3% survived. Never forget.*

About 3km away from the railway station, at what was once the Camp de Drancy, the site has changed considerably but remains recognisable as the former detention and internment centre. Immediately after the war, the Cité de la Muette was renovated and returned to its use as a housing project but throughout the following years, while France refused to accept its own history of collaboration with the Nazis, the very existence of the Cité de la Muette remained a source of awkward embarrassment. It was clear evidence of the crimes committed against the Jews by the Nazis with the complicity of the French authorities.

On 29 September 1946, the local Jewish Consistory organised a *Hazkarah* (Memory) ceremony, held on the site of Drancy camp. This took place between Rosh Hashana and Yom Kippur, the Jewish New Year holidays, and was the first commemoration ceremony to be held in the former Drancy camp. Otherwise, there was little interest in Drancy during the 1950s and early 1960s, although some inhabitants of the nearby housing development as well as some officials in the local authorities were rather ill at ease about the lack of recognition of the area's recent history.

A few associations for the victims and some religious groups held discrete ceremonies at the site during this time and organised the installation of commemorative plaques. But it was only in the 1970s that an official memorial was established. The demolition of the tower blocks in the housing complex started in 1974 and was completed in 1976. Maurice Nilès, the communist mayor of Drancy from 1959, decided in 1963 to launch a project to build a monument, which was finally inaugurated on Sunday 9 May 1976 in the presence of a large crowd.

The Memorial to the Deportation at Drancy was created by the Polish-born Jewish sculptor Shelomo Selinger, to commemorate those Jews who passed through Drancy during the Second World War. Selinger had himself survived nine German death camps and two death marches and then been discovered alive (aged 17) on a pile of dead bodies when Theresienstadt was liberated by the Russian army in 1945. His sculpture at Drancy is called *The Gates of Hell*.

The sculpture is in rose-coloured granite and took two years of carving by hand. It consists of three blocks 3m high that form the Hebrew letter *shin*. This letter has multiple meanings and can represent flame and transformation, divine revelation, or stand in for the name of God. It is usually engraved on the *Mezouzah* fixed next to the door of Jewish people's homes. In the centre of the piece, the block of ten tortured figures represents the ten men needed as a quorum for prayer. The wave-like pattern at the foot of the sculpture evokes the fire in which so many Jews died. The two lateral blocks symbolise the portals of death. Two stairs, each with seven steps, symbolise the seven degrees of suffering that a soul had to undergo before passing through the gates of death, and the seven degrees of the elevation of the soul. On one side, the man's beard forms the letter *lamed* and the woman's hair a *vav*. These Hebrew letters have a numerical value of thirty-six and so recall the thirty-six righteous individuals who, according to Jewish tradition, are necessary for the continued existence of the world.

It had taken over thirty years for a significant memorial to the events at Drancy to be installed. During the 1970s, much of the impetus and work for remembering – despite the French politicians' official position – came from the publication in 1978 of Serge Klarsfeld's *Memorial to the Deportation of the Jews from France 1942 – 1944*. Serge Klarsfeld was born into a Jewish family in Bucharest and survived the Holocaust as a child in France, but his father was murdered in Auschwitz. His massive book not only made plain the central role that Drancy played in the deportation of the Jews, it also became one of the major pillars of memory of the Jewish victims who were deported from France. It contains lists of the names of about 76,000 men, women and children, in alphabetical order and according to each of the eighty convoys. Each person is given their family name, first name, date of birth, place of birth and nationality, and a detailed history of each convoy is given.

It is an immense work and Serge Klarsfeld is rightly honoured for the pitiless, methodical and meticulous rigour with which he brought to light the enormity of the suffering endured by so many people. The dry enumeration of statistics, the lists of massacred lives, the naming of those slaughtered give – in their very precision and objectivity – a dignity to and a memory of those named. They are brought out of anonymity and made into more than a number, more than a statistic.

In Germany, the laying of *Stolpersteine* (stumbling stones) has brought the identity of individuals and communities back into those places where they were once known as members of thriving and vibrant Jewish communities. Gunther Demnig is the artist behind the idea of *Stolpersteine*. He cites the *Talmud* (the central text of Rabbinic law) as saying that 'a person is only forgotten when his or her name is forgotten'. He remembers the victims of National Socialism by installing commemorative brass plaques in the pavement in front of their last address of choice. The *Stolpersteine* in front of buildings bring back to memory the people who once lived there. Almost every stone begins with 'Here lived…' – one stone, one name, one person.

Gunther Demnig was born soon after the war ended, in 1947, in Berlin. Since 1985, he has worked from his studio in Cologne. His small, cobble-stone-sized brass memorials for the victims of National Socialism are set into the pavement in front of where the victims last lived or worked. Each one is a 10cm concrete cube with a brass plate inscribed with the name and life dates of victims of Nazi extermination or persecution. The first one was laid in Cologne in December 1992.

They are not prominent memorials and could easily be discovered just by chance. They do not require you to 'stumble', as the name might suggest, as they are set flush into the surrounding area, but they do require you to bend down to read the engraving carefully. As Demnig himself sees it, 'You do not stumble and fall. You stumble with your head and your heart.'

The *Stolpersteine* invite the passer-by to stop and look, to reflect, and consider their meaning. In Hermann's birthplace of the market town of Aurich, there are a total of 409 *Stolpersteine* in front of seventy-eight houses, and this alone brings some sense of the overwhelming scale of the Holocaust. In some streets, most houses have *Stolpersteine* set in front of them – in Wallstraße alone, where Hermann was born and brought up, they are laid in front of nineteen houses.

In Aurich – as probably happens in other places where *Stolpersteine* have been laid – each time the artist is invited to lay a number of *Stolpersteine*, the event is preceded by months of huge communal activity. A designated group of people representing those especially committed to the memory of the previous Jewish community, local historians and archivists, researchers, the local council, churches of different denominations, and youth groups, schools, and colleges meet to organise the work involved and plan the final event.

Young people at the schools and colleges work on discovering more about the people whose lives are being remembered and write biographies for each person – with the help of teachers and those with specialist knowledge and access to archives, etc. Sponsors are found to take responsibility for the cost of installing each *Stolperstein* (which is currently about 120 euros). Young people at the technical colleges are chosen to prepare the site for the actual installation and to have the correct materials and tools ready for the artist's visit. When Gunther Demnig is sure that the biographies are complete and the event can go ahead, artists from his studio manufacture each *Stolperstein* by hand.

On 21 October 2016, *Stolpersteine* were laid outside Wallstraße 46 in Aurich for Berta, Sara, and Oskar Hartog. They all follow the same wording, and the stone in memory of Berta reads:

> *Here lived*
> *Riwka Berta Hartog*
> *born 1872*
> *taken against her will*
> *1940 Emden*
> *deported 1941*
> *Łódź/Litzmannstadt*
> *1942 Chelmno/Kulmhof*
> *murdered 12.5.1942*

As local people gathered around outside the house, students from the college read out the biographies they had researched about the family, students from the vocational school for construction and technology mixed the sand and cement required for the installation, and the artist inserted the three blocks he had made – one for each member of the family who had been forced from that home by the Nazis. When completed, three white roses were laid across the brass memorials.

Where it is possible, surviving relatives are contacted about the laying of the *Stolpersteine* and invited to attend their installation. Most of the invitees travel from overseas to do so and are offered generous hospitality by the people of Aurich.

Over the months, the brass on all the *Stolpersteine* tarnishes and so twice a year, in memory of the November 1938 pogrom and in the spring, volunteers from all age groups in the town get down on their hands and knees on the pavement and clean each one – afterwards laying a white rose across it.

The *Stolperstein* symbolically brings back the victim of the Nazi genocide to their neighbourhood, to the place where they rightly belonged, and from where they had been unwillingly wrenched.

Stolpersteine are not laid in every town or place where Jewish people once lived, but they are laid in Henny's birthplace of Frankfurt. She is not remembered in this way at her old address since she had moved away from the city before National Socialism gained power. Her family had rented an apartment at number 16 Gaußstraße, and the house next door at number 14 was owned by a Jew.

During the 1920s, the apartments in this house had been large, with four or six rooms each, and were usually let to upper-middle class bourgeois Jewish families. Henny would no doubt have known Erna and Leopold Mannheimer, who moved into a large six-roomed flat on the first floor of number 14 after their marriage in 1912. Their children, Gerda and Erich, grew up in the house and were still living there when Henny moved away from Frankfurt on her marriage to Hermann. In 1920, Erna's brother-in-law bought the house and Erna and her husband took over the management of the property.

Shortly after the Nazis seized power in 1933, Erna's husband died of a heart attack. From 1938, when the Nazis required all Jews to live together in a designated 'Jew House', local Jews were crammed into the house at Gaußstraße 14. Erna had to hand over the property management to an administrator appointed by the tax authorities, and she was no longer allowed to accept rent or other money.

From 1941, Erna and her son were forced to share their house and apartment with numerous other Jewish people who were sent to live in their home. For example, Judge Karl Maas had to move under duress (and with no warning) from his 4½-room apartment at 41 Gaußstraße to 1½ rooms at number 14. He was later moved to yet another address.

Erna May was already living at 14 Gaußstraße when her father joined her from Czechoslovakia in 1936, as he had been forced out of his home and business there. At the same time, the sister of Erna's husband Jakob joined them in the apartment.

Jakob already needed to use one room in the house to store textiles as he tried to continue his business.

Thus, families who were strangers to one another had to live together in a confined space. When one Jewish resident was deported, another was brought to take their place. *Stolpersteine* are laid in front of 14 Gaußstraße for the several people who were finally forced from this address to their deaths – Erna Mannheimer and her son Erich, Erna and Jakob May and Erna's father Nathan Gottlieb, as well as Hugo Moses, Helene, Justin and Peter Neuhaus, and Salomon Wald.

On 20 March 1946, a commemorative plaque for the destroyed synagogue at the Börneplatz in Frankfurt was ceremoniously unveiled by the US military government. The plaque was installed on the rear wall of an office building of the city works department. The inscription is in German and English and reads: 'Here stood the Börneplatz synagogue which was destroyed by Nazi criminals on the 9th day of November 1938'.

This whole area, where a synagogue and cemetery had once stood, has been a memorial site since 1990. During the 1980s, excavation work prior to anticipated city centre development discovered the foundations of houses and *mikvehs* from the earlier Jewish ghetto, the *Judengasse*. There was fierce public protest against the destruction of the remains of the Jewish community buildings and the building site was occupied by demonstrators. The planners were forced to compromise with a partial reclamation of some of the Jewish properties, which became the heart of a new museum built above them – the *Museum Judengasse*, which opened in 1992.

Outside the museum, the outline of the synagogue walls is marked on the ground with slim steel rails, and nearby is a large cube made of the stone remains of the former ghetto. It is set in the middle of a grove of plane trees.

The ancient Jewish cemetery, which is immediately adjacent, is surrounded by a new wall, which is a memorial to members of the Frankfurt Jewish community who were victims of the Holocaust. It was inaugurated in 1996 and contains a frieze of name blocks, one for each individual. Each block gives one name, date of birth, and date and place of death, if known. There have since been additions and in 2023 there were 11,908 blocks on the wall.

Each block is a cube that stands proud of the wall, allowing visitors and mourners space to place on top a pebble or small stone in remembrance of the named person – as is the Jewish custom. When my husband and I were last there, we had a pocketful of pebbles to have sufficient to place on the name blocks for Henny, her father Adolf, his sister Rosalie, and Henny's uncle and aunt, Louis and Hedwig Bodenheimer. We spoke their names. There are so many Scheuers, so many Bodenheimers, so many inter-related names of people who might once have become living relatives.

Before the 'Wall of Names' was publicly inaugurated, new metal gates had been placed at the entrance to the ancient cemetery. They are modern in design and inscribed in Hebrew letters on the two wings are the words *Beth haChaim* (House of Life).

Inside the museum next door, the names of those inscribed on the blocks on the memorial wall can be researched on a database that is publicly available. It gives any further biographical information that might be known.

When Adolf Scheuer was deported from Frankfurt, he (and anyone else in the city who suffered the same fate) was required to go – with the small amount of belongings allowed – to the wholesale market hall as an assembly point. This large hall was built little more than ten years prior to Adolf Scheuer's deportation, and was a flagship building of the newly prosperous, modernist, technically sophisticated municipal authority that was the City of Frankfurt, under its popular and successful mayor, Ludwig Landmann – who was Jewish (and so removed from his position in 1933 by the new Nazi government).

The wholesale market had large modern facilities for the transportation of goods – an enormous hall, extensive cold cellars, and ramps and railways to make the movement of goods away from the city swift and easy. It became perfect for the transportation of human freight 'to the east' by the Nazis. A building that had been inaugurated by a Jewish mayor and 500 invited guests as a triumph of successful trade and modernism very soon became a vehicle for the transportation of thousands of Jews to their deaths. In 2015, this place was rededicated to the memory of those Jews who had passed through it to the trains that took them to the death camps.

By then, the European Central Bank (ECB) owned the site and became part of the decision – with the city of Frankfurt and the Frankfurt Jewish community – to construct a memorial that would engage anyone passing by on the path from the railway into town, or merely walking along the nearby busy street. It was to be a space where people could not be indifferent to the fate of those who had walked that way before them. The ramps and the paths, the nearby railway track, and the walls and buildings along the way had to bear witness to people whose experience should never be forgotten, and whose names should be known.

The memorial uses statements and quotations and thus emphasises the power of the written word, which is valued in Jewish tradition. The recollections of survivors, descriptions written down by non-Jewish observers, and extracts from letters written by deportees before they were forced to leave are carved on to the walls around you, imprinted on the paths under your feet as you wander around the site, and engraved on the large glass doors leading you into the cellar. The somewhat unobtrusive nature of the design emphasises the incidental way that deportees were gathered into the cellars under the market hall – as the usual trading casually continued overhead – and were then eventually ushered into trains to take them away. Once they had been taken away, crates of fruit and vegetables could again be stored in the cellars.

This memorial in Frankfurt is a powerful reminder of what could and did happen to ordinary people. It seeks to involve the onlooker – giving information, posing tacit questions, implying that some extra thought or a different course of action or activism is required by the viewer – by all of us.

The continuous work that has been undertaken in Jever over many years to restore memory, engage empathy and action, and ensure a commitment for the future is still an ongoing memorial to the Jewish community that once lived there – the community that Henny and Hermann had so much enjoyed being a part of.

On 24 April 1984, almost forty years after the end of the Second World War, there was an extraordinary meeting in the teachers' room at the Mariengymnasium, the secondary school in the centre of Jever. Hartmut Peters, one of the teachers at the school, welcomed a group of Jews to Jever. They were the survivors and relatives of Jewish families from Jever and had grown up in (and had managed to flee) the city, in spite of the Nazis. Their presence in Jever in 1984 was both the end result of a student-led research project by pupils at the Mariengymnasium into the earlier Jewish community in their home town, and the beginning of a new era of growing understanding, continuing visits, and constant conversations between those who stand as representatives of that former Jewish community and those who have to reconcile themselves with their city's past and work with honesty to create an inclusive future for everyone.

In 1978, some students at the Mariengymnasium had begun to ask searching questions about Jever's history during the Second World War – questions not generally welcomed by their families, relatives or neighbours. But Hartmut Peters supported and encouraged their research and, together with them and later students, eventually put together their research results into a book – *Verbannte Bürger. Die Juden aus Jever – Dokumente und Darstellungen zur Geschichte der Juden Jevers 1698 – 1984,* (*Banished Citizens. The Jews from Jever – documents and an account of the history of the Jews of Jever 1698 – 1984*).

In 1982, the research materials were made into an exhibition that was open to the public in Jever and also taken to other places in the surrounding area. The activities of the students during these research years brought consternation and upheaval to the town as people were brought face to face with events, attitudes and actions of the Nazi era that many of them had hoped would continue to remain in the dark silence of the post-war years. Some people in Jever supported the students and what they were working to do, but there was also considerable resistance and hostility throughout the city.

Meanwhile, the students were curious about the people whose lives they had discovered and who now lived all over the world, far away from Jever. They wanted to meet them, talk to them in person, and invite them back to Jever for a visit, hosted by them, the city, and some religious communities. Not all the Jewish people they invited wanted to visit their former home city, but some did – and were particularly swayed to do so by the fact that it was the young people of a new generation who wanted to meet them and who were offering the invitation. The landmark visit took place in April 1984.

The first person who arrived in Jever for the occasion was Professor Rolf Sternberg, who as a boy had lived on the opposite side of Schlosserstraße from

Henny and Hermann, and after emigration via Argentina was then living in New York. His attitude – that people should not meet each other with hatred but as human beings, because hatred can destroy oneself – immediately impressed the students and set the open, positive and conciliatory tone for the rest of the week. It was an important week for everyone involved and laid the ground for future contact between former members of the Jewish community in Jever and present-day residents. The young people of Jever had committed themselves and their city to continue to deal with the past, to reach out to the former Jewish community, and to take any possible action to make amends.

Hartmut Peters and his students had an impressive ally during their work. This was the pastor of the Lutheran church in Jever – Volker Landig. He had arrived in the city in 1976, a couple of years before the first students started their research. He knew, even before his arrival, of the once flourishing Jewish community that had existed in Jever forty years previously and was astonished to find nothing to show of its existence there. He discovered that the large Jewish cemetery was wildly overgrown and set to work with young members of his congregation to clear and clean it. Two years later – against some local opposition – Volker Landig worked with the mayor to have a commemorative brass plaque, inscribed in German and Hebrew, installed on the wall of the building that now stood on the site of the demolished synagogue. A ceremony for its unveiling took place on 9 November 1978, exactly forty years after the synagogue was deliberately destroyed by fire. The plaque states that it is there 'as a reminder and a warning'.

> *If my head were a well, my eyes would be sources of tears.*
> *I would weep day and night for the slain of my people (Jeremiah 8:23)*

Volker Landig and Hartmut Peters began to work together in 1983, and they were both involved with the visit of the former Jewish residents the following year. Over the ensuing years, they have worked to promote the importance of the Jewish tradition in the area, to help the local population to understand the history of the Jews who once lived there, to inform and involve young people so that they know and share an interest and empathy with those former residents, and to welcome back survivors and relatives from that earlier Jewish community. On International Holocaust Memorial Day, 27 January, in 2017, they were awarded the Obermayer German Jewish History Award for their work.

The understanding behind the presentation of the award is that, 'combating hate starts with a shared understanding of the past'. The award is given annually:

> *...to honour people and organisations in Germany that have worked creatively and selflessly to raise awareness of Jewish history and*

culture in their communities, and to fight the rise of hate, prejudice and anti-Semitism.

By the time Volker Landig and Hartmut Peters were given the award, they had also created the 'GröschlerHaus' on the site of the synagogue in Jever. In 1954, the site had been granted to a plumber who had a business and residential buildings constructed there. They still remain and in 2014 the working party called 'Jews in Jever' (that would soon become the GröschlerHaus) was able to rent the vacant ground floor of the property for its educational work.

Only when they moved into the building did Volker Landig, Hartmut Peters and their co-workers discover remnants of the original wall and window in the area where Hermann Hartog's schoolroom had once been, a 'cellar' that proved to be the old *mikveh* (a bath for ritual purification), fragments of slate slabs from the roof, cornices of the façade, and charred beams from the 1938 destruction. Renovation of the building took place, with the floorplan of the synagogue indicated on the floor, the original wall and one window of the schoolroom preserved, the *mikveh* viewed through a glass panel, and fragments of masonry conserved. The GröschlerHaus – named after the brothers Hermann and Julius Gröschler – is now a centre for education, an event venue, and a meeting place for people rediscovering the Jewish heritage of Jever and the surrounding area. It also hosts a website and an archive of articles, books, documents, photographs, etc.

A short walk from the old synagogue site is a memorial installed in 1996. It stands in the centre of the town, near other memorials for citizens of Jever, and against the wall of the city's old prison yard – the same prison where all the Jews of the Jewish community were held on the night the synagogue burned in 1938, before the men were later taken to the concentration camp at Sachsenhausen. The memorial shows three piles of books, each book dedicated to a life of one of the murdered Jews of Jever. There are sixty-four books, plus an unnamed one that stands for all the unknown names of Jews who died, each with their year of birth, year of death or deportation, and place of death or deportation. The names of Henny Hartog and Hermann Hartog are inscribed on the spines of two of the books.

The walk around Jever can actually take quite a long time, since you can follow the route researched and described by the working group and volunteers of GröschlerHaus. It is written as a pocket-sized leaflet, with short descriptions of each Jewish person's life and work against their address, photographs of the people, and explanations of events. This community is not nameless. It has been brought vibrantly to life as a result of years of careful research, a massive commitment to the responsibility to answer for the past, and the necessity for us all to move forward with humility and respect for the wellbeing of people of all nationalities, philosophies and identities.

Henny and Hermann's names are also inscribed on a memorial at the site of the destroyed synagogue in Wilhelmshaven, and in 2024 plans were being made for the future laying of *Stolpersteine* to commemorate members of the former Jewish community in the city, including the Hartog family.

When a person loses their memory, they are no longer the same person. A nation that forgets is in danger of losing its identity. The past can never be fully remembered but it should not be fully forgotten. The accounts of survivors, the testimonies of those who witnessed events, and the documents from those who did not survive may be unfinished or fragmentary, but together they build a monument to the memory of people caught up in one of the worst catastrophes that the world had hitherto known.

Creating an active collective memory requires younger people to be part of the memory-making. The need for relevant information and ways of transmitting it to new generations, the participation of young people in establishing a bank of memory against a loss of identity, and their involvement in civic life remain crucial if a nation does not lose its memory and run the risk of repeating horrors from the past.

In both Aurich and Jever, young students are a large part of the memorial events in their towns, and also of the continuing work of those who wish to keep alive a history of their communities that includes the Jews who were once driven from them. Young people who keep alive these memories and who are active in their communities will, hopefully, be better equipped and able to act against any rise in right-wing radicalism and protect their country's democracy.

It took a long time for many communities in France to accept any level of complicity in the Holocaust, or *Shoah* – partly because of the position taken by their political leaders. The word *Shoah* is the Hebrew word for 'catastrophe'. The *Mémorial de la Shoah* is the Holocaust Museum in Paris. It is in the local district of the Marais, which had been home to a Jewish community for nearly nine centuries and still had a large Jewish population at the beginning of the Second World War. Not everyone living in the Marais has accepted their leaders' position on collaborative responsibility over the years. After a few minutes' walk into the heart of the old Jewish community, we come across a large stone memorial above an imposing door to a large residence. The engraving reads:

> *Here lived Baruch and Dora Matykanski, their daughter Esther (9 years), deported in 1942 by the Nazis with the active complicity of the Vichy government and exterminated at Auschwitz Camp because they were born Jews. In their memory.*

The foundations of the present-day *Mémorial de la Shoah* in Paris were created during the Second World War when, as early as April 1943, a Jewish Russian-born industrialist living in Grenoble, Isaac Schneersohn, set up an organisation to collect evidence of anti-Jewish persecution in order to bear witness and also to demand justice after the war. He and the forty activists he invited to share with him this risky venture set up the *Centre de Documentation Juive Contemporaine* (CDJC), (the Contemporary Jewish Documentation Centre), and began collecting documents.

In September 1943, the Germans invaded the Grenoble area so Schneersohn joined the local French Resistance. When the fighting to liberate France began, he went to Paris to prevent the records of the Vichy government and the German occupiers from being destroyed or sent elsewhere. He and his co-worker Léon Poliakov (a Russian Jew living in France) managed to acquire papers from the Commissariat-General for Jewish Affairs (CGQJ), the German embassy in Paris, the German general staff, the Vichy government's representatives and (crucially) the Gestapo anti-Jewish departments. Immediately after the war, the CDJC started to process the documents and was asked by the new French government to assist with evidence for the Nuremberg trials.

In 1950, Schneersohn created a memorial tomb in Paris for the Holocaust victims – the *Mémorial du martyr juif inconnu* (Memorial of the Unknown Jewish Martyr). In the forecourt to the building surrounding the tomb is a large bronze cylinder listing the names of the death camps and the Warsaw ghetto. On the wall nearby are bas reliefs that symbolise the camps and the persecution of the Jews. The memorial was inaugurated in October 1956, and the following year the chief rabbi of France deposited ashes from the extermination camps and the Warsaw ghetto, mixed with soil from Israel, in the crypt. The memorial crypt also houses the 'Jewish Files', which were created by the Vichy government to identify Jewish citizens, and which were later used to locate Jews for deportation. The files of both Henny Hartog and Hermann Hartog are amongst them.

France is a country that, over decades, has had to come to terms with its fascist past during the war years. Vichy was a police state that affected every single life. Yet, until the mid-1990s, this was erased from the collective memory in an amnesia that French historian Henri Rousso calls the 'Vichy Syndrome'. It was not until a speech on 16 July 1995 that Jacques Chirac broke the taboo of silence, recognising the responsibility of the French state, and particularly the French police, admitting that 'the French government had given support to the criminal madness of the occupiers'.

When the Memorial of the Unknown Jewish Martyr was built, the CDJC moved into the same premises and the memorial was able to expand. The later extension, which then created the *Mémorial de la Shoah*, was completed in 2004. It currently offers spacious reading rooms, a permanent exhibition on the history of the Holocaust, a multi-media learning centre, and an auditorium. Outside the building is the 'Wall of Names', on which are inscribed the names of all the Jews who were deported from France. The names of Henny and Hermann are among the 76,000 recorded there.

The completed memorial was opened by President Jacques Chirac on 27 January 2005 – International Holocaust Memorial Day and the 60th anniversary of the liberation of Auschwitz concentration camp.

Nowadays, the Mémorial includes a bookshop, changing exhibitions, an extensive programme for outreach to everyone, the documentation centre, and a programme committed to education about the Holocaust. Every time we are there, the place is teeming with students of all ages, engaging seriously with historical events, ideas concerning humanity, and questions of political engagement. Since most of Henny and Hermann's letters were written while they were in France, and as we are both impressed and reassured by the easy access to research there, and the emphasis on an education programme at the Mémorial, this will be the future home for Henny and Hermann's original letters so that they can be read and understood by a much wider group of people.

Genocide is facilitated by ordinary people. Ordinary people turn a blind eye, believe propaganda, join murderous regimes. And those who are persecuted, oppressed, and murdered in genocide aren't persecuted because of crimes they have committed, they are persecuted simply because they are ordinary people who belong to a particular group.

And ordinary people are the ones who make brave decisions to rescue, to hide, or to stand up. But ordinary people also make decisions to ignore what is going on around them, to be bystanders, to allow the genocide to continue. How can ordinary people, such as ourselves, play a bigger part than we might imagine in challenging prejudice today?

The wrongs that were committed in the past cannot be undone. Those sent to the gas chambers cannot be returned to life. We cannot adequately fix or compensate those who survived the horrors of Nazi genocide. But if we research and document what happened, if we record what we know for posterity, if we act on what we know in a way that will carry on the work of active and critical remembering, and maybe reduce the possibility of another Holocaust; if we remember and say the names of those murdered, then we can perhaps offer a shadow of the justice that they should have experienced for themselves.

Henny Hartog (née Scheuer) was born on 21 July 1897
in Frankfurt am Main.

Hermann Hartog was born on 22 February 1887 in Aurich.

Henny and Hermann were murdered in
September 1942 in Auschwitz.

May their memory be a blessing.

Acknowledgements

Writing this book has been a huge journey of discovery – of places, events and (most importantly) people. As the title of the book indicates, my husband and I have followed in the footsteps of his grandparents to discover their lives, and it is no cliché to suggest that the book could not have been written without the very generous support of the many people whom we have met on our journey.

Although I have used the original letters exchanged between Henny, Hermann and their daughters as a guide for the details of the last few years of their lives, I have – of course – needed much more objective historical documentation as a solid framework for the entire period. I am extremely grateful to the archivists in many museums for their patient and painstaking trouble in digging out any records of relevance. In London, the Wiener Library has been a wonderful place to work, with so many resources and so many extremely knowledgeable and sympathetic librarians to share their wisdom. What a joyous surprise it was to come across 11-year-old Inge's message to her mother and grandfather from the *Kindertransport* in 1938 while sifting through papers in the library one gloomy day in London about eighty years later!

In the Jewish Museums of Frankfurt, I have been able to access biographical details of some of Henny's relatives and learn of their fates through the database that has been developed there. The museums have also been a great source of very useful information about the former Jewish communities in Frankfurt and about Jewish culture in general. Their information made walking the walk through a previous Jewish neighbourhood in the town much more relatable – the ghosts of the past came to life.

I would like to thank Astrid Parisius and her colleagues for their great help on our visit to the archives in Aurich. Astrid had selected all the relevant material prior to our visit and continued to find extra materials throughout the day while we were there. I will forever be grateful to her for finding a stunning photo of Oskar Hartog (how can anyone have such piercing eyes?), and I only wish that she and I could have had longer to continue our conversations together.

When I first arrived at the archives at Oldenburg, I had quite a narrow but definite brief: I wanted to know in particular about Hermann Hartog's training as a teacher and a cantor, and any information about his activities in the First World War would be a welcome bonus. Thus far, I had drawn a blank on all of my investigations on this topic and I was no more successful on this visit to Oldenburg. But it was not without a great deal of thoughtful and willing research by the archivists. It is not their fault that the documents just do not exist and I am grateful to them for listening to us and for trying their very best to source the information I would dearly liked to have found. So many documents have been lost through war, fire and devastation.

I have met Stephan Horschitz twice in Neustadtgödens and on both occasions it has rained in biblical proportions. Stephan's curatorial responsibilities include the former synagogue (which was not burnt down in 1938) in this small town and he has overseen the transformation of the building into a place that reflects its Jewish heritage and informs visitors of its history. For me, Neustadtgödens will always be the place where Hermann led the choir from Jever in a rousing celebration of their faith at the last service ever held at the synagogue before the Nazis closed it for good. I am grateful to Stephan not only for his work but also for his serious and informative conversations as we sat on the stone benches in the former synagogue, with our dripping umbrellas at the entrance door, and for his commitment to the memory of the earlier Jewish community there. The display in the nearby museum, also managed by Stephan, brings to life much of that community's relevance.

It can be a strange experience, discovering quite personal documents in the reading room of an archive, and – apart from my Wiener Library experience with the short message from Inge – I have probably felt this most in the archives of Brussels and, later, at Pau. In Brussels, I am grateful to the archivists there for discovering several documents relating to both Henny and Hermann when they first arrived after fleeing Nazi Germany. In the same handwriting as we see in their letters, they answer questions on official questionnaires with the same dignity and honesty as we have come to expect. They hardly know through which entry point they arrived in Belgium. They have little or no money. They had no choice except to leave and be with each other. These banal official forms carry so much understated emotion. The officials we met at the archive in Brussels (like those in all the archives we visited) regretted the paucity of their findings, the lack of well-documented materials, the loss of materials through bombing or deliberate destruction – but those documents that we found throughout our journey generally painted a coherent and consistent picture to help us to view Henny and Hermann across the years.

The archivists working at Pau have welcomed us several times and have been consistently extremely generous with their time and efficient with finding documents. Again, we have found significantly personal documents in official records and have been glad of the sensitivity of the people working in the archives to allow us to process these materials. Henny did not write in her letters to her daughters, for example, about applying for an identity card – but here we are given all the correspondence and the actual document. The required photo can't hide the grey hairs and the effect of years of difficult living conditions, and the weight of sorrow and exile. And when we turn a page in a file, we hold in our hands the letter that Charles Castagné wrote to the commandant at Camp de Gurs after Henny and Hermann had left Arette. Many thanks to the archivists at Pau for all their help and care.

The *Musée de la Déportation et de la Résistance* in the town of Tarbes (about 100km east of Arette) is housed in an ornately decorated old building that was once a school. The exhibition was first put together in 1989 by a collection of veteran, resistant and deportees' associations and was then used as an itinerant display to remind and educate people, especially schoolchildren, about their local history during the Second World War. Many of the exhibits are documents, newspaper cuttings, photographs and artefacts that give a very personal account of those times. Seeing the wooden clogs and the radio set, in particular, brought to life for us the physical conditions that had been part of Henny and Hermann's life in France, and I am grateful to the museum staff for their readiness to explain and talk about wartime conditions in the area from a local and personal perspective. It was a very useful introduction to the Pyrénées as we first travelled there and dropped in on the museum almost by chance.

At the other end of the research timeline, we just managed to fit in a quick dash to the archives in Bayonne on our last afternoon in Arette because we had been told it was the only place to find a certain document. Torrential rain made the journey unexpectedly exciting but in such weather an archive is as good a place to spend the time as any other. The archivist was welcoming and generous with her time as she spent a great deal of the next hour searching and searching, phoning colleagues for advice and suggestions, and trying all sorts of different approaches before she was forced to apologetically explain that there was nothing at all in the archive. I don't know her name, but she was gracious and hard-working and I am very glad of all her efforts. On our way back to Arette, we passed the camp at Gurs and contemplated another visit, but the relentless rain seemed to bring the past back to life much too vividly.

Another chance visit had been to the *Kazerne Dossin* (Dossin Barracks) in Mechelen, Belgium, which we visited from Brussels when we were following the trail of Henny and Hermann immediately after they had fled Germany. Formerly part of a Second World War concentration camp, the barracks now house a memorial, museum and documentation centre and we visited the permanent exhibition that documents the wartime persecution of Jews, Roma and Sinti people in Belgium and northern France, as well as drawing attention to questions of human rights violations, discrimination and exclusion. Afterwards, we wandered around the archive building and found a solitary young archivist working after hours. She made us very welcome and, although her particular speciality did not include the plight of adult Jewish refugees in 1940, she gave us a very thorough tutorial about the situation and events of that time in Belgium and Brussels that helped enormously with understanding what I needed to know. She then pointed us in other directions for further help and recommended useful specific reading. I am extremely grateful to her.

There are particular people in Germany who have been essential to the writing of this book, partly because they have enriched our understanding and partly because for a long time they have been (and remain) committed to remembering the earlier Jewish communities in their towns and villages. In doing so, they have created places where people, events and buildings from the past are named, marked out and documented. Their educational work is ongoing and extends to future generations in the active hope that the conditions Henny, Hermann and millions of Jews endured during the 1930s and 1940s can be prevented from rising again.

Although there are many people working together in different localities, I particularly want to thank Elfriede and Günther Lübbers in Aurich, and Hartmut Peters and Volker Landig in Jever, for the extraordinary amount of time and help they gave to me as I wrote this book.

We visited Aurich first (because I was trying to write the life story chronologically) and were grateful for Günther's offer to show us around the town. What might have been an interesting hour's meeting and explanation turned into a whole day of fascinating discovery as we walked the streets to learn about the *Stolpersteine* and the process involved with their laying. Günther also arranged an interesting meeting with Wolfgang Freitag, and I am grateful to Wolfgang for explaining the close links that he and a local group have forged and developed with the families of former Jewish residents of Aurich who now live in Israel.

Since that first meeting, we have returned to Aurich several times and have enriched our understanding about the earlier Jewish community on every visit. Each time, we have been welcomed with generous hospitality from Elfriede and Günther and also from their extended family. Günther continues to keep me informed about further *Stolpersteine*-laying in neighbouring villages, visits from relatives of previous Aurich families now scattered throughout the world, and relevant newspaper articles and books. Hermann and his family were hounded out of Aurich – the place of his birth – and we are pleased to be welcomed back as friends.

When I first made contact with someone in Jever through searching the internet, I had no idea there was already a strong group of people in the town who had been remembering, researching and documenting the earlier Jewish community for decades. They had, in fact, been trying to trace relatives of Teacher Hartog for a long time. We hastily rearranged our travel arrangements to be able to accept their invitation to the re-opening of the GröschlerHaus in Jever.

On our first evening, we were invited into the home of Volker Landig and his wife Marie-Luise, and we met Hartmut Peters and other members of the volunteer group who give so much time and energy to the work of the GröschlerHaus. Other invited relatives were also there and it was extraordinary to meet people who knew so much more about our own family history than we did ourselves.

Over the following few days, amongst a whirlwind of other meetings and activities, Volker showed us around the places in Jever that are particularly significant for the Hartogs. Having the retired pastor as our guide – someone who had been well-known in the town for many years – literally opened doors for us as we walked through the streets. He knocked on the door of the house where Henny and Hermann had lived when they first married and the kind owner showed us around, describing how the former kosher kitchen would have been set up and pointing out features that were unchanged. And as we walked through the streets, Volker explained so much about the earlier Jewish community and brought those early years to life for us. On a different later visit, I was again able to ask him so many questions and I am grateful to him for sharing his knowledge, and to him and Marie-Luise for all their generous hospitality.

On the day the GröschlerHaus was formally opened, the building was crowded with visitors and well-wishers. We were glad to have been able to see inside the building the previous evening, to view the exhibition created by Hartmut Peters, and to absorb the fact that we were standing on the site of the synagogue. As we moved through the space, we found ourselves standing in the room that had once been Hermann's schoolroom, by the side of the one remaining wall of the original synagogue, looking through the one window that had survived the destruction. Hartmut joined us, and we were glad to stand quietly and thoughtfully together with him – the one particular person who has refused to allow the people of Jever to bury the memory of the Jewish community, and who continues to use his time, scholarship and creative energy to ensure that an active memory lives on into future generations.

Hartmut also walked with us around Wilhelmshaven and pointed out significant buildings, including the memorial at the site of the synagogue. It was while we were there that the architect of the memorial, Hartmut Wiesner, stopped while passing by and explained his ideas for the design, and I am grateful for his thoughts.

On subsequent visits, Hartmut and his wife Heidrun have been generous in offering us hospitality and I am very grateful to them for their time and interest. Hartmut has been extremely helpful to me throughout the writing of this book, and I am very grateful for his knowledge and published documents, as well as his encyclopaedic information about individual members of Jever's Jewish community. I owe him a great debt of gratitude for almost every aspect of this story.

I also want to thank the volunteers at the GröschlerHaus for everything they do as part of the project. In particular, Uta Esselborn has been a welcoming friend on our every visit and a quiet and stalwart strength – often, it seems, behind the scenes. She and her husband Ewald Esselborn have also been an enormous help to me in translating letters in German that had completely defeated me. Not only were the letters mostly written by hand, some were also written in the old German script. I think that I particularly have Ewald to thank for painstakingly deciphering them.

On our most recent visit to Jever, we were particularly glad to be able to link with the local senior school, the Mariengymnasium, and I would like to thank the headteacher, Jürgen Ploeger-Lobeck, and his deputy, Katrin Finke, for organising such helpful, interesting and enjoyable events at their school. We were especially pleased to meet with some of the students and we thank them and their teacher, Britta Herzog, for talking with us and for asking such searching and thoughtful questions.

Whenever we visit Jever for an event that the GröschlerHaus has organised, the city of Jever is welcoming, generous in its hospitality, and much engaged with the programme and the returning relatives of its former citizens. We are grateful to the city officials who help to create this happy atmosphere in the place where Henny and Hermann themselves created a happy home.

In France, when we first visited Arette, we made immediate contact with the mayor, Pierre Casabonne, who is François' grandson. It seems strange to relate today that at that time we knew no one else in the village – and nothing at all about it. Pierre has been a constant support and encouragement since that first day, and we are extremely grateful to him for his friendship, organisation, and willingness to participate in our journey. He shares his grandfather's beliefs and humanitarianism, and on our very first day together he declared, 'Your family's story is mine also.' Pierre has given us a tremendous welcome whenever we have been in Arette. I am so grateful to him for all the time he has given to us to show us around the village and answer our questions, all the occasions on which he has picked up his keys to the town hall (after hours) and said, 'I will see what I can find out,' before returning shortly with copies of interesting and useful documents, and the many times that he has introduced us to the people and traditions of this beautiful Basque region. And many thanks to Pierre and his wife Viviane for wonderful hospitality in their home.

I am also extremely grateful to Pierre's mother, Rose Casabonne, for her gracious welcome to us in her home, which is the same house where Amélie Derrez once lived. We met with her in the kitchen of her house and sat at the long table in front of the range, right by the windows that looked over the garden. It was in this same room that Henny, Liesbett Preiss and Amélie had sat talking together during the afternoons. 'Why?' we asked Rose. 'Why did they come here?'

Rose looked surprised that we had asked the question, and as quick as a flash she replied, 'The radio. They listened to the radio.' When I asked whether listening to the radio was actually allowed at that time, Rose – then in her late eighties – sat up slightly straighter and taller, and replied elegantly and with some steel, 'We were free.' I am, with much humility, grateful to Rose Casabonne for giving me a glimpse of the determination, dignity and enormous kindness of the women who gave hope and friendship to others as part of the French resistance to Nazism. She also gave us a very useful practical tutorial in interpreting the records kept by Gaston Derrez for the distribution of food rations.

On that first visit, Pierre introduced us to Emile Vallès, who grew up in Camp de Gurs as a very young child of Spanish refugees. His knowledge of the camp is unsurpassable and he is a founder member of the *Amicale*. Pierre joined us when Emile showed us around the camp and we all endured the unrelenting, torrential rain that only enhanced the awful reality of this experience. It was an unforgettable few hours and I am so grateful to Emile for sharing his knowledge and experiences with us. Afterwards, we went to Emile's house near Oloron, and I apologise yet again to Emile's wife Aline for all the puddles we deposited on her kitchen floor. While we dripped at the kitchen table, she kindly made tea for everyone as Emile went in search of his copy of *Mémorial* by Serge Klarsfeld, which he then brought to the centre of the table. I had never seen this book before and was aghast at the sheer size and weight of it. I had enough information at this point in my research to know the number of the convoy that had deported Henny and Hermann to their deaths, but it was still a shock to see their names recorded in this unremitting record of extermination.

I want to say how grateful I am to Emile Vallès, not only for everything he has done to help us in our own understanding and research, but also for his extraordinary vision and commitment to creating the memorial at Camp de Gurs, including the creation of the *Amicale*.

A few months before our planned 'final' visit to Arette before the completion of this book, I had a surprise message via my website from a local historian in the village. Since that unexpected introduction, Janette Ananos has become a valued friend who has guided us through the village and introduced us to several people who have memories and family stories to share about the time when Henny and Hermann lived in Arette. I cannot thank her enough, and I am more than grateful to her and her husband, Jean-Claude, for their generous welcome.

We had a limited number of days in Arette, Janette had a book being published that same week, and yet almost every day she spent time with us and other people in the village teasing out memories and the experiences of people who had been actively connected with Henny and Hermann and the time in which they had lived in Arette. Often, it was quite mind-blowing for us and, always, the remembered anecdotes allowed us to better visualise the people who had lived in the village as refugees.

As a result, I have so many people to thank for sharing their stories and memories. First, to Elia Migazzi. We gave her quite a shock when we mentioned

'Madame Hartog', who had been 'like a member of our family'. She, on the other hand, gave us an enormous shock when she described so vividly the part that Henny had played in their domestic life, and we are extremely grateful to Elia's family for the friendship, care and concern they showed to Henny. At a time when Henny struggled to find much happiness in her life, being in the home of Louise Borau and Josephine Migazzi – and playing their piano – gave her a great deal of happiness. I thank Elia for so generously sharing her memories.

These memories are shared by Elia's brother, Gilbert, and I am grateful to him and his wife Marie-France for talking with us and for sharing photographs from their family album.

I would like to thank Jacky Tillous for his memories of a childhood in Arette, on the farm adjacent to François Casabonne's, with his unique memory of seeing Hermann working in the fields nearby. Seen through the prism of a child's experience, recounted so vividly over eighty years later, we were able to appreciate far better the life and lifestyle of the different people who lived and worked in and around Arette while a war was raging around them. It was an enormous pleasure to meet with Jacky.

Similarly, Madeleine Larragueta has on several occasions told us her memories of life in Arette during the war, when the village welcomed so many refugees from all parts of France, Belgium and Germany. She and her family have lived in the village for a long time and she remembers that 'we have always had refugees here'. Madeleine and her family have been among those who have welcomed, accepted, and helped strangers to their village. I also thank her for allowing me to use the photograph of François Casabonne that she holds – which also inspired Leo's poem at the beginning of this book.

Janette introduced us to her friend Marie-José Capdevielle, who has not only helped us as a translator on occasions but has also searched as far as possible in the archives of the town hall at Montory for information on the Hartogs. I am very grateful to her for her good company, her extensive local knowledge, and her glorious sense of the absurd.

While in Montory, we were delighted to be welcomed into the home of Robert Espelette and his wife Michelle. We spent an absolutely wonderful few hours with them and Marie-José, mostly listening to the spellbinding stories that Robert told of the activities of the *passeurs* in the nearby mountains during the time of the German occupation of the area. These are stories that have only fairly recently been told as the fear of denunciation and retribution has faded. It was a thorough explanation and description of the times, delivered with understated passion and drama, that I will remember for a very long time. I would like to thank Robert and Michelle for a fascinating morning – and for the excellent book recommendations.

The Basque-Pyrénées is a glorious area in every way, and I want to thank Sandra Ott for describing it to me from an anthropologist's point of view. Her books are a splendid read and proved to be essential for understanding so many aspects of what I found when I arrived in the area. I would like to thank her not only for writing such wonderful books but also for engaging with me in correspondence that has been helpful, encouraging and enlightening.

Books don't get published without publishers, and I am extremely grateful to the team at Pen and Sword Books Ltd for facilitating the telling of this story. My commissioning editor, Lester Crook, has been enthusiastic and encouraging from the very beginning and I am grateful to him for everything that he has done to enable this story to see the light of day. As far as I am concerned, Harriet Fielding is a miracle worker – and a friendly one at that – in accomplishing everything that is needed for a book to be a success. The book itself has been much improved by the skilful editing of Diane Wordsworth, who has reduced all the superfluity and tightened up the text with speed, professionalism and cheerfulness – as well as greatly encouraging me with her confidence and trust. And here's a shout-out to the design team that creates absolutely wonderful-looking books that go out from this publishing house. Thank you all.

Which leaves me, finally, the opportunity to acknowledge the huge support of my family. This is their story, and they have cheered me all the way in writing it. It is the story of their grandparents, great-grandparents, or great-great-grandparents, and I am grateful to them all for their interest in seeing it told. How the story continues is, to some extent, up to them. And many thanks to Leo Hepburn and his parents for permission to publish his poem *Almost*, which was inspired by this story.

I am particularly grateful to my husband, Peter Hepburn, for travelling with me on this journey of family discovery. Henny and Hermann are his grandparents and in the last few years we have, together, touched their lives more closely than we had ever thought possible. We have been able to do so through the welcome, the generosity, and the painstaking research of many, many people in Britain, Germany, Belgium, and France. Thank you all.

Bibliography

Books

Ananos, Janette, *Rue Paillassère*, (Mon Helios 2020)
Ananos, Janette, *Sur les Sentiers du Refus 1939 – 1945: Espoirs et Drames vus d'une Vallée Béarnaise et d'Ailleurs,* (Mon Helios 2023)
Arendt, Hannah, *For Love of the World*, (Yale University Press 1982)
Aubrac, Lucie, *Outwitting the Gestapo*, translated by Bieber, Konrad, (University of Nebraska Press 1993)
Barlay, Nick, *Scattered Ghosts: One Family's Survival through War, Holocaust and Revolution*, (I.B. Tauris 2013)
Berghahn, Marion, *Continental Britons: German Jewish Refugees from Nazi Germany*, (Berg 1988)
Boschwitz, Ulrich Alexander, *The Passenger,* (Pushkin Press 2021)
Broch, Ludivine, *Ordinary Workers, Vichy and the Holocaust: French Railwaymen and the Second World War,* (Cambridge University Press 2016)
Caron, Vicky, *Uneasy Asylum: France and the Jewish Refugee Crisis 1933 – 1942,* (Stanford University Press 1999)
Crowe, David M., *The Holocaust: Roots, History and Aftermath*, (Westview Press 2008)
Diamond, Hanna, *Fleeing Hitler*, (Oxford University Press 2007)
Dwork, Deborah and van Pelt, Robert Jan, *Flight from the Reich: Refugees 1933 – 1946*, (W.W. Norton and Co. 2009)
Fast, Vera K., *Children's Exodus: A History of the Kindertransport*, (Bloomsbury 2010)
Freeman, Hadley, *House of Glass: The Story and Secrets of a Twentieth-century Jewish family*, (4th Estate 2020)
Fredj, Jacques, *Drancy: An Internment Camp at the Gates of Paris*, (Editions Privat 2015)

Gérard-Libois, Jules and Gotovitch, José, *L'An 40. La Belgique occupée*, (Crisp 1971)

Gildea, Robert, *Fighters in the Shadows: A New History of the French Resistance*, (Faber and Faber 2015)

Grenville, Anthony, *Jewish Refugees from Germany and Austria in Britain 1933 – 1970*, (Vallentine Mitchell 2010)

Gröschler, Änne, *Aus dieser schwerer Zeit/About these Hard Times*, (Fuego 2020)

Gross, Raphael and Semmelroth (eds.), *The Memorial at the Frankfurt Grossmarkthalle: The Deportation of the Jews 1941 – 1945*, (Prestel 2016)

Harris, Mark Jonathan and Oppenheimer, Deborah, *Into the Arms of Strangers. Stories of the Kindertransport*, (Bloomsbury 2000)

Hoffman, Eva, *Lost in Translation: A Life in a New Language*, (Virago 1998)

Hoffman, Eva, *After such Knowledge: Memory, History, and the Legacy of the Holocaust*, (Vintage 2005)

Hunter, Rob, *Walking in France*, (Oxford Illustrated Press 1982)

Kaplan, Marion A., *Between Dignity and Despair: Jewish Life in Nazi Germany*, (Oxford University Press 1998)

Kaplan, Marion A., *The Making of the Jewish Middle Class*, (Oxford University Press 1995)

Kedward, Rod, *The French Resistance and its Legacy*, (Bloomsbury Academic 2002)

Klarsfeld, Beate and Klarsfeld, Serge, *Hunting the Truth*, translated from the French by Taylor, Sam, (Farrar, Straus and Giroux 2018)

Klemperer, Victor, *I shall bear Witness. The diaries 1933 – 1941*, (Weidenfeld and Nicolson 1998)

Laharie, Claude, *Les Basses-Pyrénées dans la Seconde Guerre Mondiale 1939 – 1945*, (Editions Cairn 2021)

Lambert, Richard Raoul, *Diary of a Witness 1940 – 1943*, translated from the French by Best, Isabel, (Ivan R. Dee, Chicago, with the United States Holocaust Memorial Museum)

Lindsey, Thérèse Gevaert, *En Béarn sous l'Occupation 1940 – 1944: Mémoires d'une jeune fille de réfugiés politiques belges*, (Marrimpoucy 2011)

Lougarot, Gisèle, *Dans l'Ombre des Passeurs*, (Elkar 2004)

Malet, Marian and Grenville, Anthony (eds.), *Changing Countries. The Experience and Achievement of German-speaking Exiles from Hitler in Britain from 1933 to Today*, (Libris 2002)

Neave, Airey, *Nuremberg. A Personal Record of the Trial of the Major Nazi War Criminals in 1945 – 6*, (Hodder and Stoughton 1978)

Ostrum, Meg, *The Surgeon and the Shepherd: Two Resistance Heroes in Vichy France*, (University of Nebraska Press 2004)

Ott, Sandra, *The Circle of Mountains: A Basque Shepherding Community*, (University of Nevada Press 1993)

Ott, Sandra, *War, Exile, Justice and Everyday Life 1936 – 1946*, (Centre for Basque Studies, University of Nevada 2011)

Ott, Sandra, *War, Judgement and Memory in the Basque Borderlands 1914 – 1945*, (University of Nevada Press 2008)

Paul, Oscar, *Farewell France*, (Victor Gollancz Ltd 1941)

Peters, Hartmut (ed.), *Verbannte Bürger. Die Juden aus Jever – Dokumente und Darstellungen zur Geschichte der Juden Jevers 1698 – 1984*, (Goldmann GmbH 1984)

Ryan, Donna F., *The Holocaust and the Jews of Marseille: The enforcement of anti-Semitic policies in Vichy France*, (University of Illinois 1996)

Sands, Philippe, *East West Street*, (Weidenfeld and Nicolson 2016)

Sands, Philippe, *The Ratline*, (Weidenfeld and Nicolson 2020)

Schwarz, Géraldine, *Those who Forget: One Family's Story – A Memoir, a History, a Warning*, (Pushkin Press 2020)

Schwertfeger, Ruth, *In Transit: Narratives of German Jews in Exile, Flight and Internment during 'The Dark Years' of France*, (Frank and Timme 2012)

Seghers, Anna, *Transit,* (Virago 2021, first published 1944)

Shirer, William, *The Nightmare Years 1930 – 1940,* (Little, Brown and Company 1984)

Sternberg, Hans, *We were Merchants*, (Louisiana State University Press 2009)

Stourton, Edward, *Cruel Crossing: Escaping Hitler across the Pyrénées,* (Black Swan 2014)

Synnestvedt, Alice Resch, *Over the Highest Mountain: A Memoir of Unexpected Heroism in France during World War II,* (Intentional Productions 2005)

Taylor, Frederick, *1939: A People's History: 'The War Nobody Wanted'*, (Pan Macmillan 2019)

Vallès, Emile, *Itinéraires d'internés du Camp de Gurs 1939 – 1945*, (Editions Cairn 2016)

Weitz, Margaret Collins, *Sisters in the Resistance: How Women fought to free France 1940 – 1945*, (John Wiley and Sons 1998)

Wyman, David S., *Paper Walls: America and the Refugee Crisis 1938 – 1941*, (Pantheon Books 1985, first published 1968)

Yelin, Barbara, *Irmina*, (SelfMadeHero 2016)

Zuccotti, Susan, *Holocaust Odysseys: The Jews of Saint-Martin-Vésubie and their Flight through France and Italy*, (Yale University Press 2007)

Zuccotti, Susan, *The Holocaust, the French and the Jews*, (Harper Collins 1993)

Articles

American Friends Service Committee, *'Activities in France to November 1942'*, (AFSC, written and produced in Baden-Baden 13.06.1943)

Bell, George K.A., Bishop of Chichester, '*Humanity and the Refugees*', (fifth Lucien Wolf Memorial Lecture, delivered at University College, London, 01.02.1939)

Bonnet, Dorothy, *'Quaker report for 1940 – 1941'*, (American Friends Service Committee in France 1941)

Cantacuzino, Marina, *'Forgiveness doesn't mean forgetting'*, (The Forgiveness Project, *The Guardian* 02.05.2015)

Fontaine, Thomas, *'Chronology of Repression and Persecution in Occupied France 1940 – 44'*, (SciencesPo 2007)

'France', (www.yadvashem.org),

Gilbert, Shirli, *'A Cache of Family Letters and the Historiography of the Holocaust: Interpretive Reflections'*, (*The Journal of Holocaust Research*, volume 36, 2022, issue 4, published online 20.11.2022)

'*HICEM*', (Shoah Resource Centre, The International School for Holocaust Studies)

Horovitz, David, '*Grappling with traces of my family's Nazi-shattered world*', (*The Times of Israel* 21.06.2012)

'*Immigration to the United States 1933 – 1941'*, (United States Holocaust Memorial Museum, Washington DC)

Joly, Laurent and Williams, Benn E.: *'The Parisian Police and the Holocaust: Control, Round-ups, Hunt (1940 – 44)'*, (*Journal of Contemporary History* 2020)

Jünger, David, *'Beyond Flight and Rescue: the migration setting of German Jewry before 1938'*, (Dubnow Institute Yearbook 16, 2017)

Kershner, Howard E., *'Quaker work. Report on work autumn 1941 – spring 1942'*. (AFSC)

Lachmanovich, Liraz, *'The Holocaust of the French Jews: A Historical Review'*, (Yad Vashem)

Matthäus, Jürgen (ed.), *'Documenting Life and Destruction, volume 1, 1933 – 38'*, (United States Holocaust Memorial Museum)

Mayer, Eugen, *'Frankfurt Revisited'*, (Association of Jewish Refugees, December 1961)

Mohaupt, Hillary, '*All in the Same Boat, Non-French women and Resistance in France 1940 – 1944'*, (a thesis submitted to the University of Delaware spring 2010)

Parisius, Astrid, *'Aurich biographies*' (the internet)

Pascal, Julia, *'Vichy's shame'*, (*The Guardian* 11.05.2002)

Peters, Hartmut, '*Der Pogrom vom 10/11 November 1938 in Jever und die Geschichte der jeverschen Synagogen'*, (In *Die Synagogen des Oldenburger Land*, pp 41 – 121, Enno Meyer, Oldenburg 1988)

Peters, Hartmut, many articles published on GröschlerHaus website, www.groeschlerhaus.eu

Tortel, Emilian, *'Marseille, City of Refuge: International Solidarity, American Humanitarianism, and Vichy France (1940 – 1942)'*, (Esboços, Florianópolis, v. 28, n. 48, p. 364 – 385, 2021)

Exhibitions

'*Law and Justice*', an outdoor installation opposite the palace in Karlsruhe, September 2022

Index